The Palgrave Lacan Series

Series Editors

Calum Neill
Edinburgh Napier University
Edinburgh, UK

Derek Hook
Duquesne University
Pittsburgh, USA

Jacques Lacan is one of the most important and influential thinkers of the 20th century. The reach of this influence continues to grow as we settle into the 21st century, the resonance of Lacan's thought arguably only beginning now to be properly felt, both in terms of its application to clinical matters and in its application to a range of human activities and interests. The Palgrave Lacan Series is a book series for the best new writing in the Lacanian field, giving voice to the leading writers of a new generation of Lacanian thought. The series will comprise original monographs and thematic, multi-authored collections. The books in the series will explore aspects of Lacan's theory from new perspectives and with original insights. There will be books focused on particular areas of or issues in clinical work. There will be books focused on applying Lacanian theory to areas and issues beyond the clinic, to matters of society, politics, the arts and culture. Each book, whatever its particular concern, will work to expand our understanding of Lacan's theory and its value in the 21st century.

More information about this series at
http://www.palgrave.com/gp/series/15116

Peter D. Mathews

Lacan the Charlatan

palgrave
macmillan

Peter D. Mathews
Department of English Language and Literature
Hanyang University
Seoul, Korea (Republic of)

The Palgrave Lacan Series
ISBN 978-3-030-45203-2 ISBN 978-3-030-45204-9 (eBook)
https://doi.org/10.1007/978-3-030-45204-9

Cover illustration: letty17/gettyimages

This Palgrave Macmillan imprint is published by the registered company Springer Nature Switzerland AG.
The registered company address is: Gewerbestrasse 11, 6330 Cham, Switzerland

For Hyunhee, whose love and support made this book possible

Acknowledgments

Because *Lacan the Charlatan* is my first published monograph, I want to acknowledge and thank the many people who made this book possible in the broadest possible sense.

First, thank you to the people at my alma mater, Monash University, who started me on my intellectual journey. Slobodanka (Millicent) Vladiv-Glover was the person who first introduced me to Jacques Lacan, for which I am most grateful. I want to thank Claire Colebrook, whose penetrating lectures on Deleuze, Foucault, and Lacan, in particular, revolutionized my ideas of what critical theory could be and do. I would also like to thank my other mentors at Monash, including Philip Anderson, Elizabeth Grosz, Kevin Hart, Michael Janover, Russ Kerr, Andrew Milner, Brian Nelson, and Walter Veit. During my time at the Centre for Comparative Literature and Cultural Studies at Monash, I was also fortunate to encounter fellow postgraduate students Angus Nicholls and Soe Tjen Marching, with whom I remain good friends all these years later.

I also want to thank the colleagues who have helped me along the way in my journey through academia. The first person to acknowledge is the late Robert F. (Bob) Bergstrom, who hired me for my first-ever academic post as a lecturer at the University of Nebraska-Lincoln, a sweet, wonderful man who lives on in my heart even though he has since departed this earth. Second, I would like to thank Bridget Keegan, who hired me for a visiting position at Creighton University, for providing my younger self with a much-needed model of scholarly rigor and academic professionalism. Third, I want to thank John R. Holt, who gave me my chance at a full-time position at Centenary. John and his wife Nancy Gable have been steadfast friends to me during my time there and beyond. Finally, I wish to thank Seongho Yoon for bringing me on board at my current institution, Hanyang University, a place where I have grown and flourished intellectually. Naturally, there are many other colleagues who have been crucial in supporting me along the way, but who are too numerous to name in this limited space. I thank you all from the bottom of my heart.

My academic life has been enriched over the journey by two scholarly societies in particular. The first is the American Association of Australasian Literary Studies (AAALS), a community of scholars working on Australian and New Zealand literature whose mentorship and generosity is second to none. Thank you to all the friends and colleagues that I have met through AAALS since I attended my first conference at Georgetown back in 2007, especially Nicholas Birns, Carolyn Bliss, Rich Carr, Mike Griffiths, Brenda Machosky, Nathanael O'Reilly, Eva Rueschmann, Sean Scarisbrick, and John Scheckter. The second, more recent connection is the Société d'Études Anglaises Contemporaines (SEAC), a French academic society focused on contemporary British fiction. Thank you to my new SEAC friends Catherine Bernard, Adèle Cassigneul, Elsa Cavalié, James Dalrymple, Camille Fort, Jean-Michel Ganteau, Benjamin Kohlmann, Marie Laniel, Miles Leeson, Sylvie Maurel, Laurent Mellet, Lucy Oulton, Ravi Rana, Frances White, and many others for welcoming me to your intellectual community.

I have read many, many books and articles about Lacan over the past three years. It was an honor to be able to correspond with some of the authors of those works, all of who were generous in responding to my messages and inquiries. Luke Thurston's work on knots was especially helpful in making sense of the later period of Lacan's work. The brilliance of A. Kiarina Kordela's connection of Lacan with Spinoza, Marx, and other thinkers is matched only by her kindness in providing me with books and sage advice. Aaron Schuster's book on Deleuze, Lacan, and pleasure was instrumental in clarifying my own ideas, and I thank him for our intellectual exchanges and his wise counsel. Todd Dufresne has proven himself the very best kind of interlocutor, not only bouncing ideas back and forth with refreshing energy and insight, but also providing much-needed help with negotiating the publishing process.

A very special thanks is necessary for my friend and mentor Nicholas Birns, whom I first met back in 2006. It is rare to meet a person who combines a prodigious intellect with such deep compassion and personal integrity. I owe a huge debt of gratitude to him for his help and influence on my life and academic career.

I also want to thank my family. My father recently passed away from an aggressive brain tumor, yet even during his illness he took the time to read the manuscript of this book. I am grateful for all their love and support.

The most important person I want to thank is my wife, Hyunhee Shin. She has been with me every step of the journey in creating this book. She has been so gracious in putting up with my intellectual ambitions, loving and caring for me even when it seemed as though all my time was being devoured by reading and writing about Lacan. Without her love, this book could not have come into existence, and that is why it is dedicated to her.

Praise for *Lacan the Charlatan*

"What authorises an analyst to analyse? *Lacan the Charlatan* makes a significant contribution to this important question and is a must read for anyone interested in the future of our praxis."

—Russell Grigg, *World Association of Psychoanalysis*

"*Lacan the Charlatan* is much more than a highly engaging study of Lacan's various critics, detractors, and would-be debunkers. It focuses in on one of the essential problems of his psychoanalytic theory: the nature of authority under conditions of modernity. Clown, guru, master, imposter, insurgent, analyst: Mathews shows how Lacan both incarnated and exposed the impasses of authority, and how his theoretical framework is crucial for understanding the charade of power and mastery we are living in today."

—Aaron Schuster, author of *The Trouble with Pleasure: Deleuze and Psychoanalysis*

"Mathews is that rarest of scholars in psychoanalytic studies: someone brave enough to consult works he disagrees with, and then able to produce smart, judicious, and fair-minded commentary and critique. Likewise, his interventions into the work and legacies of the best critics of Lacan, such as Roustang and Borch-Jacobsen, is not just overdue; it is often revelatory. *Lacan the Charlatan* is a major contribution to the literature—one of interest to scholars of literature, philosophy, and sociology—that will still be worth reading in twenty years."

—Todd Dufresne, *Professor of Philosophy at Lakehead University, author of* The Late Sigmund Freud: Or, The Last Word on Psychoanalysis, Society, and All the Riddles of Life

Contents

1

Introduction

A Genealogy of the Charlatan Label

In the introduction to *Jacques Lacan and the Adventure of Insight* (1987), Shoshana Felman recalls that she initially learned about Lacan while she was a graduate student at the University of Grenoble. 'I first heard Lacan's name mentioned by two highly respected teachers in the university,' she writes. 'One of them kept referring to Lacan with enthusiasm and admiration. The other would mention Lacan in a derogatory way, advising us, in sum, not to read him' (Felman 1987, p. 3). Felman's experience is not unusual. Lacan's audiences tend to be bitterly divided between those who loathe and oppose him, and those who become his loyal disciples and followers. Not much critical space exists, it seems, for any position in between. Felman thus writes:

> How can one comprehend a figure with such a record of controversiality? With a few exceptions, most attempts to understand Lacan have assumed the shape either of a didactic exposition of Lacan's complicated thought or of a polemical defense of Lacan's position in the context of the controversy among different psychoanalytic factions. (Felman 1987, p. 4)

P. D. Mathews, *Lacan the Charlatan*, The Palgrave Lacan Series,
https://doi.org/10.1007/978-3-030-45204-9_1

The title of my own book reflects the controversial nature of its subject. It is designed to provoke with its evident boldness, but in a way that complicates and rethinks the simplistic options of being 'for' or 'against' Lacan. In truth, I am interested neither in attacking nor defending Lacan: my real concern in this book is with problems of mastery and authority, and the unique way that Lacan's charlatanry, rather than being a purely negative phenomenon, might offer a potential solution to them.

Like Felman, my own introduction to the work of Lacan came through my university studies. In my second year as an undergraduate, I took a course titled 'Postmodernism and the Novel' with Slobodanka Vladiv-Glover, a renowned Dostoevsky scholar, who introduced Lacan as one of the key thinkers of postmodernism and an intellectual hero. I remember taking several pages of long-lost notes in the first class, headed by the two overlapping circles of the 'vel of alienation' from Lacan's *Seminar XI*. That diagram was followed by hermetic terms like 'castration' and 'signification,' all part of a complex theoretical language I had never before encountered. My eyes were opened to literature and critical theory in an entirely new way, and in subsequent semesters I took further courses like 'Freudian Fable' with acclaimed poet and Blanchot specialist Kevin Hart, which focused on the connections between psychoanalysis and narrative theory, 'Introduction to Critical Theory' with Elizabeth Grosz, author of *Jacques Lacan: A Feminist Introduction* (1990), and two courses, 'Deleuze and Foucault' and 'Lacan and Subjectivity' with Deleuze scholar Claire Colebrook. Lacan was a constant touchstone during this period of my education. When the time came to write my undergraduate honors thesis, I chose Lacan's use of mathemes as my topic. In what would turn out to be a fatal move for my youthful interest in Lacan, however, my extracurricular reading that year also included the two volumes of Gilles Deleuze and Félix Guattari's *Capitalism and Schizophrenia*, *Anti-Oedipus* (1972) and *A Thousand Plateaus* (1980). Upon finishing the former, my impressionable mind had already been firmly swayed: psychoanalysis was a neurotic system of control mired in a hopelessly blind form of philosophical idealism. Reading *Anti-Oedipus*, in particular, persuaded me that Lacan was wrong, perhaps even a charlatan, a judgment that was just becoming prevalent in theoretical circles.

When I began this project, some twenty years later, the accusation of charlatanry had become commonplace in the critical literature about Lacan. I refer here not to the infighting and schisms that characterized Lacan's school, the École Freudienne de Paris (EFP), in which the divisions were primarily about questions of allegiance rather than the inherent value of Lacan's teaching. Nor am I referring to the various thinkers who have performed sophisticated intellectual critiques of Lacan's ideas, such as Deleuze and Guattari in the *Capitalism and Schizophrenia* books, Jean-Luc Nancy and Philippe Lacoue-Labarthe in *The Title of the Letter* (1973), Luce Irigaray in *Speculum of the Other Woman* (1974), or Jacques Derrida in *The Post-Card* (1980). Although these works take Lacan to task in various ways, they always assume that he is to be regarded seriously as a thinker. Instead, what has emerged more recently is a discourse that is openly hostile to the work of Lacan not at the level of ideas, but of authority. For the critics who hold this position, Lacan is not just wrong or mistaken about this or that concept—he is a fraud and a charlatan whose oeuvre should be stripped of its validity and dismissed entirely as an act of pure deception.

One of the precursors of this discourse was brought to my attention by Jean-Michel Rabaté's essay 'Lacan's Turn to Freud' in *The Cambridge Companion to Lacan* (2003), which recalls Lacan's skirmish with the linguist Georges Mounin. Mounin's attack, widely known at the time but now largely forgotten, took the form of an article titled 'Some Features of Jacques Lacan's Style,' which he published in 1969. Since Mounin's text is relatively obscure and has never been translated into English, Rabaté provides a helpful summary:

> To describe what had already often been called Lacan's 'mannerism,' a labyrinthine syntax that its author had preemptively defended as 'Gongorism,' a poetic manner that would force his readers to be attentive while immersing them in the fluid equivocations of unconscious discourse, Mounin listed a number of oddities in the psychoanalyst's use of vocabulary and syntax. [...] On the whole, Lacan, so Mounin continued, loved nothing more than obscure archaisms, poetic inversions, or unusual turns of phrase borrowed either from German or Latin. (Rabaté 2003, p. 4)

Rabaté notes the accuracy of Mounin's analysis of Lacan's unusual grammatical choices, recounting humorously how, even after Lacan's death, it was still possible to identify his French disciples by the peculiarly tortured sentence structures they had copied from him. Mounin is one of the first to notice how Lacan's style had changed over time, becoming ever more dense and difficult. 'Mounin observed a dramatic increase in the frequency of these circumlocutions'; writes Rabaté, 'for him, the 1966 preface to *Écrits* verged on self-parody' (Rabaté 2003, p. 4). Rabaté makes the case that Mounin's concerns were grounded primarily in the disparity he saw between 'the excessive theatricality of a fustian style suggesting the image of a hamming buffoon' and the professionalism he otherwise witnessed in Lacan's work (Rabaté 2003, p. 5). 'Mounin's worry seemed justified, even inevitable,' concludes Rabaté. '[W]as Lacan a frustrated poet, a post-Heideggerian thinker progressing by opaque epigrams, a psychoanalyst wishing to revolutionize a whole field of knowledge, or just a charlatan?' (Rabaté 2003, p. 5). Rabaté contends that Mounin, as a linguist, had little real interest in psychoanalysis, and was mainly concerned with the way structuralist ideas were intruding on his academic turf. Still more concerning for Mounin was the possibility that Lacan was *becoming* a charlatan, a performer leading astray his ever-growing crowd of followers. Mounin's attack achieved what it set out to do, putting enough pressure on the head of the École Normale Supérieure, where the weekly seminar had been held since Lacan's departure from the Sainte-Anne Hospital in 1963, that Lacan was denied access to this venue and forced to relocate to his third and final seminar location at the Faculty of Law across from the Panthéon.

Although the history of the EFP was beset by rifts and schisms, during Lacan's lifetime attacks on his authority were rare. Critics were willing to criticize him at the level of ideas, or for his authoritarian leadership style, but seldom did it occur to them that he was an outright fraud. A notable exception comes from the Italian critic Sebastiano Timpanaro, who writes in his book *The Freudian Slip* (1974):

> I must confess that I am incurably committed to the view that in Lacan's writings charlatanry and exhibitionism largely prevail over any ideas of a comprehensible, even if debatable nature: behind the smoke-screen, it

> seems to me, there is nothing of substance; and it is difficult to think of a pioneer in the encounter between psychoanalysis and linguistics who has more frequently demonstrated such an erroneous and confused knowledge of the latter, whether structural or not. (Timpanaro 2011, p. 58)

Although Timpanaro's reproach bears all the hallmarks of the later charges of charlatanry, *The Freudian Slip* is a book that is concerned mainly with Freud's *The Psychopathology of Everyday Life* (1901) rather than Lacan. As such, Timpanaro's comment only appears as a passing footnote to that discussion, and Lacan is barely mentioned again in the rest of the text. Another example is François George's 1979 book *L'Effet 'Yau de poêle: De Lacan et des lacaniens*, in which he accuses Lacan of being a charlatan who bamboozled his disciples by deploying a hermetic discourse that consists mainly of nonsense and word play. Despite its initial flash of scandalous success, George's book has since sunk into relative obscurity, out of print and untranslated.

Lacan's death in 1981 resulted in bitter infighting among his followers over who had the authority to carry on his legacy. In this atmosphere, factions and ideologies hardened to the point where, as David Macey points out in *Lacan in Contexts* (1988), for 'a long time, the reader of Lacan has been faced with a stark dilemma: total acceptance or total rejection' (Macey 1988, p. ix). Rejection of Lacan comes in many varieties, however, and in this period it rarely equates to the kind of hostile denigration that characterizes later detractors. Monique David-Menard's pointed 1982 essay 'Lacanians Against Lacan,' for instance, is aimed at the problematic effects produced by the EFP and, in the wake of its dissolution, the attempts to forge a Lacanian orthodoxy among his most ardent disciples:

> Lacan thought he would avoid the pitfalls of university learning by correlating his teaching and his analyses, and because he marginalized or excluded the medical or university institutions that originally sheltered his seminar[.] [...] In hindsight, it can be asked if this method of teaching, ingenious as it was, did not reinforce the pitfalls of all teachings, and perpetuate a passive, spellbound relation to the discourse of an idealized Master. (David-Menard 1982, p. 100)

In the same spirit, Marcele Marini, in *Jacques Lacan: The French Context* (1986), explores the political and institutional chaos created by Lacan's passing, showing how it divided opinion about his work and legacy. 'So, who was Lacan? Was he a visionary, a shaman, or a guru?' ponders Marini. 'Was he a sorcerer's apprentice or an exemplary practitioner?' (Marini 1992, p. 3). Once again, there is little sense for Marini that this situation entails a total dismissal of Lacan's authority. If Lacan is labeled a charlatan in this period, the nuances of the epithet tend to arise from these struggles over his legacy rather than any blanket attempt to dismiss his authority as such.

The tone of the criticism changes noticeably in the late 1980s, epitomized by comments that appear in a 1989 interview in *Radical Philosophy* with Noam Chomsky. Chomsky is a groundbreaking linguist whose ideas about universal and transformational grammar are widely seen as a challenge to the structural linguistics that inspired the most famous period of Lacan's work. Chomsky is also a prominent figure of the American political left who has engaged publicly with some of the leading French contemporaries of Lacan. Chomsky's 1971 debate with Foucault, for instance, later published as *The Chomsky-Foucault Debate: On Human Nature*, is fascinating for the ideological divisions it reveals between French and American understandings of the Enlightenment and human nature. Chomsky's meeting with Lacan at MIT in 1975 was rather less successful, as Élisabeth Roudinesco reports:

> Lacan scandalized everyone with his answer to a question by Chomsky on thought. 'We think we think with our brains; personally, I think with my feet. That's the only way I really come into contact with anything solid. I do occasionally think with my forehead, when I bang into something. But I've seen enough electroencephalograms to know there's not the slightest trace of a thought in the brain.' When he heard this, Chomsky thought the lecturer must be a madman. And afterward, despite the explanations of his friend Mitsou Ronat, who did her best for several years to point out that Lacan was speaking metaphorically, Chomsky remained convinced that Lacan was so contemptuous of his American audience that he had tried to kid the MIT scientists that the seat of the human brain was in the bones or the toes. The affair gave rise to a rumor, and the rumor became a legend:

> Lacan had tried to convert America to another obscurantist 'plague' by suggesting that the source of man's intelligence was in his feet. (Roudinesco 1997, pp. 378–379)

In the intervening years, Chomsky's negative perspective on both Lacan and the French intellectual scene hardened into open contempt, as evidenced by the tone of his comments in the aforementioned 1989 interview:

> In the case of Lacan, for example—it's going to sound unkind—my frank opinion is that he was a conscious charlatan, and was simply playing games with the Paris intellectual community to see how much absurdity he could produce and still be taken seriously. I mean that quite literally. I knew him. If you took him seriously it was just embarrassing, so you had to assume something else was happening, some other level that you don't quite understand. That's the impression that I get from a good deal of this Paris-based intellectual pop culture which is, I understand, fairly popular in England and certainly is in the United States, in literary circles. But if anyone can detect any intellectual content in that, I'd like to see it. (Chomsky 1989, p. 31)

These sentiments are not a one-off statement—they are repeated, for instance, in the discussion following a lecture that Chomsky delivered in 1996, subsequently published as *The Architecture of Language* (2000). Asked about Lacan's theories of language and sexuality, Chomsky brushes off the question by again dismissing Lacan as an intellectual fraud. 'I knew Lacan personally and I never understood a word he was talking about; so I can't answer the question,' he says. 'In fact I have a rather strong feeling that he was playing jokes, that he was trying to see how crazy he could be and still get people to take him seriously' (Chomsky 2000, p. 47). Chomsky's comments about Lacan set a new tone, one that does not even attempt to tackle the question of whether Lacan is wrong or mistaken. Instead, Lacan's authority is simply rejected out of hand, without any intellectual or analytical engagement, as nothing more than fraudulent nonsense.

Imperious dismissals such as Chomsky's become increasingly prominent in the years that follow. In the preface to *Key Concepts of Lacanian*

Psychoanalysis (1998), for instance, Dany Nobus notes how 'Lacan's numerous personal idiosyncrasies are often used as arguments *ad hominem* to minimize the value of his theoretical contributions' (Nobus 2018, p. v). These attacks noticeably alter the tone of Roudinesco's writing on Lacan. In contrast to the magisterial style of her biography, the slim volume she published in 2011 titled *Lacan: In Spite of Everything* is a comparatively gloomy apology for a figure who has lost a considerable amount of his former luster. Like Nobus, Roudinesco contends that Lacan is not so much under attack for his ideas as for the extravagance of his character and acknowledged taste for luxury:

> A fetishistic collector, passionate about rare or original editions, over his lifetime Lacan had collected all sorts of objects—paintings by masters, water colours, designs, sculptures, archaeological figurines, valuable furniture, extravagant clothing made in accordance with his instructions: furs, suits in unusual materials, hard collars without flaps or collars twisted and turned up, lavallières of various sizes, made-to-measure shoes in rare skins, gold pieces, ingots. (Roudinesco 2014, pp. 111–112)

An important part of Lacan's appeal during his lifetime was his personal charisma, and these *ad hominem* attacks may be read, in part, as a backlash against this aspect of his success. It is impossible to defend the integrity of such tactics, although Roudinesco has hardly helped matters by sometimes resorting to such attacks herself.[1]

There has been a steady production of this anti-intellectual mode of criticism in recent years. In his book *Fools, Frauds and Firebrands: Thinkers of the New Left* (2015), for instance, Roger Scruton refers to Lacan as a 'criminal charlatan' (Scruton 2015, p. 177) and a 'crazy charlatan' (Scruton 2015, p. 241). Once again, his book makes only the most cursory attempt to engage with Lacan's ideas, with his argument framed by bewilderment as to why they are seen as important or influential by anyone at all. 'The influence of these seminars [...] is one of the

---

[1] See Todd Dufresne's article 'The Making of a "Freud Basher," or Reflections of a "Supercilious Neurotic..."' (Dufresne 2014, p. 81). Citing a private email from Borch-Jacobsen, Dufresne points out, in particular, Roudinesco's use of the words '*révisionniste*' and '*négationniste*,' which he argues are terms that in French apply to Holocaust deniers, in her attacks on *Le livre noir de la psychanalyse*.

deep mysteries of modern intellectual life,' contends Scruton. 'Their garbled regurgitation of theories that Lacan clearly neither explored nor understood, is, for sheer intellectual effrontery, without parallel in recent literature. [...] Lacan discovered the infinite power of the meaningless, when the meaningless is used to exert a personal charisma' (Scruton 2015, p. 177). In a chapter from the collection *Desire in Ashes: Deconstruction, Psychoanalysis, Philosophy* (2016), similarly, Herman Rapaport writes that 'we see this seamy side of transference love in the lecture hall as well, for example, in the charge that Lacan was a Char-Lacan (charlatan), something that a French journal once announced on its cover' (Rapaport 2016, p. 86). This emerging tendency causes John Forrester to deliver, as early as 1990, the following rebuke to critics deploying this line of attack:

> It is still common for discussions of Lacan to mention him only to dismiss him as a crank and a charlatan. Given that premise and conviction, the only thing that needs to be said about him is that he is impossible to read (and therefore must be a charlatan) and is of importance only because he is dangerous, owing to the fawning followers who disseminate his foolish theories and distort the general public's understanding of what psychoanalysis really is. The fact that he is French, the fact that he writes difficult prose in a highly idiosyncratic manner, is taken to be yet more self-evidently conclusive proof of his insignificance. Criticism of this calibre would not normally need to be rebutted. It is more properly material for the historian and sociologist of chauvinism and philistinism. (Forrester 1991, p. 112)

The problem that Forrester highlights is not that Lacan is being questioned or attacked, but that these attacks do not constitute intellectually valid forms of critique. Lacan was, in reality, a formidable critic of his own ideas, and it is a central thesis of this book that he was engaged in a vigorous and self-conscious interrogation of his own authority. There is strong evidence that Lacan saw his authority—and indeed, *all* forms of authority grounded in the symbolic order—as a kind of charlatanry, a charade of power and mastery from which there is much to be learned.

The Turn Against Psychoanalytic Authority

The recent tendency to reject Lacan's authority in this manner may be understood as a backlash against the success not only of Lacanian psychoanalysis in France, but also a reaction to the larger impact of French critical theory on Anglophone humanities departments during the 1970s and 1980s. The British novelist A.S. Byatt, herself a former academic, captures the mood of these times in novels like *Possession* (1990), in which postmodern cultural critiques inspired by Lacanian psychoanalysis and French feminism focus on the smallest specks of perceived orthodoxy while ignoring the log of serious material abuses of the rising neoliberal order, and *The Biographer's Tale* (2000), which shows how the appropriation of French theory by the Anglophone academy has drained that discourse of many of its most insightful, critical aspects and turned it into just another ideology. The forceful way these theories penetrated into fields such as literary and film studies is a key part of this backlash, for in many cases this hegemony was achieved not through rational persuasion, but by a kind of hostile takeover. The deployment of esoteric language and elitist assumptions about philosophical learning further helped to alienate and intimidate those not swept up by its current.

In *Lacan in Contexts*, Macey provides some useful historical background for how Lacanian theory was appropriated by Anglophone literary and film studies. 'A variety of agencies ranging from *New Left Review* to *Yale French Studies* were involved in the initial importation of Lacan, the one thing they all have in common being that they are far removed from the psychoanalytic community and from any clinical practices,' he observes. 'Indeed, *New Left Review* implies that it is *because* "Lacan's work is widely influential outside his own discipline" that "it is time it received its due international recognition"' (Macey 1988, p. 15). The ridiculousness of this claim, Macey points out, is reflected in the complete 'hostility or indifference' to Lacan's work in the British psychoanalytic establishment (Macey 1988, p. 15). The most influential medium for importing Lacan (and other high theory) into the Anglophone world during the 1970s was the film studies journal *Screen*, which established a pattern of imposing the authority of Lacan's ideas onto its readers.

> *Screen*'s approach to Lacan is from the outset strikingly instrumental. The point is never to read Lacan as such, or to situate him within the history of psychoanalysis, but to use him to consolidate the theoretical project of elaborating a theory of the subject and of ideology that can supplement Marxism. To that extent, Lacan is regarded as a pre-given theoretical entity whose concepts can be appropriated, deployed and applied quite unproblematically. The fact that Lacan displays no enthusiasm for being articulated with Marxism and has little of interest to say on that subject is simply ignored. (Macey 1988, p. 16)

Macey argues that it was strategies such as these that set the arrogant—even authoritarian—tone that marked the importation of Lacan into Anglophone academia. '*Yale French Studies* introduces an element of intellectual terrorism in its "French Freud" issue, and *Screen* refines the climate of terror by failing to resolve the contradiction between its supposed pedagogic aims and its reliance upon decontextualized theories for the furthering of its theoretical project,' he continues. 'In so doing it establishes an unfortunate precedent' (Macey 1988, p. 17). In an unwitting inversion of Lacan's concept of the 'subject who is supposed to know,' this strategy places the reader in the position of one who is 'presumed to know' (Macey 1988, p. 17). The editors of *Screen* complete their Marxist agenda by citing Louis Althusser's essay 'Freud and Lacan' (1969) in sealing their approval of Lacan, a move that Macey rightly characterizes as 'a classic appeal to authority' (Macey 1988, p. 18). Given the largely authoritarian way in which Lacan and French theory were imposed on Anglophone academia, it is not surprising that there has been such a strong backlash against both discourses.

Alongside this reaction is a growing body of criticism interrogating the validity of psychoanalysis itself. While disagreements and critiques of psychoanalysis have always been a part of its discourse, the more recent skirmishes are distinguished by their intense focus on the authority of its founder. Jason Glynos argues in *Lacan and Science* (2002) that the so-called 'Freud Wars' have predominantly been waged in the name of a scientific logic in which psychoanalysis, because it does not fit the parameters of a narrowly-defined mode of rationalism, has been stripped of its authority. Glynos provides a useful historical summary of the key touchstones of this development:

> Of course, psychoanalysis was the subject of critique [...] from its very inception. But science's onslaught over the last three decades or so has been relentless. And, finding himself on the receiving end of most of those attacks, Freud has not fared well. Either Freud mistook the shadows cast by grammar as an 'inner' unconscious (Bouveresse); or subscribed to a crypto-evolutionary biologism (Sulloway); or adopted a faulty scientific method and dubious epistemology (Popper, MacMillan, Crews, Esterton); or compromised his intellectual integrity through a self-deluded descent into pseudoscience (Cioffi, Webster, Humphrey); or if one granted him proper scientific methodology, he lacked sufficient evidence to substantiate his hypotheses (Grünbaum); or if one excused him from recognized scientific methods by reason of the peculiarly private and non-reproducible nature of the psychoanalytic encounter his personality, for the very same reason, was not: his character became fair game (Masson, Thornton, Swales, Cioffi). (Glynos 2002, pp. 14–15)

The book that consolidated this movement is Richard Webster's *Why Freud Was Wrong: Sin, Science and Psychoanalysis* (1995), which rehearses what will become a familiar accusation: that Freud's brand of psychoanalysis is a pseudoscience, the success of which can be attributed primarily to a cult of personality. In *Freud: The Making of an Illusion* (2017), Frederick Crews thus writes:

> My main concern here [...] is with Freud in person—and indeed, with only one question about him. How and why did a studious, ambitious, and philosophically reflective young man, trained in rigorous inductivism by distinguished researchers and eager to win their favor, lose perspective on his wild hunches, efface the record of his mistakes, and establish an international cult of personality? (Crews 2017, p. 3)

The repetition of this accusation continues in Mikkel Borch-Jacobsen and Sonu Shamdasani's *The Freud Files* (2012), in which they also refer to Freudian psychoanalysis as a 'personality cult' (Borch-Jacobsen and Shamdasani 2012, p. 192).

Attributing Freud's appeal primarily to his charisma opens the possibility of explaining Lacan's success in the same way. In *Returns of the 'French Freud'* (1997), for instance, Todd Dufresne attributes Lacan's allure mainly to personal appeal rather than his ideas: 'Like other intellectual trends in France, psychoanalysis thrived as a cult of personality, one centered around the name and legend(s) of Jacques Lacan' (Dufresne 1997, p. 3). Lacan staked his reputation and authority on the 'return to Freud,' so that toppling Freud is sufficient to bring down the entire enterprise. 'For my money, Freud's "discoveries" were projections seasoned with a dash of scientific preconceptions, most of which have been (conveniently) forgotten,' Dufresne reiterates in *Killing Freud* (2003). 'Like other analysts after Freud, Lacan's innovations were mostly Freud warmed over—with, mind you, a very serious dash of whatever intellectual fashion blew his way or fell into his lap' (Dufresne 2003, p. 99). The Freud Wars have seen the further hardening of positions for and against psychoanalysis. In a poignant article about the state of Freud Studies, Dufresne laments the way that vitriol too often eclipses critique. 'Spend enough time in Freud Studies and the abyss called psychoanalysis infects one's soul,' he writes in the conclusion of that essay. '[A] few decades in psychoanalysis may be fine, but one risks one's health in a field so thoroughly and deeply troubled' (Dufresne 2014, p. 81). The world of Lacan studies is not so different when it comes to the bitterness of its entrenched positions.

The pinnacle of the Freud Wars in France was the publication, in 2005, of the *Le livre noir de la psychanalyse* (*The Black Book of Psychoanalysis*), a collaborative work that sets out in detail the many problems and abuses that have darkened the history of psychoanalysis. The *Livre noir* is an interesting barometer of the difference between the French and Anglophone legacies of Lacan. Because Lacan is still considered a major figure in France, with an ongoing cadre of ardent followers, the appearance of this book caused a major controversy, whereas in the English-speaking world the *Livre noir* has not yet even been translated. One of that book's key contributors, Mikkel Borch-Jacobsen, whose work will be examined in detail in Chap. 6, is an important long-time critic of psychoanalysis. In an excerpt from the *Livre noir* titled 'A Zero Theory,' Borch-Jacobsen complains, with some justification, about the tactics of Lacan's supporters in response to the book's publication.

> The vehement attacks on *Le livre noir* in France won't end anytime soon. In January Éditions du Seuil will publish an *Anti-Livre noir de la psychanalyse*, edited by Lacan's son-in-law Jacques-Alain Miller and featuring forty Lacanian authors. Meanwhile, the same publisher is about to issue another book-length riposte, *Pourquoi tant de haine?: Anatomie du livre noir*, by the most intellectually prominent advocate of Lacanian views, Élisabeth Roudinesco. Her already published comments in the press and on websites sufficiently indicate the tenor of her forthcoming critique: it will be an *ad hominem* assault on the book's contributors as neofascists and anti-Semites. The same line of argument has been vigorously advanced by other defenders of the therapeutic status quo. Needless to say, it constitutes a libel on the contributors, some of whom are Jewish and/or members of the political left, and none of whom write about psychoanalysis with a political agenda in mind. What is totally missing from the discussion thus far is any objective challenge to *Le livre noir*'s factual assertions about psychoanalysis. From the Freudian/Lacanian side there has been *nothing but* character assassination. (Borch-Jacobsen 2005)

Borch-Jacobsen's lament about the unwillingness of the psychoanalytic community to confront difficult home truths about their discipline strikes a chord. Yet while the Freud Wars have produced some important scholarship that provides a more critically and historically accurate perspective on the origins of psychoanalysis, the truth is that *both* sides have helped to normalize the use of *ad hominem* attacks and other similar tactics that have no place in serious intellectual discourse.

Borch-Jacobsen also points out that the foolish behavior of Lacan's disciples is frequently to blame for the perception that his theories are the product of a personality cult, a point also made by Daniel Bougnoux. '[T]he contrast is sharp between Lacan's sparkling intellect—his incredible cultural receptivity to the intellectual innovations of his time—and the mental restriction or lack of curiosity of his followers, which verges on stupidity,' notes Bougnoux. '[K]nowledge in this field has turned into an apparatus of power and intimidation. Despite the reflux of ideologies, or perhaps because of it, Lacanism is one of the last bastions of arrogance, and few domains today remain so jealously guarded' (Bougnoux 1997, p. 93). Even Roudinesco admits that Lacan's disciples have often been willfully blind to his human frailties:

> When Lacan went deaf, some of his pupils refused to admit that the great and idolized ear could have failed: 'He's not deaf,' they said. 'He's just pretending not to hear.' Similarly, when the first signs of cardiovascular troubles appeared in 1978, Lacan's 'blanks,' his silences, his sudden rages and thumpings with his fist were sometimes regarded as subtle 'interpretations' (in the technical sense of an analyst's attempt to convey to a patient the latent meaning of what the latter has said or done), sometimes seen as signs of fatigue stemming from old age. The mere presence of the master, together with nostalgic invocations of what had made his true greatness, were enough to weld together a fragile group overshadowed by the presage of death. (Roudinesco 1997, pp. 391–392)

As with the revelations about Lacan's personal and professional shortcomings, it would be pointless to deny the foolishness and dishonesty of such followers. At the same time, it is important to balance this perspective by observing Lacan's actual responses to the phenomenon of blind discipleship and the way it shapes his critique of mastery. There is a marked difference between Lacan's often-jocular attitude toward his audience in the early seminars, for instance, and the deep frustration he exhibits in the later seminars, when celebrity has transformed these events from an intellectual forum into a public circus. 'I dreamt last night that when I arrived, no one was here,' he remarks bitterly in *Seminar XX*. 'That confirms the wishful character of the dream' (Lacan 1999, p. 118).

Two Untenable Modes of Mastery

As the head of the EFP, Lacan was known as the '*Maître*' ('Master'), a special title conferred on him by his followers as a sign of his superior standing as a leader and thinker. The status of being a master, in general, carries with it a double connotation. In the first instance, it refers to someone who has obtained an outstanding level of skill and achievement in their chosen field, allowing them to stand apart from the everyday crowd and proclaim, as it were, their own *self*-mastery. In this first connotation, the primary source of authority of the master comes from within, from an internal sense that they have achieved the necessary competence to claim that title. It is from this perspective, for instance, that Lacan, in the 1976 preface to the English translation of *Seminar XI*, insists that an analyst does not require official recognition from an organization or authority-figure to be considered a legitimate practitioner of psychoanalysis. 'For no one can call anyone an analyst and Freud did not do so,' insists Lacan. 'Handing out rings to initiates is not to call by a name. Hence my proposition that the analyst hystorizes only from himself: a patent fact. Even if he is confirmed in doing so by a hierarchy' (Lacan 1994, p. viii). Lacan's position is grounded in psychoanalytic logic, but it is also informed by his troubled relationship with the International Psychoanalytical Association (IPA). Lacan's time in the IPA was marked by repeated concerns about his integrity as an analyst, especially the infamous practice of holding variable-length analytical sessions. Lacan was eventually expelled from that organization in 1963, a move that prompted him to cut short his planned seminar on the topic of the Names-of-the-Father, a concept central to Lacan's understanding of authority.

When Lacan addresses his 'excommunication' from the IPA in the opening session of *Seminar XI*, the attentive reader can detect a new sense of direction and purpose in his thought. It is from this point that, without ever abandoning Freud, he nonetheless leaves behind the slogan of the 'return to Freud' that defined his early seminars and begins to develop a distinct set of ideas of his own. Just as important to this shift is the pressing need that Lacan feels, in the wake of his excommunication, to interrogate the nature of authority. In *Seminar XI*, the centerpiece of this examination is his newly-developed concept of the 'subject who is supposed to know' ('*le sujet-supposé-savoir*'). In the session dedicated to this concept, Lacan again frames its importance in the context of what authorizes a person to be called an analyst.

> It is clear, in the experience of all those who have passed through this training, that in the absence of adequate criteria, something that is of the order of ceremony is put in their place and—since for the psycho-analyst there is

> no beyond, no substantial beyond, by which to justify his conviction that he is qualified to exercise his function—the substitution, in this instance, can be interpreted in only one way—as simulation. (Lacan 1994, p. 230)

While Lacan's words may be read, correctly, as a rejection of the authority of institutions like the IPA, they also carry the seed of a subversion that not only questions the parameters of the analytic situation, but also challenges the very notion of authority itself.

That challenge is contained in the unresolved tension between the two possible meanings of 'the subject who is supposed to know.' On the one hand, it may be read as a synonym for the master in the sense described above. The master is 'supposed to know' insofar as the claim to mastery (and self-mastery) ought to rest not on ignorance and incompetence, but on the assurance that the master/analyst knows what they are doing. It is the professional and ethical obligation of the analyst to ensure that this condition is met. On the other hand, Lacan's use of the word 'supposed' allows a degree of doubt and uncertainty to enter this situation. For while the initial meaning of the word 'supposed' refers to an obligation, it also has the sense of an assumption—that is to say, of 'the subject who is *assumed* to know.' In analysis, this situation represents the typical dilemma of the analysand, for when a patient first comes to see an analyst they have little choice but to suppose that the latter knows how to help them. This judgment is necessarily grounded in faith and authority rather than experience and knowledge. While the analyst is professionally obliged to know what they are doing, the patient can only guess whether the analyst actually has that knowledge based on the authority of the latter's position.

Guessing games have long been a part of Lacan's work, most memorably the games of 'Even or Odd' that the seminar participants play in *Seminar II*, an homage to the childhood pastime that Edgar Allan Poe describes in 'The Purloined Letter' (1844). It is not the notion of analysis as a kind of bluff that is new in Lacan's developing view of psychoanalysis in *Seminar XI*, therefore, but a deepening of the implicit challenge to the master's authority that 'the subject who is supposed to know' represents. For whereas the game of 'Even or Odd' at least gives the person guessing an occasional chance of being right (provided they are skillful or lucky enough), the emerging suspicion in Lacan's concept of the 'subject who is supposed to know' is that the answer is *always* wrong—wrong, that is, in the sense that authority is only ever accepted as valid on the basis of the imagination of those who submit to it. Authority is a working concept only because there are people who want to place their faith in the make-believe of a master figure. While those who trust in the Name-of-the-Father are the dupes of an authority built on this false premise, Lacan also becomes increasingly fascinated with the idea that those who reject all forms of authority, the so-called 'non-dupes,' are just as deluded. The fruit of this later direction can be seen, for instance, in the topic for *Seminar XXI*, '*Les non-dupes errent*,' a play on words that translates into English as 'the non-dupes are wrong' but sounds, in French, exactly the same as 'the Names-of-the-Father' ('*Les Noms-du-Père*'). This homophonous resonance is Lacan's way of signaling that, despite their apparent divergence, the 'non-dupes' ultimately end up being just as deceived as the 'dupes' from whom they hoped to distinguish themselves.

Another subversive aspect of the master as 'subject who is supposed to know' is that the effectiveness of the process does not depend in any way on the knowledge of the analyst. The analyst presents a silent, impassive mirror to the patient's discourse, with the usefulness of whatever knowledge they do possess being set aside entirely. The effectiveness of this strategy, for Lacan, derives from the patient's erroneous assumption that the analyst knows how to cure them. The closest thing to a 'cure' in this scenario lies in the analyst's strategy of triggering a feeling of disillusionment in the patient, thus creating a growing realization that the 'subject who is supposed to know' is a fraud, a bluff, a charlatan who does not, in fact, know all the answers. This experience is meant not only to terminate any feelings of transference the patient may have for the analyst, but also to ensure that this pattern of sublimation is not then repeated. That way, the patient does not simply end up exchanging one idealized master for another. Elsewhere, Lacan compares the analytic situation to a game of bridge in which the analyst plays the role of the 'dummy' ('*le mort*') (Lacan 2006, p. 492). Theoretically, it makes no difference to the outcome whether the analyst is a genuine master or an outright charlatan. So long as the patient buys into the illusion that the analyst is a 'subject who is supposed to know,' the identity of the person installed in that symbolic position is functionally irrelevant, so that even a silent, dummy-like analyst will suffice.

With the development of the concept of the 'subject who is supposed to know,' therefore, Lacan comes dangerously close to undermining the foundations of psychoanalysis as a social practice. If the role of the analyst is arbitrary, a position that can be filled by literally anyone, then the authority of psychoanalytic training falls apart. The downfall of that authority would mean, in turn, that psychoanalysis will not be taken seriously as a privileged field of knowledge capable of producing masters (or 'subjects who are supposed to know'). Lacan thus finds himself caught precariously between two imperatives, two different modes of mastery that come to define his discourse from *Seminar XI*. As his clashes with the IPA show, Lacan insisted on defining his mastery in its first connotation as self-mastery, in which his authority as an analyst derives from his own insight and experience. His theories are similarly directed toward teaching both analysts and patients how to attain this self-mastery for themselves, a path that begins with seeing through the illusion of the 'subject who is supposed to know.'

Lacan's desire for self-mastery is undermined by the second connotation of mastery, the more conventional kind of authority that is conferred not by the self, but by something *outside* the subject, such as an institution, a discourse, or a certification: in short, by what in Lacanian terms is referred to as the Other. This concept of Otherness makes true self-mastery impossible, since for Lacan the subject only comes into existence through its own alienation. This process is illustrated by the human experience of language, for instance, which, although we use it to express our most intimate thoughts, nonetheless comes from outside our own being, from the Other. Lacan thus finds himself at an impasse, trapped between two untenable modes of mastery. On the one hand, he regards the idea of the analyst as an external authority, as 'subject who is supposed to know,' as a tyrannical farce, a charade, in much the same way that he refuses the interference of the IPA in his own practice as an analyst. This mode of mastery has no validity, as far as Lacan is concerned, and is reserved for disciples and dupes. On the other hand, Lacan increasingly comes to understand that, far from being liberated by his rebellion, he has become caught in the trap of the non-dupe, for in turning against the master discourse he has cut off the source of his own symbolic power. Lacan is thus caught between two equally unsatisfactory choices: either he must toe the line of a master discourse in which he finds it impossible to believe, or else insist on the authority of his own teachings at the risk of no longer being recognized as a master.

There is an implicit interplay between Lacan's theoretical discussions of mastery in his writings and seminars, and the difficulties and paradoxes he dealt with in his professional life. After being 'excommunicated,' Lacan's vision in founding the EFP was to set up an institution that would avoid the rigid orthodoxy that plagued the IPA. In *Psychoanalytic Politics* (1978), Sherry Turkle considers how this attempt 'to create a nonauthoritarian, nonhierarchical psychoanalytical structure' suffered from its contradictory aim of 'subvert[ing] all "truths" and the need for organizational discipline' (Turkle 1992, p. 119). Particularly problematic for the EFP was its initial decision to allow analysts to authorize themselves as qualified analysts.

> From the very start, membership in the Freudian School was open, informal, and without prerequisite. Anyone could join[.] [...] There were no required courses for analysts in training. People simply participated in those study groups that interested them. [...] Lacan sees the decision to become an analyst as analogous to the act of becoming a poet. It is the assumption by the individual of a new, particularly intimate relationship to language. (Turkle 1992, pp. 121–123)

Allowing people to evaluate their own status as qualified analysts was an experiment that failed because the EFP faced pressure, especially from within, to conform to 'the organizational imperatives of the psychoanalytic establishment' (Turkle 1992, p. 126). As early as December 1965, less than two years after its inauguration, François Perrier, one of the co-founders of the EFP, resigned from the Board in protest over the school's training methods, a gesture that would culminate in the 1968 schism that led to the creation of the Organisation Psychoanalytique de Langue Française, better known as the 'Fourth Group' ('*Quatrième Groupe*').

The root of these issues was Lacan's equivocal position as the *Maître* of the EFP, a role he initially adopted as a way of breaking with the orthodoxy of the IPA, but in which he selectively took on the attributes of an absolute ruler. The problem of the two untenable modes of mastery that Lacan faced before his 'excommunication,' rather than being solved by the creation of the EFP, was instead displaced onto his school. As *Maître*, Lacan considered himself to have a self-mastery that made him accountable to no one. At the same time, he also played the role of the authorizing master, as reflected in a number of EFP practices. Chief among these was Lacan's 'Proposal of October 9, 1967,' which ended unregulated self-authorization and instituted the controversial practice known as 'the Pass' ('*le passe*'), a procedure that elevated those who underwent it to the status of officially-certified analysts. A kind of lip service was still paid to self-authorization, since 'the Pass' could only begin when the aspiring analyst identified themselves as being 'ready' to two 'passers,' who then referred the case to a jury, but in reality it was Lacan who always had the final say. A similar inconsistency can be seen in the practice of the EFP's main publication, *Scilicet*, of publishing all its articles anonymously—except those written by Lacan.

In her biography of Lacan, Roudinesco quotes at length from a revealing letter written in January 1965 by Perrier that highlights, early on in the EFP's existence, the problems of Lacan's contradictory role:

> You are in the process of destroying what you claim to found, [...] whether it be a school or a treaty of trust with your friends. [...] You think you're putting societies of analysts and their 'structure' on trial, but in fact you're only bringing out the fact that your own relationship to any collegiate body is that of a loner, one who excludes himself voluntarily and rejects all groups. [...] And so you always divide but never rule. [...] What we expect of you is serene authority based on a theory already largely worked out, not reckless skirmishes that might be the work of ex-guerrillas turned desperadoes. (Perrier in Roudinesco 1997, p. 318)

The skirmishes and rebellions against Lacan's authority would continue over the coming years. In 1967, for instance, Lacan's former pupil Didier Anzieu denounced him in an article pointedly titled 'Against Lacan,' while in 1968 the aforementioned 'Fourth Group' schism occurred. Lacan then fell out with Félix Guattari, formerly one of his closest followers, who went on to co-author *Anti-Oedipus* with Gilles Deleuze, a scathing critique of psychoanalysis's abuses of power. Even the faithful Serge Leclaire expressed his doubts about the direction of Lacan's teachings in the 1970s, once describing the mathemes as little more than 'graffiti' (Leclaire in Turkle 1992, p. 182).

Lacan's position as *Maître* of the EFP placed him in a problematic state of exception, the result being that, while in his teachings he engaged in an incisive critique of mastery, in his professional life he effectively played the part of a tyrant. '[T]he EFP, a republic made up of elites and directed by a master who gave all his disciples equal rights but never renounced a jot of his own power, was a very fragile edifice,' observes Roudinesco. 'At once the school of a mass ideology and of resistance to mass ideology, it had a life as brief and doomed as a tragedy' (Roudinesco 1997, p. 317). Lacan nonetheless gained some important theoretical insights into the nature of power and mastery from these institutional skirmishes. Such practical issues are reflected in the content of his seminars, which move from a critique of analytical authority in the 'subject who is supposed to know' from *Seminar XI*, to the development of the 'four discourses' in *Seminar XVII*, and culminate with the self-authorizing notion of the 'sinthome' in *Seminar XXIII*. In order to achieve this critique, Lacan has to break with Alexandre Kojève's reading of Hegel's master/slave dialectic in *Introduction to the Reading of Hegel* (1947), the original model in Lacan's work for the theorization of mastery. The central question of my book concerns Lacan's success in resolving this philosophical problem. Was Lacan simply another master—and Lacanism simply another master discourse—that draws its authority, as his most strident detractors would have it, from a group of deluded followers who were tricked into believing him to be a 'subject who is supposed to know'? Is Lacan a charlatan in this entirely negative sense, or is there a larger purpose to his charlatanism, a greater lesson in which charlatanry plays an essential part in solving the double bind of dialectical mastery?

The Work of Critical Sacrilege

Lacan's ambivalent attitude toward his own mastery, which pits his practical desire to perpetuate the psychoanalytic discourse against his critique of authority, is a recurrent theme in his seminars, up to and including the dissolution of the EFP in 1980. Indeed, when reading the documents relating to the dissolution, it is hard not to feel that Lacan's critique of authority is what eventually led him to shut down his school. In 'The Other is Missing,' for instance, a text published ten days after the dissolution, Lacan writes:

> I have no more School. [...] Now I have a pile—a pile of people who want me to take them. I am not going to make a totality out of them. No whole. I don't need many, I said, and it's true—but of what use is it to say so, if there are many who need me? At least who believe it (that they need me). Who believe it enough to tell me so in writing. And why shouldn't I myself believe it too? Since I count myself among the number of dupes, as everyone knows. (Lacan 1990, p. 133)

This melancholy document shows Lacan still trapped between the two untenable modes of mastery. Yet throughout his long career Lacan repeatedly challenges his audiences not to take his teachings on authority. 'I'm not going to try to convince people who want nothing to do with me,' he says in *Seminar XX*. 'One must not convince (*convaincre*). What is proper to psychoanalysis is not to vanquish (*vaincre*), regardless of whether people are assholes (*con*) or not' (Lacan 1999, p. 53). Or consider the opening of *Television*, on the first page of which this crucial sentence is inscribed: 'He who interrogates me also knows how to read me' (Lacan 1990, p. 1). Lacan always demands that his audiences be actively critical of his ideas.

Following through on such a demand is another thing altogether, however, since a critical mindset can easily fall prey to so many things: economic pressures, institutional politics, the behavior of disciples, the egoism of the *Maître*, and so on. That is what prompts Oliver Harris, in *Lacan's Return to Antiquity* (2017), to highlight the compromises that can occur in the gap between theory and practice.

> Cherish the impasses, Lacan suggests. Beware answers. This, of course, is difficult when teaching relates to a body of knowledge like psychoanalysis, with institutions, examinations, qualifications, dictionaries, conferences, associations. This is where the style of the seminar comes in: always promising, never handing over anything predigested. (Harris 2017, p. 32) In *The Lives and Legends of Jacques Lacan* (1981), Catherine Clément argues that the responsibility for the integrity of a thinker's legacy comes from neither master nor disciple, but instead lies in the authority of the work itself.

> A thinker cannot be put to death. He survives his idolators. Not because he is the master and they are the disciples—no, not that. What could possibly be more deadly than all those disciples dedicated to immortalizing Lacan, who repeatedly told them that he was not their master and wanted no part of their adoration? A thinker cannot be put to death if he has really done his job of thinking. No matter how his life comes to an end, whether by old age, accident, suicide, madness, or crime, his thought will have lived and will go on living. In spite of his disciples, in spite of itself. (Clément 1983, p. 2)

The spirit in which Clément aims to conduct her investigation of Lacan—on the same page she reveals that her 'intention was to write a sacrilegious work' (Clément 1983, p. 2)—is close to my own. 'In the end we forgot Lacan's thought and thought Lacan,' she points out. 'This is how a dogma is born' (Clément 1983, p. 13). My book, similarly, aims to be a 'sacrilegious' work, not only in its investigation of Lacan's possible charlatanry, but also in its rigorous evaluation of the arguments of his most vocal critics.

Although film studies and literary theory were two of the main avenues by which Lacan entered into academic discourse, many of the most important commentators on his work in the 1970s and 1980s were feminist theorists: Luce Irigaray, Julia Kristeva, Juliet Mitchell, Teresa de Lauretis, Nancy Chodorow, Jane Gallop, and Elizabeth Grosz, to name but a few. In the second chapter of *Jacques Lacan and Feminist Epistemology* (2004), Kirsten Campbell provides a helpful historical overview of the conflicting opinions about Lacan in second-wave feminism, which found itself torn between the patriarchal assumptions of psychoanalysis and the revolutionary potential that many critics saw in Lacan's revisions of the Freudian tradition. 'These mutual narratives of the difficulties of feminism/psychoanalysis continue to haunt contemporary feminist and Lacanian movements,' observes Campbell (Campbell 2004, p. 25). Grosz's *Jacques Lacan: A Feminist Introduction* is particularly attuned to the importance of regarding Lacanian theory as a critical tool, so long as its limitations are carefully moderated by a feminist mindset. Grosz explains her methodology with typical precision:

> To preserve what is of insight or strategic use in his work, while maintaining a critical distance from what is problematic would be the aim of a deconstructive reading of Lacan. At the same time, such a reading would need to show, not how separable and delimitable the problems and insights are, but rather, how the insights are necessarily dependent on what is problematic. In other words, such a reading would need to show how psychoanalysis both participates in and departs from phallo(logo)centrism in ways that are not clearly distinguished. Feminist critiques need to occupy its internal 'intellectual space' but always from a perspective outside its parameters. What I am suggesting is the cultivation of a critical ambivalence, a simultaneous love and distance, a paradoxical inhabiting yet living outside of its precepts. (Grosz 1990, p. 190)

Grosz warns in particular against the danger of the feminist critic becoming a 'dutiful daughter'—the reference is to Simone de Beauvoir's autobiography *Memoirs of a Dutiful Daughter* (1958)—by learning how to use Lacan and psychoanalysis without succumbing to the authority of the symbolic Father, a lesson that informs my own work.

Another critic who has influenced my methodology is Jane Gallop, whose groundbreaking writing on Lacan is made all the more extraordinary by the relative paucity of primary sources, in both French and English, that were available at the time she was writing. In *Feminism and Psychoanalysis: The Daughter's Seduction* (1982), Gallop simultaneously praises and criticizes Juliet Mitchell's *Psychoanalysis and Feminism* (1974), a work that was instrumental in making psychoanalysis a central discourse in feminist theory. Reflecting on the differences between French and American feminism, Gallop emphasizes the importance of using psychoanalysis as a critical tool in the service of feminism, a process in which Lacan's discourse must be deployed in an 'unauthorized' way. 'What is this feminist practice of unauthorization?' she asks. 'The authorized partakes of the legal and the name. The authorized, legitimate thought bears the author's name: the unauthorized, the illegitimate lacks the Name-of-the-Father' (Gallop 1982, p. 47). The Lacanian concept of the Name-of-the-Father that Gallop speaks of here, also sometimes called the 'master signifier' in his theory, refers to the second mode of mastery outlined above. To speak with authority, for Lacan, is to direct the basis of power for your words outside the subject—to speak with authority means to speak *in the name of* someone else—and because in the Freudian metaphor of the Oedipus complex the law is associated with the father, Lacan combines these two terms into the Name-of-the-Father:

> Infidelity then is a feminist practice of undermining the Name-of-the-Father. The unfaithful reading strays from the author, the authorized, produces that which does not hold as a reproduction, as a representation. Infidelity is *not* outside the system of marriage, the symbolic, patriarchy, but hollows it out, ruins it, from within. Unlike such infidelity, a new system, a feminist system, one constant, faithful to the tenets and dogmas of feminism would be but another Name-of-the-Father, feminism as a position and a possession. (Gallop 1982, p. 48)

In this passage Gallop brilliantly captures the danger that shadows every act of critique, resistance, revolution: while opposing the authority of the Name-of-the-Father is important, there is an imminent risk that a revolutionary discourse, such as feminism, will undermine its own critical position by becoming a new discourse of authority and mastery.

In her next book *Reading Lacan* (1985), Gallop turns her attention from writing directly about feminism to provide some genuinely innovative readings of selections from Lacan's *Écrits*. Nonetheless, as she reminds the reader in her introduction, her interest in Lacan is rooted in his ability to call 'into question the phallic illusions of authority,' a 'project [that] is profoundly feminist' (Gallop 1985, p. 20). Central to this mode of critique is Lacan's concept of the 'subject who is supposed to know' from *Seminar XI*:

> What does it mean to invoke authority in order to legitimate an attack on authority? This ambiguity, I believe, is what promises the most. To speak without authority is nothing new; the disenfranchised have always so spoken. Simply to refuse authority does not challenge the category distinction between phallic authority and castrated other, between 'subject presumed to know' and subject not in command. One can effectively undo authority only from the position of authority, in a way that exposes the illusions of that position *without renouncing it*, so as to permeate the position itself with the connotations of its illusoriness, so as to show that *everyone*, including the 'subject presumed to know,' is castrated. (Gallop 1985, p. 21)

Gallop touches here on what is also a core concern of my own book, which is that the key to Lacan's critique of authority lies in recognizing the misstep of simply renouncing authority. As Gallop points out, even though such a move may create the impression of a moral high ground, it does nothing to challenge the actual paradigm of mastery. The alternative strategy that Gallop recognizes in Lacan's discourse is to understand the extent to which he is *performing* the role of the master. Many times Lacan takes on the appearance of a charlatan, not for the sake of tricking his disciples, but in order to reveal that the power of the symbolic order is an illusion. Such a reading is, of course, deeply 'sacrilegious' for the way it undermines the authority of the *Maître*. 'To give a reading of Lacan that is faithful to this ethic means that the reading must not always side "with" Lacan, that it must be suspicious of the imaginary (egotistical or adversarial) dimension of his work,' argues Gallop (Gallop 1985, p. 60). For this reason, I reject the idea of my work being labeled as 'Lacanian': like Gallop's, my reading resists both the name and the authority attached to it.

One other critical reflection on Lacan worth noting comes from the eminent British scholar Malcolm Bowie that, while hardly 'sacrilege,' points in a similar critical direction to Gallop's. There is an interview with Bowie, conducted by Michael Payne and Harold Schweizer, which appears at the end of *Psychoanalysis and the Future of Theory* (1993), a book that reproduces Bowie's contributions to the Bucknell Lectures in

Literary Theory series. In that interview, Payne notes how, in 'a significant departure,' Bowie's recent work has become more critical of Lacan's 'theoretical and stylistic excesses,' and as such he asks Bowie whether this latest direction is 'a continuation of his [Lacan's] correcting of Freud from within' or if it is operating 'from a position outside Lacanian theory' (Bowie 1993, p. 141). Bowie replies by condemning the dogmatism that has become pervasive in Lacanian circles:

> I have great difficulty with the status of disciple and with the state of mind of discipleship. So much so that I find certain Lacanian enthusiasts and loyalists difficult to engage with. It seems to me that they're creating out of his works an impossible coherence, a grand system, that is then beamed with menaces at other people who may be hesitating on the threshold. Or they bring a workaday dogmatism, born of this intimacy with the System, to a whole range of non-clinical questions. It's not that I'm setting myself up as occupying any kind of morally superior position: it's just that loyalty of that kind makes me uncomfortable. There are, of course, powerful systematic elements in Lacan's thinking, and these should be got right. (Bowie 1993, p. 141)

Bowie is rightly suspicious of the seriousness of Lacan's disciples, a gravity that tends to harden into dogmatism. For while Lacan is indeed a serious thinker, to regard him only in this light is to overlook the humorous, even satirical elements of his performance. That is why Bowie is correct to point out, as part of his response to Payne's question, how important it is to appreciate the ironic aspects of Lacan's rhetoric. 'Being ironic about Lacan is, I think, a Lacanian thing to be, although it may be, as one twists and turns with him, that one finds oneself rejecting quite large swathes of his output,' says Bowie. 'So all I'm saying here is that there's a way of being loyal to Lacan that has to do with adhering to his mobility of mind and to his powers as an ironist, rather than to the dogma that he also sometimes offers' (Bowie 1993, p. 142). Lacan's irony is what makes his performance of mastery so ambiguous, since we can never distinguish whether he is speaking with the voice of authority, of the *Maître*, or whether he is playing the critical role of the charlatan, one who is merely bluffing about being the 'subject who is supposed to know.' It is this ingredient that holds the potential antidote to the critical limitations of the master's authority for, as Bowie contends, irony is a crucial weapon in countering dogma and orthodoxy.

Lacan's Accusers

For the seventeenth year of his seminar, Lacan chose the title '*L'envers de la psychanalyse*,' translated by Russell Grigg into English as *The Other Side of Psychoanalysis*, but it also has other nuances such as 'psychoanalysis turned inside-out' or 'psychoanalysis reversed.' The aim of this book is to take a similar approach: rather than restricting myself to what Lacan and his commentators have written, I also want to view these theories from the other side (*à l'envers*) by regarding them from the perspective of a select group of critics who have published arguments *against* the validity of Lacan's theories. These authors are of interest because of how the issue of authority (both Lacan's and their own) is central to the ways in which their critiques succeed and fail. Although the quality of the arguments put forward by Lacan's detractors is sometimes uneven, I think it is important to treat each one on its merits, in a way that avoids the kind of partisan bickering that has blighted the history of psychoanalysis. If this history has taught us anything, after all, it is that the most revealing and important figures for the critical integrity of a discourse are often its enemies and detractors, people who are unafraid to confront important and difficult truths in what they have to say.

Accordingly, I have arranged each of the subsequent chapters of the book around the figure of one of Lacan's accusers and the aspect in which he is charged with being a charlatan. Chapter 2: 'Lacan the Linguistic Charlatan,' for instance, examines the work of the British physician Raymond Tallis, a specialist in geriatric medicine who has regularly stepped outside of his specialty in order to write about science and the humanities. A vehement critic of postmodern theory, Tallis chiefly criticizes Lacan's theory of language and its relationship to reality, along with a scathing assessment of the 'mirror stage,' in his book *Not Saussure: A Critique of Post-Saussurean Literary Theory* (1988). Chapter 3: 'Lacan the Mathematical Charlatan' looks at Alan Sokal and Jean Bricmont's book

Fashionable Nonsense (1998) (first published in French in 1997 as *Impostures Intellectuelles*), which looks at various examples of French theorists misusing scientific and mathematical concepts in their work, with Lacan singled out in the first chapter. I will consider their arguments in light of the heated debate of the place of mathemes and formalization in Lacanian theory. Chapter 4: 'Lacan the Scientific Charlatan' focuses on the case of Dylan Evans, a former Lacanian who renounced psychoanalysis in favor of evolutionary psychology. This chapter will examine Evans's rejection of Lacan in order to understand why he came to privilege scientific and technocratic authority over other forms. Chapter 5: 'Lacan the Ethical Charlatan' looks at another former Lacanian, Stuart Schneiderman, who gave up psychoanalysis to become a 'life coach.' In *The Last Psychoanalyst* (2014), Schneiderman accuses Freud of creating psychoanalysis as a decadent social philosophy that uses sexual immorality to seduce patients into surrendering control of their lives, a cause he claims Lacan also championed. Chapter 6: 'Lacan the Absolute Charlatan' outlines the critique of psychoanalysis presented by Mikkel Borch-Jacobsen, a professor of French and Comparative Literature at the University of Washington and a key contributor to *Le livre noir de la psychanalyse*. Borch-Jacobsen's book *Lacan: The Absolute Master* (1991) argues that Lacan, far from being a master in his own right, is actually an unwitting puppet of his true masters: Alexandre Kojève, Martin Heidegger, and Claude Lévi-Strauss. Chapter 7: 'Lacan the Master Charlatan' closes the book by building on the work of François Roustang, a key member of the EFP who disavowed Lacanian psychoanalysis a few years after the school's dissolution. In *Dire Mastery* (1976), Roustang points out the built-in paradox of psychoanalysis: analytic practice creates transference in order to work through unconscious problems and bring about a cure that ultimately results in the dissolution of transference, whereas the institution of psychoanalysis, through the figure of the *Maître*, also generates a kind of transference, one that it sustains and exploits for the sake of maintaining psychoanalysis as a discourse. The common thread that connects these various detractors is the ambiguous question of Lacan's authority, of the extent to which he is to be considered a charlatan rather than a master, and the consequences that such fraudulence entails.

References

Borch-Jacobsen, M., 2005. A Zero Theory. *Butterflies and Wheels*, 5 November, p. np.

Borch-Jacobsen, M. & Shamdasani, S., 2012. *The Freud Files: An Inquiry Into the History of Psychoanalysis*. Cambridge(MA): Cambridge University Press.

Bougnoux, D., 1997. Lacan, Sure – And Then What?. In: T. Dufresne, ed. *Returns of the 'French Freud': Freud, Lacan, and Beyond*. New York and London: Routledge, pp. 91–106.

Bowie, M., 1993. *Psychoanalysis and the Future of Theory*. Oxford: Blackwell.

Campbell, K., 2004. *Jacques Lacan and Feminist Epistemology*. London and New York: Routledge.

Chomsky, N., 1989. An Interview. *Radical Philosophy*, Volume 53, pp. 31–40.

Chomsky, N., 2000. *The Architecture of Language*. New Delhi: Oxford University Press.

Clément, C., 1983. *The Lives and Legends of Jacques Lacan*. New York: Columbia University Press.

Crews, F., 2017. *Freud: The Making of an Illusion*. New York: Metropolitan Books.

David-Menard, M., 1982. Lacanians Against Lacan. *Social Text*, Volume 6, pp. 86–111.

Dufresne, T., 1997. Beyond the French Freud. In: T. Dufresne, ed. *Returns of the 'French Freud': Freud, Lacan, and Beyond*. New York and London: Routledge, pp. 1–10.

Dufresne, T., 2003. *Killing Freud: Twentieth Century Culture and the Death of Psychoanalysis*. London and New York: Continuum.

Dufresne, T., 2014. The Making of a 'Freud Basher,' or Reflections of a 'Supercilious Neurotic…'. *The European Legacy: Toward New Paradigms*, 19(1), pp. 72–82.

Felman, S., 1987. *Jacques Lacan and the Adventures of Insight: Psychoanalysis in Contemporary Culture*. Cambridge(MA): Harvard University Press.

Forrester, J., 1991. *The Seductions of Psychoanalysis: Freud, Lacan and Derrida*. Cambridge(MA): Cambridge University Press.

Gallop, J., 1982. *Feminism and Psychoanalysis: The Daughter's Seduction*. Basingstoke and London: Macmillan.

Gallop, J., 1985. *Reading Lacan*. Ithaca(NY) and London: Cornell University Press.

George, F., 1979. *L'Effet 'Yau de poêle: De Lacan et des lacaniens*. Paris: Hachette.

Glynos, J., 2002. Theory and Evidence in the Freudian Field: From Observation to Structure. In: J. Glynos & Y. Stavrakakis, eds. *Lacan and Science*. London and New York: Karnac, pp. 13–50.
Grosz, E., 1990. *Jacques Lacan: A Feminist Introduction*. London and New York: Routledge.
Harris, O., 2017. *Lacan's Return to Antiquity: Between Nature and the Gods*. London and New York: Routledge.
Lacan, J., 1990. *Television: A Challenge to the Psychoanalytic Establishment*. New York and London: W.W. Norton & Company.
Lacan, J., 1994. *The Four Fundamental Concepts of Psycho-Analysis*. Harmondsworth: Penguin.
Lacan, J., 1999. *The Seminar of Jacques Lacan, Book XX: Encore: On Feminine Sexuality, The Limits of Love and Knowledge, 1972–1973*. New York and London: W.W. Norton & Company.
Lacan, J., 2006. *Écrits: The First Complete Edition in English*. New York and London: W.W. Norton & Company.
Macey, D., 1988. *Lacan in Contexts*. London and New York: Verso.
Marini, M., 1992. *Jacques Lacan: The French Context*. New Brunswick(NJ): Rutgers University Press.
Nobus, D., 2018. Preface. In: D. Nobus, ed. *Key Concepts of Lacanian Psychoanalysis*. New York: Routledge, pp. v–viii.
Rabaté, J.-M., 2003. Lacan's Turn to Freud. In: J. Rabaté, ed. *The Cambridge Companion to Lacan*. Cambridge(MA): Cambridge University Press, pp. 1–24.
Rapaport, H., 2016. Transference Love in the Age of 'Isms'. In: S. M. Wortham & C. Alfano, eds. *Desire in Ashes: Deconstruction, Psychoanalysis, Philosophy*. London: Bloomsbury, pp. 73–92.
Roudinesco, É., 1997. *Jacques Lacan: Outline of a Life, History of a System of Thought*. New York: Columbia University Press.
Roudinesco, É., 2014. *Lacan: In Spite of Everything*. London and Brooklyn: Verso.
Scruton, R., 2015. *Fools, Frauds and Firebrands: Thinkers of the New Left*. London: Bloomsbury Continuum.
Timpanaro, S., 2011. *The Freudian Slip: Psychoanalysis and Textual Criticism*. New York: Verso.
Turkle, S., 1992. *Psychoanalytic Politics: Jacques Lacan and Freud's French Revolution*. 2nd ed. New York and London: The Guilford Press.

2

Lacan the Linguistic Charlatan

Linguistic Idealism

In the preface to his book *Theorrhoea and After* (1999), Raymond Tallis reflects on the reception of two books he published in 1988, *Not Saussure* and *In Defence of Realism*, the first being a critique of the contemporary trend for theories of literature grounded in structural linguistics, the second a denunciation of the move away from literary realism that Tallis sees as the result of these new theories. His two earlier books, he complains, were treated unjustly because they went against the hegemony of post-Saussurean theory dominating the humanities. Without offering any evidence of this mistreatment, he contends that the 'Young Turks' who led this revolution are 'now Old Profs and they occupy commanding positions in the republic of academic letters' (Tallis 1999, p. x). Corrupted by these 'vested interests,' Tallis goes on, the new establishment is willfully blind to the 'truth' that he has revealed about the shortcomings of post-Saussurean theory (Tallis 1999, p. xi). He claims that the bitter realities he describes cannot compete with the opium of counterfeit subversion offered by the proponents of literary theory, false prophets who have been

P. D. Mathews, *Lacan the Charlatan*, The Palgrave Lacan Series,
https://doi.org/10.1007/978-3-030-45204-9_2

inspired by charlatans like Derrida and Lacan, the two thinkers he singles out as the worst purveyors of post-Saussurean theory.

Tallis's wounded narrative of persecution is characterized by two dominant rhetorical features. The first is the sheer arrogance of his style of argument, which displays none of the humility that accompanies critical inquiry and investigation, but instead proceeds from the absolute conviction that he is always right. In the second chapter of *Theorrhoea and After*, for instance, he expresses his amazement that *Not Saussure* and *In Defence of Realism*, far from revolutionizing the field, more or less disappeared without a trace:

> The expectations I had when I wrote those books seem in retrospect to have been over-optimistic. I confidently anticipated that the purveyors of post-Saussurean 'theory' would be stopped in their tracks. After all, I thought I had demonstrated [...] beyond doubt [...] [that] the most important ideas of post-Saussurean theory are mistaken[.] [...] I expected a scandal to result and the post-Saussureans to die of shame or to apply for retraining as useful citizens. I was astonished when the arguments of both books were largely ignored and it was business as usual. (Tallis 1999, p. 29)

As this quotation demonstrates, Tallis's style is adversarial and condescending, notable for the way he looks down on his intellectual opponents as little more than academic parasites who, in language borrowed from oppressive, authoritarian regimes, ought to be retrained as 'useful citizens.'

The second dominant feature of Tallis's style of argument, one that grows out of his arrogant tone, is its blatant rudeness. His disrespect manifests itself in numerous petty insults and acts of dismissal against ideas and critics that he considers beneath his contempt. These tactics are already present, in slightly milder form, in his earlier books: in *Not Saussure*, for instance, he argues that the rise of post-Saussurean theories 'in the Groves of Hackademe' has contributed to the rise of a 'talentless anti-realism' in the field of serious fiction (Tallis 1988b, p. 1). A few years later, these insults have become the basis of a confrontational style that is remarkable for its vulgarity and disdain. Consider the term 'theorrhoea' that appears in the title of Tallis's 1999 book, a portmanteau word that combines 'theory' with the British spelling of 'diarrhea'—such is the level of childish ridicule that characterizes Tallis's prose. In a similar manner, Tallis has a habit of giving contemptuous epithets to thinkers with whom he disagrees: Terry Eagleton, for instance, is referred to as 'the most accomplished ram-raider in the shopping mall of ideas, the ultimate Critic of Bray' (Tallis 1999, p. xii), Derrida is sarcastically dubbed 'the High Priest of Theory' (Tallis 1999, p. vi), and Lacan is described as an 'old charlatan' who became 'increasingly reminiscent of L. Ron Hubbard,' with Tallis eventually settling on the hilarious nickname 'Jacques Zen Hubbard' (Tallis 1999, pp. 79–81). His 1997 review in *The Times Higher Education Supplement* of Roudinesco's biography of Lacan, titled 'The Shrink From Hell,' is a mixture of hostility and cynicism, devoid of any intellectual engagement with Lacan's ideas, and bristling with personal attacks. Tallis writes in the conclusion to that piece:

> Lacanians may argue that the great edifice of the *Écrits* is not undermined by revelations about his life. The Master's thoughts should be judged on their own merits. However, in the absence of any logical basis or empirical evidence, the authority of the thought has derived almost completely from the authority of the man. The discovery that Lacan was the shrink from hell is not, therefore, irrelevant. Roudinesco's biography is consequently an act of liberation on behalf of those students, forced by uncritical teachers who do not know Stork from butter, to try to understand and make sense of his nonsense. This act of liberation is all the more compelling for being the work of a disciple and thus in part involuntary. (Tallis 1997, p. 20)

This paragraph exemplifies Tallis's strategy of dismissing Lacan's authority by attacking his character, highlighting personal shortcomings that, by some mutation of logic, also invalidate his theoretical ideas. Not only does this tactic constitute the most blatant form of *ad hominem* argument, it also blends together a mixture of cynicism (the concluding slander that Roudinesco, as a disciple, can only 'involuntarily' speak the truth about Lacan's flaws, as though she has no intellectual integrity or agency of her own) and appeals to authority. Tallis thus enacts that most perverse of paternal prohibitions, in which it is decreed not only that one *cannot* find anything of value in Lacan's work, but also that one *must* not.

Despite the arrogance and lack of professional courtesy that Tallis displays in his public writings, it is important not to allow these shortcomings to obscure the genuine concerns he raises in the course of his work. Tallis's main skirmish with Lacan occurs in *Not Saussure*, a critique that is framed by that book's larger engagement with post-Saussurean literary theory. As his arguments in favor of literary realism reveal, this distaste extends not just to theory, but to experimental writing in general, especially the French modernist tradition that begins with Stéphane Mallarmé. It was Mallarmé, argues Tallis, who directed attention away from the psychology of the author toward the structure of language, a move that opened the door to psychoanalysis and the surrealists—and thus to Lacan. Lacan, after all, was a close associate of the surrealists, publishing several pieces in their journal *Minotaure* during the 1930s. Tallis thus correctly traces Lacan's lifelong interest in language and its effects to the influence of the surrealist movement:

> Surrealism—or at least the Surrealist project of subverting ordinary consciousness and the order of everyday life by yielding to the genius of language—was an important intermediate step between Mallarméan and structuralist poetics. […] The most explicit connection between the Surrealist preoccupation with the unconscious and systematic linguistics was in the work of Lacan who also revelled, like the Surrealists, in mischief and abuse. (Tallis 1988b, pp. 6–7)

Although Tallis gets this first step in Lacan's interest in theories of language right, he appears to be ignorant of other important influences (apart from Saussure) on the development of Lacan's work, a crucial lacuna that shall be addressed in the course of this chapter.

The central thesis of *Not Saussure* concerns an important question about the relationship between language and reality. In contrast to the tradition of literary realism, in which authors wrote about the world from the perspective of lived experience, Tallis argues that the rise of post-Saussurean literary theory has created an artificial separation between language and reality. By arguing that language is not referential, that the signifier does not point to anything in reality but only ever refers to another signifier, with language never touching anything but itself, Tallis argues that post-Saussurean theory constitutes a kind of linguistic idealism:

> The thesis that literature is a closed system thus expands until it changes imperceptibly into the thesis that language is a closed system—so that it does not refer even in ordinary daily life to an extra-linguistic reality. This in turn shades into the position that there is no extra-linguistic reality. Consciousness, reality and society become conterminous with language. The constraints of genre reflect the prison-house of language which in turn constrains consciousness. Consciousness, the world, reality, society become a single closed system. At its limit, where there is nothing but language [...] intertextualism becomes a linguistic version of neo-Kantian idealism. (Tallis 1988b, p. 48)

Tallis is referring here to Kant's separation between noumena and phenomena, the idea that reality (noumena) is functionally inaccessible to human experience because we only ever have access to limited perceptions of that reality (phenomena) rather than reality itself. Whereas neo-Kantian idealism regards humans as trapped in the bubble of their own perceptual apparatus, Tallis charges post-Saussurean theorists with having built a 'prison-house of language' (the allusion is to Fredric Jameson's *The Prison-House of Language* [1972]), an endless labyrinth of signifiers that forever shuts humanity off from reality.

In *Not Saussure*, therefore, Tallis puts forward some genuinely probing questions about the linguistic idealism on which post-Saussurean literary theory, if his reading is correct, seems to be based. What is more, Tallis argues that such theories are constructed not only on a basic philosophical error about the inaccessibility of reality, but also on a misinterpretation of Saussure. 'The most powerful arguments in favour of the idea that natural languages are closed systems—so that they can only apparently be used to make true (or false) referential statements about extra-linguistic reality—originate from popular misreadings of Saussure,' he contends (Tallis 1988b, p. 66). Tallis's position is that even though 'much of what Saussure says in his *Course in General Linguistics is* hypothetical rather than empirically proven,' many contemporary theorists have blindly taken those hypotheses as proven facts (Tallis 1988b, p. 66). Tallis's biggest criticism, however, concerns the 'most revolutionary aspect of Saussure's theory—and the one that has generated the most misinterpretation—[which] is the denial of the pre-linguistic reality of the signified' (Tallis 1988b, p. 67). Despite the supposed prevalence of this kind of error, Tallis does not provide examples from Lacan or any of the other post-Saussurean thinkers he discusses to prove his point.

Indeed, Tallis dedicates a whole section of *Not Saussure* to a dismissal of Lacan's theory of the 'mirror stage,' but a closer inspection reveals that his overall rejection is based on an extraordinarily thin array of sources. Apart from the essay on the 'mirror stage,' the only other references to Lacan in Tallis's books are two brief allusions to the 'Seminar on "The Purloined Letter,"' together with a single repeated quotation from 'The Function and Field of Speech and Language in Psychoanalysis' (often referred to as the 'Rome Discourse,' so named after the city where Lacan first delivered it). The quotation from that essay runs as follows—'the world of words creates the world of things'—and constitutes the centerpiece of Tallis's charge of Lacan's linguistic idealism (Tallis 1988b, p. 51). At no point does Tallis attempt to locate this quotation in the larger context of the text from which it is taken, even though this seminal paper occupies some eighty-six pages in the original French edition of *Écrits*. As such, a mere handful of words, stripped of all context, is deemed a sufficient basis for Tallis to dismiss the entire body of Lacan's work as a naïve and insidious form of linguistic idealism. Even if Lacan's appropriation of Saussure really is a wrong step, such a slim textual foundation is hardly the stuff of scholarly rigor.

The Place of Saussure

Another problem with Tallis's arguments is that there are numerous passages in Lacan's work where he explicitly rejects idealism in any form, linguistic or otherwise. In *Seminar V*, for instance, Lacan says that 'not everything is reducible to language. I have always said so, of course, but I haven't been heard' (Lacan 2017, p. 362). In the first and only session Lacan delivered of his abandoned seminar on the Names-of-the-Father, he laments how people frequently misunderstand the consequences of his teaching. After listening to Lacan's ideas, for instance, one of his more naïve students came to the erroneous conclusion that truth is inherently inaccessible:

> In one of those confused debates in the course of which the group—our group—has shown itself truly, in its function as a group, buffeted about by blind whirlwinds, one of my students [...] thought he should say that the meaning of my teaching was that the true hold (*prise*) of the truth is that one can never grab hold of it. What an incredible misunderstanding! At best, what childish impatience! (Lacan 2013, p. 89)

As for the charge of philosophical idealism, Lacan states in no uncertain terms where he stands on this issue. 'Idealism asserts that what is involved is *que de pensées*, nothing but thoughts' he says in *Seminar XIX*. 'It is in this respect that I include myself in the class of realists' (Lacan 2018, pp. 97–98). As these quotations demonstrate, the phrase 'the world of words creates the world of things' hardly constitutes the full scope and variety of Lacan's thought, and to present it as such is at best ignorant, and at worst dishonest.

Although these quotations show that Lacan's work transcends the idealist limits that Tallis attributes to him, their larger significance in the development of Lacan's ideas still needs to be clarified. In his insightful essay on the 'mirror stage,' Nobus rightly insists that 'reconstructing and examining the historical context of Lacan's works is essential in order to understand some of the allusions they contain, and provides an excellent framework to grasp the meaning and the importance of his wording' (Nobus 2018, p. 102). Lacan's career, after all, spans more than fifty decades of writing and teaching, including thirty years of a public seminar that functioned as an intellectual laboratory in which Lacan honed and refined his ideas so extensively that, as with Marx or Freud, it is necessary to acknowledge its different phases rather than treat it as a consistent whole. By considering Lacan's work in the context of its development, we can avoid such glaring chronological errors as Tallis's railing against Lacan's use of Saussure, and then making the paper on the 'mirror stage,' a work that predates Lacan's engagement with structural linguistics and does not mention Saussure even once, the centerpiece of his critique.

Different narratives of the importance of Saussure and structural linguistics on Lacan's intellectual development have emerged among his commentators. Roudinesco, for instance, argues that Lacan came across Saussure relatively early in his career. She claims that his initial discovery of Saussure occurred in 1931 while working on a case involving a young woman named Marcelle, who had delusions that she was Joan of Arc. Lacan and his two collaborators on this case focused their report, in particular, on linguistic anomalies that resulted from Marcelle's psychosis. As such, they cite the work of Henri Delacroix who, Roudinesco contends, was the first to bring Saussure to Lacan's attention:

> But the most interesting reference is to a work by Delacroix published in 1930, because it is a valuable indication of what the young Lacan was reading at this period. In support of his thinking on aphasia, Delacroix, who taught Sartre philosophy, drew on Ferdinand de Saussure's *Cours de linguistique générale* (*Course in General Linguistics*), published in Geneva in 1915. So there can no longer be any doubt about it: it was in this now forgotten writer that Lacan first came across Saussure's theory of language, of which he was to make such fruitful use two decades later. (Roudinesco 1997, p. 27)

This passage from Roudinesco's biography of Lacan is an implicit riposte to Macey's *Lacan in Contexts*, in which he criticizes a claim made in her earlier two-volume work *Jacques Lacan & Co.: A History of Psychoanalysis in France, 1925–1985* (1982–1986). 'According to Roudinesco,' writes Macey, 'Lacan began to read Saussure in about 1946, but whilst this seems probable, there is no direct textual evidence to support the suggestion' (Macey 1988, p. 129). Roudinesco's discovery of the Marcelle case thus 'wins' the argument as to when Lacan first encountered Saussure.

Yet the establishment of this initial date of 1931 is not of any great importance, as it turns out, for Saussure and structural linguistics had no significant impact on Lacan's work until much later in his career. In his introduction to *Reading Seminars I and II* (1996), Miller provides an insightful summary of the main influences on Lacan's thought up until 1953, the year of his first public seminar:

> In the *Écrits*, Lacan provides a clue as to his intellectual trajectory in saying that he considers that his work, the work associated with his name, began in 1952: what came before counted in his mind as his 'antecedents.' He doesn't thereby cancel out what came before, but stresses a cut in his own intellectual development that occurred around 1952–1953. The starting point of his teaching was 'Function and Field of Speech and Language in Psychoanalysis,' a paper written for a 1953 conference in Rome. (Miller 1996, p. 4)

Because the work that Lacan produces in the period immediately after this 'cut' is so well-known, it is easy to overlook the fact that 'up until 1953' he 'may be deemed an existentialist,' not a post-Saussurean Freudian (Miller 1996, p. 7). 'Nineteen fifty-three was not the year he abandoned existentialism/phenomenology for structuralism,' explains Miller, 'but rather the year he blended the two[.] […] Lacan's theory of speech at that time is, in a sense, existentialist and phenomenological, while his theory of language is structuralist' (Miller 1996, p. 7). This tension between phenomenology and structuralism in Lacan's work would become increasingly strained in subsequent years.

The initial idea of applying structuralist logic to fields beyond linguistics, a process that Lacan undertakes in works like 'The Instance of the Letter in the Unconscious, or Reason Since Freud' (1957) in order to create a groundbreaking new marriage of Saussurean linguistics and Freudian psychoanalysis, was a strategy borrowed from the anthropologist Claude Lévi-Strauss. Lacan's 'real initiation into Saussure's system and the principles of structural linguistics dates from his encounter with the works of Claude Lévi-Strauss,' writes Roudinesco. 'For Lacan, as for a whole generation of philosophers who would come into prominence in and around the fifties, the appearance in 1949 of Lévi-Strauss's *The Elementary Structures of Kinship* was a major event' (Roudinesco 1997, p. 206). Despite its apparent success, this marriage between linguistics and psychoanalysis would not prove to be an entirely comfortable combination. Anne Durand notes in her article 'Lacan and Lévi-Strauss,' for instance, that there is something troubling in Lévi-Strauss's influential essay 'The Effectiveness of Symbols' 'that attacks psychoanalysis' (Durand 1996, p. 104). This ambivalence arises from the fact that appropriating

Lévi-Strauss in this way casts the psychoanalyst as a practitioner of magic who offers a 'shaman's cure, an operation on an imaginary object using signifiers,' a problem that Lacan returns to in 'Science and Truth' (1965) 'where he brings up the problem of the efficiency of magic and *magical thinking*' (Durand 1996, p. 105). The figure of the shaman/analyst is deeply ambivalent because charlatanry is a necessary aspect of its always-fraudulent performance of mastery. Durand argues that Lévi-Strauss had been wrestling with a similar problem in his attempts to define the line between nature and culture:

> But the whole point is that a line cannot be drawn between nature and culture, as they are two imaginary agencies: they cannot be equated with the different levels of the real and the symbolic. It is the dynamic opposition between the real and the symbolic that Lacan designates, at the end of Seminar I, as the structuralism proper to Freud. The symbolic is the network of language thrown over the real. It does not give the subject any sure signifying prey or bond, except for the truth of castration that is the absence of all significations. (Durand 1996, p. 107)

Despite his debt to Lévi-Strauss, in other words, what Durand sees Lacan as resisting is the reduction of the world to a form of structuralist idealism. Lacan finds himself repeatedly caught in a tension between the powerful logic of linguistic idealism, on the one hand, and the exigency of a real that is grounded in the beyond of the pleasure principle, on the other. According to this reading, Tallis has it entirely the wrong way around: far from giving in to linguistic idealism, Lacan, as his thought develops, actively struggles against the illusions of the imaginary and symbolic in order to address the problem of the real.

While the bulk of the credit usually goes to Lévi-Strauss's influence for introducing Lacan to structuralism, the importance of another of his intellectual friends, the philosopher Maurice Merleau-Ponty, also deserves to be acknowledged here. Roudinesco, for instance, points out that although Lacan had already begun the process of connecting subjectivity and language, it was Merleau-Ponty who provided the chief inspiration for bringing together Freud and Saussure in a systematic way.

> In France, Merleau-Ponty was the first to declare, in his inaugural lecture at the Collège de France, that a philosophy could be derived from Saussure's *Course in General Linguistics* [...] Lacan had got the message. He had first linked together the subject, language, and speech in his 'Rome Discourse,' on the basis of Heidegger's philosophy and the elementary structures of kinship. Thereafter he set out, using a logical method and abandoning all ontology, to formulate a theory concerning the relationship between subject and signifier. The work was carried out gradually, over a period of time, and in a baroque and convoluted style. Lacan never traveled in a straight line. (Roudinesco 1997, p. 267)

Nonetheless, it is also Merleau-Ponty, claims James Phillips in 'Lacan and Merleau-Ponty,' who recognized the philosophical hazards inherent in such a move. 'Merleau-Ponty perceives in contemporary (i.e. Lacanian) psychoanalysis a triumph over crude Freudian biologism,' writes Phillips, 'but notes the danger, with the predominance of linguistics, of a veering in the opposite direction, toward a psychoanalytic idealism' (Phillips 1996, pp. 70–71). Far from being a blind advocate of linguistic idealism, Lacan finds himself repeatedly confronted by the philosophical dangers of this path, which increasingly lead him away from Saussure and structural linguistics rather than toward it, as Tallis wrongly assumes.

The history of Lacan's engagement with structural linguistics is not, therefore, a straightforward one, and this layering of different influences (Lévi-Strauss, Jakobson, Merleau-Ponty, Heidegger) causes Roudinesco to divide the initial period of his interest in Saussure (1949–1954) from a second period (1954–1961) when, 'for the first time, instead of merely referring to ideas of language, speech, or linguistics, Lacan commented on Saussure's theory of signs' (Roudinesco 1997, p. 268). Macey agrees with Roudinesco on this point, arguing that 'The Freudian Thing' (1955) is the moment when Lacan truly began to appropriate Saussure, a strategy rendered visible by the new and extravagant claim that the latter is the 'founder of modern linguistics' (Macey 1988, p. 130). The success of this phase of Lacan's work, Macey argues, created the false impression that his idiosyncratic version of Freudian linguistic structuralism is the centerpiece of his thought.

> Imaginary constructs typify many English-language presentations of Lacan, as a fundamental assumption of unity and systematicity transforms *Écrits* into a conceptually homogeneous text rather than a collection of papers written over a considerable period of time, with all the shifts and modifications that implies. Thus, the alleged importance of structural linguistics—as opposed to an interest in language—constructs Lacan into the child of Freud and Saussure. (Macey 1988, p. 13)

Macey dedicates a superb chapter of *Lacan in Contexts* to an assessment of the history of Lacan's dubious engagement with linguistics, from the 'surprisingly slow and hesitant' (Macey 1988, p. 130) appropriation of Saussure to another shift in the late 1960s when 'linguistics finally gives way to *linguisterie* as the charms of positive linguistics fade in the face of those of psychotic language' (Macey 1988, p. x). '*La linguisterie*,' a term introduced in *Seminar XX*, is linguistics performed by a charlatan, a series of word games that eschews the linguist's attempt to formalize language and instead explores its faults and slippages—Bruce Fink translates it as 'linguistricks' (Homer 2006, p. 69) to try and capture this nuance.

A finer historical sense of the development of Lacan's ideas highlights the narrowness and inadequacy of Tallis's choice of representative texts, all of which are drawn from a period of Lacan's work when he had not yet even begun his second, more influential engagement with Saussure. Indeed, Lacan's article on the 'mirror stage,' which Tallis boldly claims in *Not Saussure* can be 'regarded as the cornerstone of Lacan's *oeuvre*,' was first formulated in 1936 (this earlier version has since been lost) and reworked into its current form in 1949, both versions of which belong to a period that predates his engagement with structural linguistics (Tallis 1988b, p. 133). It is difficult to see how Lacan can be considered a 'post-Saussurean' theorist at a point in his career when he is yet even to engage properly with Saussure's ideas. Tallis thus falls for the common misconception that Macey identifies, in which the intense academic focus on Lacan's linguistic structuralism obscures the importance of the phenomenological period that precedes it, as well as the eventual rejection of both linguistics and structuralism that marks the final period of his work.

Regimes of Truth

In addition to the historical development of Lacan's work, Tallis also appears to be unaware of the critical divisions that separate the various theorists he considers: Lacan, Derrida, Barthes, Foucault, and others are all lumped together without any meaningful distinction under the rubric of 'post-Saussurean' theory. By indulging in such broad generalizations, Tallis makes some curious blunders, such as his misplaced disdain for Jean Baudrillard, who might have been considered a potential ally in the 'defense of realism.' In *Theorrhoea and After*, for instance, Tallis observes sardonically that the 'post-Saussureans have [...] been discomforted by recent evidence, both within and without the universe of theory, that the world is not just "wall to wall text,"' such as the wars in the former Yugoslavia, Africa, and the Persian Gulf (Tallis 1999, p. xii). The theoretical response to these events, argues Tallis, led to 'the most absurd textualisation of the universe by one of the Old Hands (Baudrillard) who claimed that the Gulf War had never happened (it was merely the sum of its representations)' (Tallis 1999, p. xii). Tallis's interpretation is a misreading not only of *The Gulf War Did Not Take Place* (1991), but of Baudrillard's project in general. Baudrillard is not celebrating the rise of postmodern simulation and the concomitant disappearance of reality because his work, on the contrary, is a scathing critique of that phenomenon. If anything, Baudrillard, like Tallis, is looking to defend the importance of reality in a postmodern world defined by empty and unsatisfying simulacra.

Tallis also suppresses many of the important theoretical differences that separate Lacan from Derrida. Just as he draws from a tiny, inadequate pool of Lacan's writings, so too Tallis omits from his critique any serious discussion of other texts that might throw light on the dispute between the two thinkers, such as Derrida's essay 'Le Facteur de la Vérité' from *The Post Card*. In that text, Derrida provides an influential critique of the way Lacan reads Poe in the 'Seminar on "The Purloined Letter,"' arguing that Lacan strips away Poe's careful 'framing' of the story through the narrator in order to impose his own 'regime of truth' onto the text. Derrida's essay constitutes one episode in a long history of tension between the two thinkers, yet in *Not Saussure* Tallis basically treats Lacan and Derrida as though there are no discernible differences or conflicts between them. Tallis does briefly touch on the ripples generated by their clash in *In Defence of Realism* while criticizing the reductive methods of postmodern critics:

> Clearly the aim of the critic is not to submit to the text but to dominate it; not to try to extract what can be got out of it but to go beyond it—to see it for all it is, to put it in its place, to reduce it to an example, an illustration of a principle, grist to the theoretical mill. A paradigm case here is Poe's *The Purloined Letter*. Lacan makes it into a French letter to be filled with his semes. Derrida then takes Lacan's piece and uses it for his purposes. Next, Barbara Johnson grinds her own theoretical axe on Derrida's theories. Then Culler uses it as an example of a deconstructive reading. Finally, I have used it here to show how critics expropriate works of art rather than explicate them. *The Purloined Letter* becomes a purloined text[.] (Tallis 1988a, pp. 163–164)

With exquisite lack of insight, Tallis fails to grasp that what he objects to in these readings is the very thing that is at stake in them. Derrida's criticism of Lacan's reading of Poe, for instance, is precisely that Lacan tries to impose his own theoretical apparatus, his 'regime of truth,' onto the literary text. Lacan's putative assertion of interpretive authority sits uneasily with the Derridian principles of deconstruction.

Whether Lacan's reading really does claim for itself such authority is open to question, however, as two examples from Felman's work on this topic help to show. The first is her chapter on 'The Purloined Letter' in *Jacques Lacan and the Adventure of Insight*, in which she distinguishes Lacan's interpretation of the story from the reductive readings made by Joseph Wood Krutch (1926) and Marie Bonaparte (1933). The earlier Freudian analyses of Poe's text were built on an implicit critical hierarchy, in which the work of literature was made subservient to the psychoanalytic theory that 'unlocked' its meanings. Felman argues, by contrast, that Lacan allows these two discourses to reflect on each other, a process she calls 'implication': 'The methodological stake is no longer that of the *application* of psychoanalysis *to* literature but, rather, of their *interimplication in* each other' (Felman 1987, p. 49). Lacan's revolutionary interruption of the usual hermeneutical hierarchy aims instead to reveal the outlines of authority in the text, Felman explains:

> The history of reading has accustomed us to the assumption—usually unquestioned—that reading is finding meaning, that interpretation can dwell only on the meaningful. Lacan's analysis of the signifier opens up a radically new assumption, an assumption that is an insightful logical and methodological consequence of Freud's discovery: that what *can* be read (and perhaps what *should* be read) is not just meaning but the lack of meaning; that significance lies not just in consciousness but, specifically, in its disruption; that the signifier can be analyzed in its effects without its signified being known; that the lack of meaning—the discontinuity in conscious understanding—can and should be interpreted as such, without necessarily being transformed into meaning. (Felman 1987, p. 45)

The Lacanian method of reading is thus focused on mapping the distinctions between those parts of the text that involve rationally-explicable knowledge and those that are the arbitrary expressions of a master signifier. What is new in this style of reading is that the latter are allowed to stand, in all their irrational authority, rather than being subsumed by the new master signifier of the story's interpreter. Lacan's mode of interpretation involves creating a map of discursive power, not a hermeneutical key.

The second example from Felman is her essay on Henry James's *The Turn of the Screw* (1898) in *Writing and Madness* (1978). As in her chapter on Poe, Felman again compares an earlier Freudian reading—in this case, Edmund Wilson's famous 1934 interpretation of James's story—to her own Lacanian reading of the text. Wilson is an exemplary case of a critic who wants 'to be a *non-dupe*,' who seeks mastery over the text by refusing to be misled by James's narrative tricks so that, 'by remaining himself *exterior* to the reading-errors that delude and blind both characters and author, the critic thus becomes the sole agent and the exclusive mouthpiece of the *truth* of literature' (Felman 2003, p. 229). The particular genius of *The Turn of the Screw*, argues Felman, is that it is constructed as a double trap that is designed to catch the naïve reader, on the one hand, and the sophisticated critic, on the other. 'The trap, indeed, resides precisely in the way in which these two opposing types of reading are themselves inscribed and comprehended in the text,' writes Felman. 'The reader of *The Turn of the Screw* can choose either to *believe* the governess, and thus to behave like Mrs. Grose, or *not to believe the governess*, and thus to behave precisely *like the governess*. [...] To demystify the governess is only possible on one condition: the condition of *repeating* the governess's very gesture' (Felman 2003, p. 231). It is only when we begin to understand Lacan's critique of masterly authority, contends Felman, that we can avoid this double trap of trying to impose a regime of truth on a literary text:

> In seeking to 'explain' and *master* literature, in refusing, that is, to become a *dupe* of literature, in killing within literature that which makes it literature—its reserve of silence, that which, within speech, is incapable of speaking, the literary silence of a discourse *ignorant of what it knows*—the psychoanalytic reading, ironically enough, turns out to be a reading that *represses the unconscious*, that represses, paradoxically, the unconscious it purports to be 'explaining.' To *master*, then (to become the Master), is, here as elsewhere, to *refuse to read* the letters; here as elsewhere, to 'see it all' is in effect to 'shut one's eyes as tight as possible to the truth[.]' (Felman 2003, p. 234)

Lacan's work strongly resembles James's literary double trap because it, too, lures naïve readers into believing him to be a 'master,' while 'non-dupes' like Tallis, who see through the charade of the 'subject who is supposed to know,' of this Emperor with no clothes, use this insight to impose their own regime of truth, to install themselves as a new master.

Diversion and Strategy

Felman's critique of the hierarchy between literature and psychoanalysis opens up an even more difficult theoretical question about the relationship between the multiple kinds of discourses deployed in Lacan's thought. After all, Lacan regularly borrows from fields such as literature, philosophy, theology, science, and linguistics in formulating his psychoanalytic theories. Commenting on Lacan's paper 'Presentation on Psychical Causality' (1946) in *Freud, Proust and Lacan: Theory as Fiction* (1987), Malcolm Bowie writes:

> The multitude of writers appearing elsewhere in Lacan's paper includes Fontenelle, Flaubert, Schiller, Molière, Montaigne and Plato. Each of them, considered alone, is a multiplier of local meanings, a supplier of knots to Lacan's own discourse. But a procession of writers moving at speed through the text, and striking up unhistorical relationships with each other as they move, creates within the argument strong cross-currents of association that have their own lessons to teach. (Bowie 1987, p. 142)

This promiscuity is a problem mainly because, as Bowie notes, these 'unhistorical relationships' are made 'at speed' in a way that strategically avoids the question of by what *authority* these heterogeneous ideas and texts are brought into contact with each other. Such moves are only made possible, it would seem, by the arbitrary power of Lacan the master—a point that Tallis also makes about the (mis)appropriation of Saussure.

This issue is the cornerstone of Jean-Luc Nancy and Philippe Lacoue-Labarthe's *The Title of the Letter: A Reading of Lacan*, one of the most penetrating early critiques of Lacan, an essential book that is notably absent from Tallis's discussion. Strongly influenced by deconstruction, Nancy and Lacoue-Labarthe have been particularly important in the critique of Lacan and psychoanalysis in France—Borch-Jacobsen, for instance, is one of their most famous pupils. '[M]y mentors […] Philippe Lacoue-Labarthe and Jean-Lucy Nancy happened to be more Derridian than Lacanian—which probably saved me from becoming just another Lacanian clone,' he recalls in one interview. 'Together they wrote a little book on Lacan, *The Title of the Letter*, which was the first rigorously philosophical reading of Lacan; this gave me the critical distance I needed' (Borch-Jacobsen 1997, p. 214). Lacan himself read *The Title of the Letter*, commenting in *Seminar XX* that although the book is 'written with the worst of intentions,' he nonetheless 'cannot encourage its circulation strongly enough'—a typical example of his paradoxical sense of humor (Lacan 1999, p. 65).

The Title of the Letter not only provides a pertinent analysis of Lacan's ideas, focused primarily on 'An Instance of the Letter in the Unconscious, or Reason Since Freud' (1957), it is also one of the few books that addresses in a meaningful way the issue of Lacan's style, from the manner in which Lacan's reading of Freud and Saussure positions itself as an implicitly philosophical (rather than purely psychoanalytic) text, to his problematic integration of other thinkers and philosophers so that they reflect his own concerns. One of the most innovative aspects of Nancy and Lacoue-Labarthe's reading is their opening rejection of the idea that Lacan is building a philosophical or theoretical system. This disclaimer is important because some commentators on Lacan approach his thought as though it is a carefully constructed unity—one marked by various revisions, new developments, and changes of direction, certainly, but a system nonetheless that, for all its faults and crevices, can be treated as an integrated whole.

Nancy and Lacoue-Labarthe, by contrast, use Lacan's reading of Saussure to show the problematic but creative way that Lacan borrows and adapts outside ideas into his work. Their initial term for how he achieves this appropriation with regard to Saussure is 'diversion.' Even though Lacan's reading of Saussure contains numerous elements that contradict Saussure's theories, unlike Tallis they claim that Lacan does not misread Saussure in the conventional sense. Instead, he 'diverts' Saussure to his own ends, taking the ideas that he finds useful, foregrounding and adapting them, while omitting those parts that are not. In 'An Instance of the Letter,' therefore,

> a *diversion* of linguistics has never ceased. However, nothing in fact authorizes this diversion, except for a certain use of Freud, a certain way of projecting, more or less explicitly, an entire psychoanalytic conceptual framework into Saussurian linguistics in order to disrupt its operation. (Nancy and Lacoue-Labarthe 1992, pp. 84–85)

Lacan rereads Saussure, in other words, as though the latter were a psychoanalyst, and in a reciprocal move, rereads Freud as though he were a structural linguist. He thus diverts the work of both thinkers in order to open a new channel whereby these two thinkers, once separate, are brought into an unexpected dialogue. Nancy and Lacoue-Labarthe argue that while Lacan is not actually creating a unified philosophical system, this 'strategy' (the second term they introduce to describe his way of interpreting texts), by which he brings a heterogeneous group of thinkers into the orbit of his own thought, is what gives his work the impression of unity. '*Strategy* will [...] designate the inevitable twisting (*tournure obligée*) of what has been left in the margins of Lacan's text,' they write—in other words, the only way that Lacan can bring these thinkers into dialogue with one another is by a careful 'twisting' that artificially removes the contextual barriers that would normally separate them (Nancy and Lacoue-Labarthe 1992, p. 87). The parts that do not fit the exchange of ideas he seeks to create are pushed into the margins, so that the overall interaction is artificially made to look seamless.

Nancy and Lacoue-Labarthe ask what it is that authorizes Lacan to divert thinkers in this way, to create homologies between such apparently heterogeneous systems of thought. Lacan did not invent this method of reading, according to Nobus, but borrowed it from two of his most important intellectual precursors in Roman Jakobson and Lévi-Strauss:

> Lacan initially read Saussure through the eyes of Lévi-Strauss, whose own reading had passed through the critical filter of Roman Jakobson. [...] When Lévi-Strauss dipped into Saussurean theory in *The Elementary Structures of Kinship*, and more markedly in his extraordinary *Introduction to the Work of Marcel Mauss*, his was already much more a critical re-interpretation of Saussure's ideas than an accurate presentation of their impact. (Nobus 2003, pp. 54–55)

The diversion of Saussure noted by Nancy and Lacoue-Labarthe therefore has its own marginalized history of theoretical appropriation, by way of Lévi-Strauss, which Lacan then extends.

> In light of Lévi-Strauss's singular espousal of structural linguistics, Lacan's alleged distortion of the Saussurean sign becomes evidently more considerate and less idiosyncratic, less erratic and more deliberate. In defending the

> 'primordial position of the signifier' and defining the line separating the signifier and the signified as a 'barrier resisting signification,' Lacan simply reiterated and formalized the ideas that Lévi-Strauss had already professed some seven years earlier. Although he did not mention his friend-anthropologist by name in his seminal 1957 article on the value of Saussure's theory for psychoanalysis, Lacan attributed to the Swiss linguist what was in reality a Lévi-Straussian conception of the relationship between the signifier and the signified. (Nobus 2003, p. 56)

Lacan's 'strategy' is therefore not an original technique, borrowing its main impetus from the critical interventions he witnessed not only in Lévi-Strauss, as Nobus traces in this essay, but also in the influential work undertaken by Kojève, whose lectures on Hegel were regularly attended by Lacan. These earlier examples of diversion exemplify for Lacan a creative technique that is the most obvious intellectual motive for his own homologies.

The strategic diversion that Nancy and Lacoue-Labarthe identify in Lacan's work differs, they argue, from a system of philosophy. Its unity emerges from this repeated procedure of diversion rather than from the development of a consistent architecture of concepts. As such, Lacan's thought is closer to a collage, an assemblage of ideas that leaves it to the audience to interpret the deeper meaning of the connections being made.

> [T]he Lacanian 'system' [...] is a system made of borrowings or rather, a system of borrowings, which we have seen illustrated in the constitution of a signifying tropism, assembled or fabricated from classical rhetoric, Jakobson's linguistics, post-symbolist or surrealist poetry, etc. Thus, strategy is here to be understood as a technique, or an 'art' of systematization—a systematization that does not reveal its own law of composition as an architectural law. [...] As a general rule, his discourse does not posit itself as needing to be defined—rather it seeks to avoid all definitions along with all the difficulties they entail. (Nancy and Lacoue-Labarthe 1992, p. 88)

Nancy and Lacoue-Labarthe identify this strategy of diversion and appropriation as a key characteristic of Lacan's thought, a heterogeneity that, sutured together in this artificial way, comes bundled with its own problems and contradictions. The strategy of borrowing constantly from other thinkers can make it seem as though Lacan is a mere commentator, erasing himself in order to facilitate a dialogue between other thinkers. 'This is why [diversion] [...] instead of presenting itself straightaway as a new theoretical area, sets itself up, if one may say, in an intermediary space, in an intersection of areas or in a permanent circulation between areas,' write Nancy and Lacoue-Labarthe. 'The diverted concepts thus retain the weight of plural reference' (Nancy and Lacoue-Labarthe 1992, p. 89). Despite the constant introduction of seemingly heterogeneous elements, Lacanian thought is nonetheless held together by 'a *connotative sliding*' that, operating in the margins of the text, makes it possible for Lacan to twist and turn these concepts until they join together smoothly in a way that suits him (Nancy and Lacoue-Labarthe 1992, p. 89).

This strategy is important for Lacan's work not only because of the rich creativity it generates with regard to other discourses, but also because it allows him to position himself as the ultimate philosophical intermediary. Lacan opens up a space for dialogue between other voices not so they can eclipse his own, but so that he can present his version of psychoanalysis as a kind of universal discursive 'glue.' In order to do this, Nancy and Lacoue-Labarthe contend that Lacan employs a rhetorical opposition that seeks not to tear down but to rescue and rehabilitate a psychoanalytic discourse seen as corrupted, even endangered, by its own institutional orthodoxy:

> The fact that Lacan seeks to rescue psychoanalysis from a certain orthopedics does not prevent, on the contrary, his project as a whole from being orthopedic. It is, if you will, an *anti-orthopedic* orthopedics, or a counter-pedagogy, which is not unrelated, in its clinical intention as well, to perhaps the most fundamental aim of philosophy as a whole, at least since Socrates. Lacan's *formation* would thus be nothing else, presumably, than παιδεία itself, or its revival in the *Bildung* of the Enlightenment (with which Lacan explicitly affiliates himself) and of German Idealism. [...] This explains why psychoanalysis could appear, here, as a sort of *generalized* medicine, the *paideia* of all *paideiai*[.] (Nancy and Lacoue-Labarthe 1992, p. 90)

Lacan's strategy, claim Nancy and Lacoue-Labarthe, is to present himself as the ultimate philosophical mediator, to erase himself strategically from being the subject who speaks to one whose role is to channel the discourse of others (and so, by implication, the discourse of the Other). That, for instance, is why Lacan presents his work as a return to Freud, for it is Freud who forms the frontline of this strategy in which Lacan plays the part of a mirror, a specular that is outwardly empty of content, so that all that remains is his style:

> What matters here, no doubt, is that this motif of formation [...] allows the Lacanian strategy to be presented according to a *specular* model [...] or even according to the just as rigorously and profoundly philosophical model of the *mise en abyme*—a *mise en abyme* where Lacan's *style* is necessarily implicated. The path of the 'return to Freud,' as is said at the end of 'La psychanalyse et son enseignement,' is 'the only formation that we could claim to transmit to our followers. It is called a style.' And why a 'style' if not by virtue of a 'circuit' whose course we could drily reconstitute by invoking the notion that if theory engenders the concept of a subject which regulates the subjects of psychoanalysis, the latter consequently is able to institute itself as the subject of discourse, in other words, to take the place of Lacan himself, or if you will, of the one who trains the subject of psychoanalysis. When Lacan speaks it would thus be the Other who speaks and speaks about him. (Nancy and Lacoue-Labarthe 1992, pp. 90–91)

Lacan uses this rhetorical strategy to distance, even erase himself from the content of his work. It is not he himself who speaks, but a series of figures such as Freud, Descartes, Hegel, Augustine, Saussure, and so on, with Lacan as the intermediary whose masterful style allows these diverse thinkers to enter into a conversation with each other. Such mediation is the essence of Lacan's style, the distinctive strategy he seeks to impart to his students and disciples rather than any particular concept or ideology.

Nancy and Lacoue-Labarthe contend that Lacan's interventions are not critical misreadings of the thinkers he is using, but rather strategic diversions of philosophical concepts. One must be aware, therefore, that when Lacan cites Saussure, for instance, he does so in a 'strategic' manner that does not adhere to the letter of Saussure's text. Whenever we read Lacan's texts, we ought to ask ourselves in what way he is diverting the thinkers he is addressing, and what his strategic purpose is in performing such a diversion.

> [O]ne must necessarily *read* the text according to the demands or requisites of strategy itself. This is why it is out of the question to *criticize* Lacan, which is to say, to exercise the systematic jurisdiction of *discourse* itself on his discourse. We will see that this excludes, in particular, reproaching him for any unfaithfulness to epistemological rigor or holding the liberties he takes with scientific linguistics against him. On the contrary, our reading should follow the diversions and displacements with which Lacanian discourse is woven, following or accompanying them, adhering to their complex design as closely as possible. This is not to say that we should purely and simply repeat them (devoutly), but rather that we should interrogate the logic of his discourse, that is, its strategic intention, in order to measure its 'displacing' efficacy and the excess which emerges there in relation to science and philosophy. (Nancy and Lacoue-Labarthe 1992, pp. 91–92)

To illustrate this principle at work, Nancy and Lacoue-Labarthe show how Lacan brings together Freud, Descartes, and Saussure, joining them in an interlocking 'repetition' that transforms their separate ideas into an apparently unified train of thought. Once Lacan has built this connection between the thinkers he wishes to join, he is then able to draw further resonances and associations with seeming ease in a way that accentuates the appearance of a system.

> The system of repetition can now be considered to be in place. This is precisely why the mechanism of repetition will accelerate. The comings and goings between the three texts (linguistics, psychoanalysis, and philosophy) will accelerate as if by the effect of a rapid oscillation between the two edges of a gap. In a way, nothing new will occur. But this 'nothing new' actually contains the possibility of a proliferation of philosophical references. (Nancy and Lacoue-Labarthe 1992, p. 99)

Nancy and Lacoue-Labarthe thus identify two basic movements that make up Lacan's stylistic strategy: a diversion of rereadings, borrowings, and combinations, which are then joined together by the deployment of a 'turning movement' that creates the semblance of a unified system.

This logic is the hallmark of the Lacanian style, an ability to create 'homologies' between different systems of value and, by a selective process of evaluation, translate them into each other. Lacan begins from the ahistorical assumption that all thinkers and philosophers are addressing the same basic questions as himself, that their ideas and concepts are merely differently-shaped tools that he can deploy to his own purposes (since his purposes, by this logic of equivalence, are ultimately shared by all thinkers). As Alain Badiou observes:

> Whoever the author he is speaking about may be, Lacan initiates a process of incorporation: he thinks the other is stating the same thing at the same time as he is. He often judged earlier thinkers or writers to have anticipated his own reflections. We've seen how he was able to argue, not without humor, that Plato was *already* Lacanian. This sort of assimilation has given rise among certain Lacanians to some comic discourses. Some think, for example, that Freud was Lacanian in advance, and that the concepts of Lacan are already found in his work. (Badiou and Roudinesco 2014, pp. 47–48)

This work of 'incorporation,' as Badiou puts it, is often clever and persuasive, so that it is only when an intervention like Nancy and Lacoue-Labarthe's is staged that the reader realizes the extent to which Lacan diverts Saussure and other thinkers for his own purposes. There are times, as Badiou points out, when Lacan can seem positively outlandish in his translations. In *Seminar III*, for instance, he makes the claim that Saint Augustine 'is as much of a linguist as Monsieur Benveniste' (Lacan 1993, p. 32). This assertion goes unchallenged because, while Lacan's claim is clearly ridiculous if taken at face value, his example from Augustine's *Confessions* is masterfully integrated into the modern context that Lacan is exploring. Lacan is thus able to make it appear that, although the discipline of linguistics did not even exist during Augustine's time, this anachronism is justified by the implication that Augustine is dealing with 'universal' philosophical problems of language, meaning, and existence.

Although Nancy and Lacoue-Labarthe ultimately conclude that Lacan does not create a philosophical system in the traditional sense, his consistent use of the critical strategy of 'diversion' effectively turns his commentary into a master discourse, an improvised system of authority that is concealed by its apparently centrifugal character. 'In all these respects,' they argue, 'Lacan composes a system in the most classical sense of the term. The Lacanian revolution, which borrows the image of the "Copernican revolution" from Kant via Freud, perhaps *also* proceeds contrary to that revolution' (Nancy and Lacoue-Labarthe 1992, p. 113). Lacan thus invests his authority in the creation of a strategy of thought, a reproducible master style that can bring any other discourse, regardless of its content, into line with its principles. *The Title of the Letter* anticipates Derrida's conclusion in *The Post Card* that Lacan, despite his apparent skill at critical disruption, surreptitiously reworks the margins of the text in order to impose a regime of truth. The brilliance of Nancy and Lacoue-Labarthe is how they show, in detail, the diversions and strategies Lacan deploys to reorient the ideas, such as Saussure's structural linguistics, that stray into the orbit of his thought.

From the Symbolic to the Real

In spite of the conspicuous differences in scholarly rigor and critical sophistication separating Tallis from Nancy and Lacoue-Labarthe, they each draw similar conclusions about the problems and limitations of Lacan's appropriation of Saussure. A shared shortcoming of both projects, however, is that they are restricted to a single, limited version of Lacan, one that is focused too narrowly on the structuralist period of his work. There are extenuating circumstances in Nancy and Lacoue-Labarthe's case, because at the time they were writing *The Title of the Letter* the only major published work by Lacan was *Écrits* (the first of his seminars to be transcribed and published, *Seminar XI*, came out in French in 1973). As they explain in the introduction, their original intention was to write an essay-length piece on 'An Instance of the Letter,' but the breadth of the argument grew until it justified a book-length study. While Tallis also had relatively limited access to Lacan's published work in English when composing his work, the rigor and insight of his critique pales in comparison with Macey's superb *Lacan in Contexts*, for instance, even though their books came out in the same year. There is no indication, either, that Tallis has read crucial texts, such as *Seminar XI*, which was translated into English in 1977, nor that, in his later work, he has looked at the newly available editions and translations of Lacan's seminars that have been published in the intervening years.

The crucial thing to keep in mind, though, is that it is not only Nancy and Lacoue-Labarthe and Tallis who have concerns about the limitations of structural linguistics—Lacan himself is *also* profoundly aware of these problems, so that the trajectory of his thought, as reflected in the themes of his seminars, shows him repeatedly struggling to address the idealist tendencies of structuralist thought. The inadequacy of adhering too closely to one period of Lacan's work is the hurdle at which both *Not Saussure* and *The Title of the Letter* ultimately fall, for limiting their critique in this way is like restricting oneself to *The Birth of Tragedy* (1872) or *The Communist Manifesto* (1848) without acknowledging the expansions and revisions that enrich the legacy of Nietzsche and Marx. '[I]t is [...] an effect of the illusion that Lacan's work is a whole which is entire unto itself, that it has no basis in five decades of French intellectual life, that it is the result of some immaculate theoretical conception,' warns Macey. 'If his work is to be evaluated critically, rather than being rejected out of hand or reproduced with filial piety, that illusion must be dispelled' (Macey 1988, pp. ix–x). Falling into the trap of considering only the structuralist version of Lacan is a false step that critics have become increasingly conscious of avoiding.

Macey's warnings about the false impression that there is a settled version of Lacanian thought—a 'final state,' he calls it—together with the historical background he provides in *Lacan in Contexts*, have helped to change the direction of the field away from the reductive psychoanalytic readings that dogged the age of high theory. John Forrester, who translated *Seminar I* into English in 1988, similarly cautions his readers about the swiftly evolving nature of the seminars. 'Anyone familiar with Lacan is aware of the rapidity with which he changed his theories,' he writes. 'The seminars of the 1970s read very differently from those of the 1960s and are even more estranged from the language of those of the 1950s' (Forrester 1991, p. 107).[1] In his essay 'Sociology Before Linguistics: Lacan's Debt to Durkheim' (1996), Stephen Michelman identifies two erroneous assumptions about reading Lacan that have placed unnecessary restrictions on how to understand his theories. First, Michelman points out, there is 'the idea that his work forms a *self-standing theoretical system* which must be approached on its own terms. This may be called the *timeless system* view' (Michelman 1996, p. 125). The second wrong assumption is largely a product of the first:

> In a similar fashion, many commentaries have been vitiated by the assumption that Lacan's work must be expounded whole cloth, like Euclid's geometry. If anything, these accounts prove that the more assiduously one tries to weave *Desire*, the *signifier*, the *Other*, the phoneme, the *mirror-stage*, and the Moebius strip into a theoretical whole, the more forced, artificial, and abstract Lacan's ideas become, and the more a charlatan he appears. (Michelman 1996, p. 125)

Michelman credits the labor of those critics and intellectual historians who have helped to contextualize Lacan's thought—'Clément, Roudinesco, Macey, and Borch-Jacobsen' are the four he identifies—as crucial for the revolutionary shift toward a more historical understanding of the different phases of Lacan's work (Michelman 1996, p. 126).

Equally notable in Michelman's overview is his reiteration of another point made by Macey about the place of structural linguistics in Lacan's work. Michelman states that while the prevailing image in the academy of Lacan is that his 'uniqueness and importance derives largely from an application of *structural linguistics* to the material of psychoanalysis' so 'that Lacan saves Freud from the pitfalls of biology and classical psychology through the intervention of a Saussurean theory of the sign,' this understanding—which 'Lacan repeated [...] frequently enough for it

[1] Such observations about Lacan's evolution as a thinker were still innovative in 1990, whereas they are now commonplace—see, for instance, James M. Mellard's chapter 'Which Lacan?' in *Beyond Lacan* (Mellard 2006, pp. 47–73).

understandably to have become dogma'—of the creation of a supposedly 'unprecedented yet preordained marriage of Freud and Saussure' is false and misleading (Michelman 1996, p. 126). Even though this misconception has dominated the wider reception of Lacan's work, the problem is that this frequently promised marriage never actually took place. 'The irony of this story is that, after twenty years of flirtation, Lacan finally called off the marriage to Saussure, or at least admitted that it had never been properly consummated,' points out Michelman. 'As is by now well known, in his 1969–1970 seminar he conceded that his linguistic formulations are not to be confused with those of linguists in the strict—that is, the scientific—sense' (Michelman 1996, p. 127). Lacan's reputation in the academy, especially in the Anglophone world, was initially built on the theory of the 'mirror stage' and the integration of psychoanalysis and structural linguistics, as Tallis claims, but these ideas belong to the early to middle parts of his career. The concepts that have revitalized Lacan's reputation over the past quarter-century, by contrast, have mainly come from the difficult later period of his work when, in order to formulate the four discourses that describe the entanglement of language and the real, he felt that he had to turn *away* from Saussure.

In his introduction to *Lacan, Politics, Aesthetics* (1996), Richard Feldstein announces the dawn of a new era in the reception of Lacan. 'By the end of the 1980s the first phase in the reception of Lacan's work by the English-speaking audience drew to a close,' he pronounces. Feldstein goes on to argue that 'in the 1990s, we have entered into a second phase in the transmission of Lacan's work,' the main task of which is to apply 'Lacan's theories to cultural studies—to issues of race, gender, and class,' an action led 'by philosophical and literary activists like Slavoj Žižek and Juliet Flower MacCannell' (Feldstein 1996, p. xi). In *Beyond Lacan* (2006), James M. Mellard provides a more extensive list of the loose cohort of thinkers leading the revival of Lacanian thought in the twenty-first century: like Feldstein, he cites not only Žižek and MacCannell, but also Joan Copjec, Mladen Dolar, Renata Salecl, Elizabeth Cowie, Parveen Adams, and Alenka Zupančič (Mellard 2006, p. 179). Far from indulging in forays into cultural studies and identity politics as Feldstein foretold—Žižek, for one, expresses contempt for these fields, even though he regularly engages in analyses of popular culture—these thinkers instead 'emphasize Lacan's late notions of drive, *jouissance*, and the Real at the expense of his early concepts of "desire," the "Imaginary," and the "Symbolic"' (Mellard 2006, p. 180). Lacan's move away from structural linguistics in his later work leads him to turn his focus from the symbolic to the real.

Although the critics mentioned by Michelman were instrumental in creating a new, historically-nuanced way of reading Lacan, by far the most influential figure in the revitalization of Lacanian thought has been Žižek. From early in his career, Žižek launched a determined campaign to do away with the prevailing image of Lacan the structural linguist in favor of a Lacanian theory that is based around the notion of the real. For instance, in 'The Limits of the Semiotic Approach to Psychoanalysis' (1990), Žižek launches a bold and unprecedented attack on Lacan's pronouncement that 'the unconscious is structured like a language':

> Lacan's best-known proposition is surely the famous 'unconscious structured like a language,' which is usually understood as pointing towards a semiotic reinterpretation of psychoanalytical theory and practice. The aim of the present paper is to demonstrate that, contrary to this widely assumed proposition, Lacan's theory, at least in its last period, is far from endorsing any kind of language reductionism: his central effort is precisely to articulate the different modes of the real kernel (*das Ding, object petit a*) which presents an irreducible obstacle to the movement of symbolization. (Žižek 1990, p. 89)

Given both its time and intellectual context, this statement was an extraordinary turn against the conventional way of reading of Lacan, a daring reversal that confirmed the advent of a new voice on the Lacanian scene. More intriguing still was Žižek's emphasis on the later period of Lacan's theories. Much of that material was not only unpublished but also, especially when Lacan became obsessed with knots, could seem eccentric to the point of madness. Nonetheless, Žižek writes:

> Now, here is our thesis. It is only the Lacanian passage from the signifier to the object, 'from the symptom to the fantasy' (J.-A. Miller), which makes it possible to take the advent of post-modernism outside the field of an ideology of authenticity, instillment, etc. Post-modernism marks the rising in the middle of the modernist space of language and its interpretative auto-movement to the infinite, of a 'hard' nucleus, of the inertia of a non-symbolizable real. (Žižek 1990, p. 105)

Notice how Žižek uses the same language as Tallis while turning the latter's commonplace assumptions upside-down. Unlike Baudrillard, who laments the loss of reality amid the rise of postmodern simulacra, Žižek sees postmodernism, once it has been armed with the ideas of the late Lacan, as opening precisely *onto* the domain of the real.

Žižek's campaign against the structuralist Lacan in favor of the later period of his work has been relentless and prolific, and in its early years it led to some paradoxical situations. Consider, for instance, his contribution to *Lacan and the Subject of Language* (1991), a book that takes as its central theme the way in which, in accordance with the prevailing theories of the time, language shapes human subjectivity. Žižek's chapter in that collection, 'The Truth Arises from Misrecognition,' explicitly rejects this idea and so places itself in explicit tension with the rest of the essays in the book. A similar instance occurs with Žižek's essay in *Reading Seminars I and II* (1996), a piece titled 'Hegel With Lacan, or the Subject and Its Cause' in which, following the collection's theme, he is supposed to be reflecting on the importance of Lacan's first two seminars. Žižek begins obediently enough by observing that 'Lacan's opening gesture consists of an unconditional espousal of hermeneutics,' and noting how this aspect of his work extends from his faithful adherence to Freud's ideas (Žižek 1996, p. 397). By the second paragraph, however, Žižek is arguing that 'already in the mid-1950s, this hermeneutic attitude'—and its implicit reliance on the symbolic order of language—'is undermined by a worm of doubt' (Žižek 1996, p. 397). The unfolding of Lacan's thought is framed by Žižek as a series of restless attempts to theorize '*how this gap between the real and the symbolic affects the symbolic order itself*,' a question that causes Lacan to accept—and then reject—structural linguistics in his relentless search for an answer (Žižek 1996, p. 398). Žižek, more than any other critic, has reframed the Lacanian discourse as one that must be considered from the perspective of the later period of Lacan's work, which takes as its central problem not language, but the register of the real.

In a similar vein, in *The Capitalist Unconscious* (2015) Samo Tomšič argues that there are two different phases of the 'return to Freud.' 'The first return famously read Freud with structural linguistics and culminated in the claim that Freud's theories anticipated the Saussurean and Jakobsonian theory of language,' explains Tomšič. The second return occurs after Lacan's 'excommunication,' from which point 'Lacan progressively elaborated an alternative reading of the Freudian discovery that found its new privileged alliance in Marx's critique of political economy. The move away from the linguistic paradigm was accomplished immediately after May '68' (Tomšič 2015, p. 16). These new directions in Lacan's work are not only a response to the events of May '68, argues Tomšič, but also an attempt to formulate a 'psychoanalytic materialism' that can overcome the idealism of structuralist logic (Tomšič 2015, p. 19). The urgency of such a move is epitomized by a slogan written by one of the May '68 protesters: 'Structures do not march in the streets.' Reflecting on this catchphrase in the opening chapter of *Read My Desire* (1994), Joan Copjec argues that 'Lacan's diagrams'—she is referring here to the four discourses from *Seminar XVII*—'bear no resemblance to the scientistic maps drawn by the structuralists; his diagrams are offered to the audience as *anti*structuralist' (Copjec 1994, p. 11). The problem is that for most audiences, Lacan's four discourses actually *do* bear a strong resemblance to logic at its most abstract and impractical.

How, after all, can these four *discourses*—with this term 'discourse' so deeply rooted in language—also, at the same time, be real? The parameters of this problem can be understood more easily by returning to a crucial earlier point in Lacan's work, the text 'The Symbolic, the Imaginary, and the Real' (1953). Lacan presented this talk on July 8, 1953, a significant date because, as Miller notes, it was delivered 'immediately before writing the so-called Rome Report on "The Function and Field of Speech and Language in Psychoanalysis" during the summer of 1953, a paper that marked the public debut of "Lacan's teaching," as it was later called' (Lacan 2013, p. vi). This presentation is notable as much for its content as for what it excludes, as two of Lacan's interlocutors remark in the course of the discussion that followed the talk. 'You spoke to us about the symbolic and the imaginary,' points out Leclaire. 'But you didn't talk to us about the real' (Lacan 2013, p. 42). Lacan responds that he 'did talk about it a little bit,' adding that the 'real is either totality or the vanished instant,' but gives no further clarification (Lacan 2013, p. 42). A little later, Françoise Dolto also notes: 'We always arrive at the same question, "What is the real?" And we always manage to move away from it' (Lacan 2013, p. 49). The register of the real is a problematic, unresolved question in Lacan's early to middle period that he only defines, unsatisfactorily, by insisting that it goes beyond the symbolic and the imaginary. The unintended result of this theoretical shortcoming in the early to middle periods of Lacan's work is indeed, as Tallis claims, a kind of linguistic idealism that separates language from reality. This division is also why the word 'discourse' sounds like just another move in the structuralist game.

Yet *Seminar XVII* really is the breakthrough moment in Lacan's struggle to articulate the real. Gone is the implicit *opposition* between reality and language, and in its place is the insistence that the real and the symbolic are inextricably entangled, and that to imagine otherwise is to engage in a utopian fantasy. Indeed, that is the critique that Lacan articulates at his meeting in 1969 with a group of revolutionary students from the university at Vincennes, as Tomšič explains:

> 'Structures do not march on the streets.' The agents and the supporters of May '68 opposed structure and the event, or structure and politics, and herein lay one of their key failures. Instead of thinking the events as an outburst of the structural real, they were guided by the fantasy of a pure real outside structure, thereby overlooking the fact that the demanded liberalisation, for instance of education, initiated a more direct commodification of knowledge. (Tomšič 2015, p. 21)

Lacan recognizes that the error of the students rests on the same opposition between structure and reality that had been haunting his own work, and which he abolishes by collapsing the dichotomy into the single notion of the 'structural real.' Like Žižek, Tomšič drastically reworks Lacan's claim that 'the unconscious is structured like a language' by arguing that 'the second return to Freud did not simply equate the unconscious with the structure of language but with the structural real, the intertwining of representation and production, the two faces of the causality of the signifier. Lacan thereby problematises the transcendentalism of the symbolic order that had marked his earlier teaching as well as the entirety of classical structuralism' (Tomšič 2015, p. 22). The four discourses are not, therefore, purely an act of language, abstracted from reality. Instead, they are Lacan's attempt to describe the different ways in which any discourse about reality is formed by the indissoluble symbiosis of symbolic authority and material power.

The first of the four discourses, the discourse of the master, is the most ancient and autocratic. Its interpretation of reality is filtered through the arbitrary social divisions of power that separate, for instance, a free man from a slave, or a king from a subject. Since the discourse of the master is grounded in authority, it is through this authority that reality is constructed: in short, 'reality' is arbitrarily determined to be whatever the tyrannical master decides that it is. The slave goes along with the master's discourse because the latter, according to Lacan's formula, is assumed to be the 'subject who is supposed to know.' Yet this kind of master is, in reality, a charlatan, an ignoramus whose contempt for the study of reality derives from the fact that knowledge is not required to keep the system of power working. A king is a successful ruler so long as his kingdom runs smoothly, regardless of how much of a fool he may actually be.

The true purpose of Tallis's book is supposedly to stage a kind of Jacobin coup d'état in the name of 'restoring' literary studies, of taking back hegemony from Napoleonic usurpers like Lacan, whom he suspects of having royal ambitions. However, the charge of linguistic idealism launched in *Not Saussure* seems, on closer inspection, more like a fig leaf for Tallis's revolt against the existing authority than a genuine critical challenge to it. Does it make any difference, for instance, that Lacan *himself* turned away from Saussure and structural linguistics? Not to Tallis who, in attempting to justify the legitimacy of his own method of interpretation, demonizes Lacan as a charlatan who has bamboozled humanities scholars into believing that his manipulations are immune to critique. 'This is particularly true in the USA, where the all-powerful Modern Language Association has been in the grip of post-structuralism and its successors for decades,' claims Tallis. 'Passive persecution of the non-believers by offering them unemployment is supplemented by active persecution' (Tallis 1999, p. xiii). Reading Tallis with the benefit of hindsight makes proclamations like these laughable, particularly in the wake of an abundance of recent books—Terry Eagleton's *After Theory* (2004), Nicholas Birns's *Theory After Theory* (2010), and D.N. Rodowick's *Elegy for Theory* (2014), to name but a few—confirming that the brief dominance of literary theory, at least in the form Tallis is talking about, is already long gone. Unable to launch an effective critique of Lacan on intellectual grounds, Tallis's alternative strategy is to launch his own transparently imperious case for Lacan's dismissal so that his own regime of truth might reign in its place as the new master signifier.

References

Badiou, A. & Roudinesco, É., 2014. *Jacques Lacan: Past and Present.* New York: Columbia University Press.

Borch-Jacobsen, M., 1997. Basta Così! Mikkel Borch-Jacobsen on Psychoanalysis and Philosophy. In: T. Dufresne, ed. *Returns of the 'French Freud': Freud, Lacan, and Beyond.* New York and London: Routledge, pp. 209–227.

Bowie, M., 1987. *Freud, Proust and Lacan: Theory as Fiction.* Cambridge: Cambridge University Press.

Copjec, J., 1994. *Read My Desire: Lacan Against the Historicists.* Cambridge(MA) and London: The MIT Press.

Durand, A., 1996. Lacan and Lévi-Strauss. In: R. Feldstein, B. Fink & M. Jaanus, eds. *Reading Seminars I and II: Lacan's Return to Freud.* Albany(NY): State University of New York Press, pp. 98–108.

Feldstein, R., 1996. Introduction I. In: W. Apollon & R. Feldstein, eds. *Lacan, Politics, Aesthetics.* Albany(NY): State University of New York Press, pp. xi–xviii.

Felman, S., 1987. *Jacques Lacan and the Adventures of Insight: Psychoanalysis in Contemporary Culture.* Cambridge(MA): Harvard University Press.

Felman, S., 2003. *Madness and Literature: Literature/Philosophy/Psychoanalysis.* Palo Alto(CA): Stanford University Press.

Forrester, J., 1991. *The Seductions of Psychoanalysis: Freud, Lacan and Derrida.* Cambridge(MA): Cambridge University Press.

Homer, S., 2006. *Jacques Lacan.* London and New York: Routledge.

Lacan, J., 1993. *The Seminar of Jacques Lacan, Book III: The Psychoses, 1955–1956.* London: Routledge.

Lacan, J., 1999. *The Seminar of Jacques Lacan, Book XX: Encore: On Feminine Sexuality, The Limits of Love and Knowledge, 1972–1973.* New York and London: W.W. Norton & Company.

Lacan, J., 2013. *On the Names-of-the-Father.* Cambridge UK and Malden MA: Polity.

Lacan, J., 2017. *The Seminar of Jacques Lacan, Book V: Formations of the Unconscious.* Cambridge UK and Malden MA: Polity.

Lacan, J., 2018. *The Seminar of Jacques Lacan, Book XIX: …or Worse.* Cambridge UK and Malden MA: Polity.

Macey, D., 1988. *Lacan in Contexts.* London and New York: Verso.

Mellard, J. M., 2006. *Beyond Lacan.* Albany(NY): State University of New York Press.

Michelman, S., 1996. Sociology Before Linguistics: Lacan's Debt to Durkheim. In: D. Pettigrew & F. Raffoul, eds. *Disseminating Lacan.* Albany(NY): State University of New York Press, pp. 123–150.

Miller, J.-A., 1996. An Introduction to Seminars I and II. In: R. Feldstein, B. Fink & M. Jaanus, eds. *Reading Seminars I and II: Lacan's Return to Freud.* Albany(NY): State University of New York Press, pp. 3–14.

Nancy, J.-L. & Lacoue-Labarthe, P., 1992. *The Title of the Letter: A Reading of Lacan.* Albany(NY): State University of New York Press.

Nobus, D., 2003. Lacan's Science of the Subject: Between Linguistics and Topology. In: J. Rabaté, ed. *The Cambridge Companion to Lacan.* Cambridge: Cambridge University Press, pp. 50–68.

Nobus, D., 2018. Life and Death in the Glass: A New Look at the Mirror Stage. In: D. Nobus, ed. *Key Concepts of Lacanian Psychoanalysis.* New York: Routledge, pp. 101–138.

Phillips, J., 1996. Lacan and Merleau-Ponty. In: D. Pettigrew & F. Raffoul, eds. *Disseminating Lacan.* Albany(NY): State University of New York Press, pp. 69–106.

Roudinesco, É., 1997. *Jacques Lacan: Outline of a Life, History of a System of Thought.* New York: Columbia University Press.

Tallis, R., 1988a. *In Defence of Realism*. Lincoln NE and London: University of Nebraska Press.

Tallis, R., 1988b. *Not Saussure: A Critique of Post-Saussurean Literary Theory*. Basingstoke and London: Macmillan.

Tallis, R., 1997. The Shrink From Hell. *The Times Higher Education Literary Supplement*, 31 October, p. 20.

Tallis, R., 1999. *Theorrhoea and After*. Basingstoke and London: Macmillan.

Tomšič, S., 2015. *The Capitalist Unconscious: Marx and Lacan*. London and New York: Verso.

Žižek, S., 1990. The Limits of the Semiotic Approach to Psychoanalysis. In: R. Feldstein & H. Sussman, eds. *Psychoanalysis And….* London and New York: Routledge, pp. 89–110.

Žižek, S., 1991. The Truth Arises from Misrecognition. In: E. Ragland-Sullivan & M. Bracher, eds. *Lacan and the Subject of Language*. London and New York: Routledge, pp. 188–212.

Žižek, S., 1996. Hegel With Lacan, or The Subject and Its Cause. In: R. Feldstein, B. Fink & M. Jaanus, eds. *Reading Seminars I and II: Lacan's Return to Freud*. Albany(NY): State University of New York Press, pp. 397–413.

3

Lacan the Mathematical Charlatan

Mathematical Charlatanry

The place of mathematical formalization in Lacan's work has a long and varied history. As with his theories of language, Lacan's interest in mathematics not only shifts frequently, but also holds different degrees of importance depending on the stage of his career being considered. In *Seminar II*, for instance, mathematics is mentioned several times, such as his discussion of Plato's *Meno* ('I do feel better for having a mathematician agree with me,' (Lacan 1988, p. 18) he says after consulting one M. Riguet, a mathematician in the audience), or his reflections on the 'circuit of language' and its connection to the 'entropy' of the pleasure principle ('Mathematicians qualified to handle these symbols locate information as that which moves in the opposite direction to entropy' (Lacan 1988, p. 83)). In a very different way, mathematical and logical concepts also form the basis of *Seminar XIX*, which effectively reformulates his concept of the 'subject who is supposed to know' in terms of Frege's logic (the 'subject who is supposed to know' becomes an empty set that is imagined by the analysand to possess the fullness of the 'one').

P. D. Mathews, *Lacan the Charlatan*, The Palgrave Lacan Series,
https://doi.org/10.1007/978-3-030-45204-9_3

Unlike Lacan's appropriation of structural linguistics, the status of his mathematical formalization has never been without controversy. Lacan's use of mathematical notation came under particular scrutiny with the publication of Alan Sokal and Jean Bricmont's book, which appeared in French as *Impostures intellectuelles* in 1997 and in English as *Fashionable Nonsense* in 1998. The events that led to the creation of this book, the so-called 'Sokal Hoax,' are well-known. In 1996, Sokal, an American professor of mathematics and physics, set events in motion by submitting what appeared to be a scholarly paper, replete with quotations from various postmodern writers about science and mathematics, to the journal *Social Text*. After the paper was published, Sokal revealed that his article was a nonsensical hoax and claimed that its publication was evidence of a culture of ignorance and unreason pervading the humanities and social sciences. A year later, in collaboration with Bricmont, a Belgian professor of physics and philosophy of science, he produced *Fashionable Nonsense*, a putative critique of how postmodern thinkers have misused ideas from science and mathematics in their work in a way that undermines the Enlightenment project. The book's first chapter was devoted to exposing Lacan, in particular, as a leading abuser of mathematical logic.

Placing Lacan at the beginning of the book was a strategy designed to hold him up as the prototypical charlatan, a model of intellectual fraud through which the deceptions of the other authors in the book could be refracted. For their own purposes, Sokal and Bricmont emphasize his importance—'Jacques Lacan was one of the most famous and influential psychoanalysts of this century. Each year, dozens of books and articles are devoted to the analysis of his work' (Sokal and Bricmont 1998, p. 18)—while at the same time insisting that he is really just a cult figure. 'According to his disciples, he revolutionized the theory and practice of psychoanalysis; according to his critics, he is a charlatan and his writings are pure verbiage' (Sokal and Bricmont 1998, p. 18). This strategy echoes Tallis's insofar as the authority of Lacan's works is dismissed *a priori* as a rhetorical trick, or 'pure verbiage.' 'Any attempt to "refute" Lacan's ideas would be doomed from the outset,' writes Tallis in *Not Saussure*. 'One cannot refute fog' (Tallis 1988, p. 131).

Avoiding the substance of Lacan's work on the grounds that his complex style is a cloak for a lack of genuine ideas is typical of both *Fashionable Nonsense* and its loudest supporters. Richard Dawkins's glowing review of the book, for example, titled 'Postmodernism Disrobed' and published in the prestigious scientific journal *Nature*, begins with the following meditation on the connection between academic charlatanism and a difficult writing style:

> Suppose you are an intellectual impostor with nothing to say, but with strong ambitions to succeed in academic life, collect a coterie of reverent disciples and have students around the world anoint your pages with respectful yellow highlighter. What kind of literary style would you cultivate? Not a lucid one, surely, for clarity would expose your lack of content. (Dawkins 1998, p. 141)

Dawkins begins by citing two examples of passages from postmodern theorists who have transgressed his standards of academic clarity, including one quotation from Lacan. He then stresses the necessity of unambiguous expression by quoting from the British biologist Peter Medawar, who had earlier railed against 'a certain type of French intellectual style' in the late 1960s (Dawkins 1998, p. 141). It is entirely on this basis of style, rather than any logical analysis of ideas or concepts, that Dawkins dismisses Lacan and his contemporaries as charlatans:

> No doubt there exist thoughts so profound that most of us will not understand the language in which they are expressed. And no doubt there is also language designed to be unintelligible in order to conceal an absence of honest thought. But how are we to tell the difference? What if it really takes an expert eye to detect whether the emperor has clothes? In particular, how shall we know whether the modish French 'philosophy,' whose disciples and exponents have all but taken over large sections of American academic life, is genuinely profound or the vacuous rhetoric of mountebanks and charlatans? (Dawkins 1998, p. 141)

Dawkins's review repeatedly violates its own standards as a defense of reason, from the use of his position of authority to attack his perceived enemies, to the circular logic he deploys in his treatment of the link between style and content, to his obvious inability to engage these thinkers on their own terms. Complex philosophies are swept aside as so much 'daffy absurdity' on the evidence of a handful of brief quotations devoid of all context (Dawkins 1998, p. 142).

Tallis's review of *Fashionable Nonsense* is also an explosion of rage and anger rather than a defense of reason. He lavishes praise on Sokal and Bricmont, these 'two very remarkable people' who in 'their patient, quiet examination' 'investigate with scrupulous care' the dubious claims and discursive abuses of postmodern thinkers (Tallis 1999). Tallis's hyperbolic prose is soaked with indignation and a vengeful sense of triumph:

> For all of these reasons, the publication of *Intellectual Impostures* is an event of first importance for the future of the humanities. Apart from its very great intrinsic merits, it has, on the back of the brilliant Sokal Hoax, attracted enormous publicity both within and beyond academe. Moreover, S&B have set new standards for the criticism of postmodern Theory and they bring new hope that the Castle of Untruth might at last be stormed successfully. (Tallis 1999)

Tallis concludes that Sokal and Bricmont have exposed the 'uncheckable opaque bullshit that excites the ignorant with the illusion of near-understanding,' demonstrating to the broader public that thinkers like Lacan make up 'part of the wider culture of charlatanry in postmodern Theory' (Tallis 1999). Once again, there is no attempt to engage with these ideas at an intellectual level, only a rhetorical fireworks display that claims to operate in the name of reason while violating the most basic principles of logical critique.

One of the stupidest moments in *Fashionable Nonsense* is when Sokal and Bricmont attempt to 'solve' one of Lacan's equations (Signifer/Signified = Statement). 'Even if his "algebra" had a meaning, the "signifier", "signified" and "statement" that appear within it are obviously not numbers, and his horizontal bar (an arbitrarily chosen symbol) does not denote the division of two numbers,' they exclaim in horror. 'Therefore, his "calculations" are pure fantasies' (Sokal and Bricmont 1998, p. 26). Sokal and Bricmont miss the obvious fact that Lacan's notation is being used to describe the mechanisms of language rather than to formulate a mathematical equation. Lacan's use of mathematical logic is determined by its usefulness as a tool for understanding psychoanalysis, so that he 'diverts' its terms (such as with Frege) in radical new ways that sometimes have little to do with their original context. As Lacan himself stresses in *Seminar XIX*:

> Just because I have made use of a formulation produced by the sudden emergence of mathematics in logic, this doesn't mean that I have employed it in quite the same way. […] [I]ndeed, I make use of it in such a way that on no account can it be translated into the terms of propositional logic. (Lacan 2018, p. 86)

Whatever the actual mistakes and misreadings in Lacan's deployment of mathematics, Sokal and Bricmont's rigid insistence that mathematical symbols must always be read as literal equations is simply absurd. One might as well declare that Robert Burns's description of his love as 'like a red, red rose' is an abuse of biology.

An examination of the chapter dedicated to Lacan's ideas in *Fashionable Nonsense* shows this lack of rigor to be a repeated pattern. Sokal and Bricmont include several pages of lengthy quotations from Lacan's work, without providing any context, which they then punctuate with occasional expressions of bafflement that reveal their profound ignorance of the subject at hand. Despite the absence of any meaningful engagement with Lacan's ideas, they confidently conclude that 'his analogies between psychoanalysis and mathematics are the most arbitrary imaginable, and he gives absolutely no empirical or conceptual justification for them (neither here nor elsewhere in his work)' (Sokal and Bricmont 1998, p. 36). If there is something problematic about Lacan's use of mathematical formalization, Sokal and Bricmont do not have the intellectual tools to articulate it. Rather than admitting their limitations, they express more bewilderment:

> What should we make of Lacan's mathematics? Commentators disagree about Lacan's intentions: to what extent was he aiming to 'mathematize' psychoanalysis? We are unable to give any definitive answer to this question—which, in any case, does not matter much, since Lacan's 'mathematics' are so bizarre that they cannot play a fruitful role in any serious psychological analysis. (Sokal and Bricmont 1998, p. 36)

This vague gesture in the direction of other 'commentators' is particularly intriguing—to whom, exactly, are they referring here? In their chapter on Lacan, Sokal and Bricmont make several similarly nebulous references to 'critics,' none of whom are specified. Yet the extensive secondary material on the topic of Lacan's flirtations with mathematical notation provides a crucial historical and theoretical context that presents a very different picture to the one painted by Sokal and Bricmont.

The Place of the Matheme

In the history of Lacan's engagement with structural linguistics outlined in the previous chapter, it was possible to detect a clear arc during which Saussure's ideas gained ascendancy, both in Lacan's thought and in the secondary criticism, and then fell out of favor. Lacan's fascination with mathematical formalization, by contrast, has had a very different reception. With few exceptions, his followers have tended to regard this aspect of his work with suspicion. Clément, for example, writes in 1981:

> Lacan [...] was always ambiguous about the use of his 'devices.' Were they scientific? Or merely educational? It was tempting to believe that they were science, and many succumbed to the illusion. This turn marked the real end of Lacan's discoveries. [...] What remained was a man playing with his mathematical toys. (Clément 1983, p. 161)

Stephen Melville, similarly, expresses his skepticism in this article from 1987:

> If we look back at [...] the various little letters Lacan has sent us, it should be clear that they bear little relation to any normal project of scientific mathesis. Lacan rips off bits of this and that, giving us 'notations' that have a certain validity within a highly restricted region. The manipulations to which they are submitted appear radically unprincipled, and their relevant features vary from the highly formal to the crudely pictorial. There is no ground for suspecting the existence of a systematic Lacanian algebra of some kind behind the various mathemes and charts. He is not dreaming that dream. (Melville 1987, p. 364)

There are numerous similar examples, all written before Sokal and Bricmont's book, that I could cite here, not only from well-known skeptics like Roustang[1] and Macey,[2] but also esteemed admirers of Lacan like Gallop[3] and Bowie.[4] The 'disagreement' among critics about Lacan's mathematical formalization that Sokal and Bricmont refer to looks, from this perspective, very much like a consensus.

This widespread reservation extends to Roudinesco, who provides a useful clarification of what Lacan was trying to do with his 'mathemes.' 'The word *matheme* occurred for the first time in the lecture Lacan delivered on November 4, 1971,' she writes, 'The word was derived from Claude Lévi-Strauss's *mythème* and the Greek word for "knowledge," *mathema*; it didn't belong to the world of mathematics' (Roudinesco 1997, p. 360). Sokal and Bricmont say nothing about the negative

[1] 'This plainly means that nothing of a mathematical nature can be elicited from Lacanian mathematics and no logical reasoning emerges from it; it is sheer misappropriation (*détournement*) of mathematics. What we are presented with, then, are nothing but images, metaphors, and illustrations[.]' (Roustang 1990, p. 97)

[2] 'Yet it is difficult to see how this "formalization" introduces anything new or moves towards any scientific rigour; it is largely a reworking of something already theorized, a second-degree representation. The same might be said of most of Lacan's models and attempts at formalization, despite the claim that they indicate a gesture towards the mathematicity of the model of science promoted by the rationalist epistemology of Koyré and others.' (Macey 1988, p. 166)

[3] 'These formulas are particularly intimidating to the literary student (Lacan's addressee). The assumption is that there is some logico-mathematical operation here that the reader cannot understand. But in fact these algorithms are absurd.' (Gallop 1985, pp. 118–119)

[4] 'Lacan's fascination with model-building devices borrowed from mathematics and symbolic logic is often thought of as a sign of amateurism. This is exactly how, it is suggested, an intellectual overreacher might be expected to disguise his dubious credentials. Yet judgements of this kind seem to me to miss the entire atmosphere of Lacan's theoretical project.' (Bowie 1991, p. 4)

reception of this turn by Lacan toward mathemes, topography, and knot theory in the 1970s, even though this development remains controversial. Roudinesco is particularly damning in her assessment of the later period of Lacan's work, observing that 'between 1968 and 1975 [...] [Lacan] showed a growing tendency to value formula above reasoning, slogan above proof, and neologism above argument. After 1970 the habit grew so pronounced as to change Lacan's utterance into a kind of miraculous grab bag for the use of messianic sects' (Roudinesco 1997, p. 337). These words anticipate the conclusion of Sokal and Bricmont's chapter on Lacan, in which they accuse him of cultivating a kind of 'secular mysticism':

> One is then faced with what could be called a 'secular mysticism': mysticism because the discourse aims at producing mental effects that are not purely aesthetic, but without addressing itself to reason; secular because the cultural references (Kant, Hegel, Marx, Freud, mathematics, contemporary literature...) have nothing to do with traditional religions and are attractive to the modern reader. Furthermore, Lacan's writings became, over time, increasingly cryptic—a characteristic common to many sacred texts—by combining plays on words with fractured syntax; and they served as a basis for the reverent exegesis undertaken by his disciples. One may then wonder whether we are not, after all, dealing with a new religion. (Sokal and Bricmont 1998, p. 37)

Whereas Roudinesco provides a nuanced framework for understanding Lacan's interest in mathemes and shows how, in her opinion, it detracts from his earlier intellectual achievements, the superficiality of Sokal and Bricmont's approach is manifest in their total inability to comprehend Lacan's project, leading to their final dismissal of his entire oeuvre as mystical nonsense.

Bruce Fink, another prominent Lacanian, expresses his frustration with Sokal and Bricmont's narrow and overly literal reading of Lacan's use of mathematical language. He derides, for instance, the way they misread Lacan's reformulation of the Saussurean 'algorithm' mentioned earlier, which they interpret incorrectly as the mathematical division of two numbers rather than as a diagram of the relationship between two linguistic terms. Fink contends that it is

> clear that Lacan is not using the bar to 'denote the division of two numbers,' and that no known or even unknown form of *mathematical* calculation is being carried out here[.] [...] His symbols are designed to abbreviate important psychoanalytic concepts in a way that is easy to write and remember, allowing for a form of psychoanalytic 'formalization' that is unrelated to quantification (his formulas, for example, do not allow of numerical solutions). (Fink 2004, p. 132)

Fink also undertakes a painstaking defense of Lacan's comparison of the square root of minus one (an irrational number) to the phallus (an unthinkable concept). Fink again chides Sokal and Bricmont for their literal understanding of this metaphorical comparison, arguing that Lacan 'is using this symbol *for his own purposes*, not as mathematicians use it' (Fink 2004, p. 135). Fink defends Lacan's use of formalization, not from a mathematical perspective, arguing instead that Lacan's use of this notation is meant to enhance the *psychoanalytic* concepts that he is exploring.

One of the most insightful pieces of commentary on this topic is Joël Dor's essay 'The Epistemological Status of Lacan's Mathematical Paradigms,' an in-depth exploration that was published just a year before Sokal and Bricmont's book. From the outset, Dor stresses that although Lacan flirted with mathematical formalization throughout his career, it never really transcended this preliminary stage in his overall project. 'If we remain faithful to Lacan's work, intellectual honesty demands that we recognize that he never *radically* cultivated and developed this project,' writes Dor, 'if only because he both formulated and invalidated it on several occasions' (Dor 1996, p. 110). Lacan's use of mathematical symbols, argues Dor, should be seen as an abstract version of the psychoanalytic concepts he was using in his writings and seminars. Again, there is no attempt by Lacan to 'mathematize' psychoanalysis:

> Lacan never presented—*a fortieri* defined—the matheme as a mathematical, that is, formal object. It is an abstract vehicle suited for a complete

> transmission of something germane to psychoanalysis. In other words, this rigorous transmission never meant to render psychoanalysis mathematical. Lacan, for his part, never committed himself to such a confusion. On the contrary, he attempted on several occasions to circumscribe the ambiguity of such an attempt. (Dor 1996, p. 117)

Dor's essay was written before the publication of *Fashionable Nonsense*, but there is something particularly prescient about his conclusion. 'Could one impute to Lacan, then, the aim of mathematizing psychoanalysis?' he ponders. 'It would seem that only detractors and dogmatists would entertain such a thought. [...] This obviously did not prevent some from nonetheless imputing to him such a project' (Dor 1996, p. 118). Detractors and dogmatists indeed—for all of Lacan's dubious flirtations with mathematics and formalization, there is little of substance in the charges that Sokal and Bricmont bring.

Although Lacan's use of mathematical formalization traces a very different path from his diversion of Saussurean linguistics, the ultimate outcome turns out to be analogous. In a move that echoes Lacan's notorious shift from 'linguistics' to '*linguisterie*,' in which he disavows that he is doing formal linguistics, so too Dor proposes that we think of Lacan's mathematical and topological borrowings, similarly, as '*topologerie*' (Dor 1996, p. 120). Macey proposes an even better term in *Lacan in Contexts*, ten years before *Fashionable Nonsense*:

> It might not be inappropriate to suggest, finally, that the mathemes are to mathematics what *linguisterie* is to linguistics. In both cases, elements from a rigorous discipline are appropriated in what Lacan himself admits is a casual manner. If few linguists take the *linguisterie* seriously, there must be even fewer mathematicians or logicians who view the matheme with anything but extreme suspicion or savage amusement. If a summary judgement has to be passed, it could well make use of the coinage *mathématiquerie*. (Macey 1988, p. 171)

This survey of the critical material confirms that the purported 'disagreement' among commentators over Lacan's use of mathematical symbols to which Sokal and Bricmont refer is, in fact, non-existent. What critics do agree on is that the 'matheme,' despite its misleading name and unconventional use of mathematical notations, is entirely separate from actual mathematics. Lacan's 'algorithms' cannot and should not be read according to any kind of mathematical rules or logic, as Sokal and Bricmont quixotically attempt to do. Far from being accepted on faith by Lacan's disciples, his attempts at mathematical formalization are regarded, even by many of his closest allies, as problematic and, in some cases, as outright nonsense.

'That Was Not Done'

The Sokal Hoax and *Fashionable Nonsense* generated an enormous amount of sound and fury in the academy and the media, most of it along predictable battle lines. The story of the hoax has been recorded in *The Sokal Hoax: The Sham That Shook the Academy* (2000), as well as Sokal's follow-up book *Beyond the Hoax: Science, Philosophy and Culture* (2008). On his NYU page, Sokal has assembled an extensive archive of texts related to the event. Much of this material is repetitive, so I will only touch on a few highlights from the critical response to Sokal and Bricmont's book. One of the biggest shortcomings of *Fashionable Nonsense* is that, by focusing exclusively on the negative, the book never explores the more pressing question of how science and critical theory might legitimately approach each other. This failure is the core of Derrida's brief response to the hoax. 'It would have been interesting to make a scrupulous study of the so-called scientific "metaphors"—their role, their status, their effects in the discourses that are under attack,' he writes in 'Sokal and Bricmont Aren't Serious.' 'That would have required that a certain number of difficult discourses be read seriously, in terms of their theoretical effects and strategies. That was not done' (Derrida 2005, p. 70).

What was done, argues G.M. Goshgarian in a scathing review, was that Sokal and Bricmont generated money and publicity for themselves. In his assessment, the thinness of the book's arguments is a reflection of the authors' desire to cash in on the scandal. Goshgarian argues that, while Sokal and Bricmont do indeed turn up some errors with regard to the deployment of science and mathematics in the humanities, the actual consequences of those mistakes are vastly overstated:

> No doubt about it: nearly all the defendants have made some lulus, as the prosecution has a picnic demonstrating. Why, then, does it not simply hang the culprits on this one credible charge? Doubtless because it knows that a sampler of math mistakes culled from recent French writing in the humanities, though not without interest, is the stuff of interesting *footnotes*, unless the mistakes can be shown to bear on matters of importance to the text they occur in. (Goshgarian 1999, p. 122)

Why then, asks Goshgarian, did Sokal and Bricmont not follow through on this task? If the blunders are so significant, why did they not show how these mistakes brought down the entire edifice, for instance, of Lacanian psychoanalysis?

> Sokal and Bricmont cannot show it, because they have barely read most of the writers they indict. Why in the name of logic, right reason, and 'accepted academic standards'—the very gods our authors swear by—did they not sit down and read them, you ask? Simple: because mere logic can't hold a candle to the logic of the market. And the logic of the market dictates that [...] if *x* can palm off a grab bag of footnotes as a respectable book exposing difficult, celebrated, mainly left-wing, and—for these and other reasons—widely resented thinkers as charlatans, why then *x* should do it, *fast*, whether he can actually tell if they are charlatans or not. (Goshgarian 1999, p. 123)

While Goshgarian's ruminations about the 'logic of the market' are quite cynical, he does provide a credible addition to Derrida's disappointment: 'that was not done,' he shows, because Sokal and Bricmont were *incapable* of doing it. They simply do not have the intellectual tools to understand and evaluate the complexities of the thinkers they criticize.

Indeed, another weakness of *Fashionable Nonsense* is its confused equation of thinkers who, in many cases, have little in common. Sokal and

Bricmont create a monstrous hybrid of *eight* French critics, whose theories they blend together, without care or distinction, under the rubric of 'postmodernism.' The resulting conglomeration constitutes a teratology that only ever existed in the imagination:

> *Impostures* slays a massively French postmodern dragon that has Lacan for a head[.] [...] But there *is* no such Lacanian/anti-Lacanian, Maoist/liberal, dialectical/deconstructionist beast. What, then, justifies fabricating this monster? Nothing at all, which is why we find our fast-footed physicists dancing nimbly round the question in their introduction. Their first step is to admit that French postmodernism is largely a figment of the U.S. imagination. Then, in a highly characteristic move, they unabashedly take this concession back, aware that if they cannot hang a frame on the very miscellaneous accused, their slapdash show trial will begin to look more like an experiment in particle physics than a book. (Goshgarian 1999, p. 122)

Sokal and Bricmont's lack of competence forces them to construct a straw man from their fears and prejudices, a shadowy bogeyman that has no meaningful resemblance to any of the actual thinkers they attempt to examine.

The most cogent defense of specific thinkers in Goshgarian's review is reserved for Lacan. Goshgarian returns, in particular, to the example of the Lacanian equation mentioned earlier in this chapter. Like Fink, Goshgarian emphasizes that the equation's validity must be evaluated from the perspective of its discursive context. Sokal and Bricmont's book, he points out,

> shows that a half-dozen passages in Lacan 'make no sense from a mathematical point of view,' whereas what one wants to know is whether they make sense from a *psychoanalytic* point of view; or, conversely, since our authors promise they will 'not enter into the debate on the properly psychoanalytic part of Lacan's work,' and that part of his work is, well, all of it. (Goshgarian 1999, p. 124)

In other words, Lacan's equations may indeed mean little to a mathematician, but that is hardly the point: Lacan's discourse is aimed at psychoanalysts, and the validity of his equations for *them* is surely what matters. Goshgarian makes a similar point about the irrelevance of applying the term 'postmodern' to Lacan. 'Let us also waste no time speculating about what Lacan is doing in a book that blasts postmodernism,' he writes, 'which he probably never heard of, and relativism, which he rejects' (Goshgarian 1999, p. 124). In this respect, Sokal and Bricmont are simply tilting at windmills.

In their essay 'Postures and Impostures: On Lacan's Style and Use of Mathematical Science' (2002), Jason Glynos and Yannis Stavrakakis launch their own defense of Lacan against Sokal and Bricmont's criticisms in *Fashionable Nonsense*. Some of the strategies and arguments that appear in this essay are variations on what Goshgarian, Fink, and others have had to say—indeed, this tendency toward repetition, on both sides, is one of the drawbacks of reading about the Sokal hoax. Glynos and Stavrakakis also reiterate, for instance, that Lacan's use of mathematical notation must be interpreted in the context of psychoanalysis. 'In order to judge whether a physicist is properly interpreting a domain of mathematics one cannot abstain from the experience and knowledge of that field,' they contend. 'How is it possible to judge the pertinence of certain mathematical ideas in an author's work when one can at the same time openly admit that one does not understand the rest of that author's work?' (Glynos and Stavrakakis 2002, pp. 220–221). They likewise note that the accusation of 'postmodern relativism' made in *Fashionable Nonsense* is irrelevant to Lacan's work. 'The epistemic relativism of "postmodern science," the idea that "modern science is nothing more than a 'myth,' a 'narration' or a 'social construction' among many others" [...] is not to be found in the work of Lacan' (Glynos and Stavrakakis 2002, p. 210), an argument borne out not only by a knowledge of Lacan's work, but also by the absence of any supporting evidence in Sokal and Bricmont's book to back up this claim.

The central part of Glynos and Stavrakakis's defense of Lacan, however, focuses on Sokal and Bricmont's criticism of his style. Sokal and Bricmont make the often-difficult writing style of the authors they talk about a central issue in *Fashionable Nonsense*, so that at the end of their chapter on Lacan, for instance, they speculate that his esoteric approach was a linguistic game designed to bamboozle weak-minded disciples into joining his cult of personality. Difficult style, they maintain, is a rhetorical trick that breaks the rules of good pedagogy. While Glynos and Stavrakakis agree that Lacan can be difficult to read—there is a general consensus on that particular issue—what they particularly object to is this confusion of style and substance:

> Let us assume for argument's sake that S&B make a case against Lacan on the grounds of his difficult, non-pedagogical style. To accuse Lacan of this, implying *thereby* that he has nothing of value to say about mathematics in relation to psychoanalysis, would then be to make a category mistake. It would be like ridiculing the work of an eminent physicist at the cutting edge of his or her discipline because he or she was either not willing or not capable of pedagogical delivery. S&B would effectively be collapsing an issue of style onto an issue of substance. (Glynos and Stavrakakis 2002, pp. 214–215)

Furthermore, they argue, when it comes to pedagogy, there is also the open question of who is responsible for acquiring knowledge. Sokal and Bricmont assume that it is the duty of the *teacher* to make the student understand, a pedagogy in which learning is a top-down process that proceeds from the master to their disciples. Glynos and Stavrakakis argue that Lacan's style, by contrast, deliberately subverts this model by making the *student* responsible for learning. 'It has to do with taking responsibility for one's understanding, rather than relying on a consensus of understanding,' they contend. 'In short, Lacan is not celebrating misunderstanding. Rather, he is making an argument in favour of *responsible* understanding' (Glynos and Stavrakakis 2002, p. 214). Lacan's pedagogical approach repeatedly undermines and questions the position of the master in this way.

The conclusion that Glynos and Stavrakakis come to in their paper is that the reason the Sokal hoax and *Fashionable Nonsense* gained so much attention was not that they raised important critical points, but because of the position of mastery and authority that science occupies in today's society. This argument offers a more measured explanation than Goshgarian's accusation that Sokal and Bricmont were simply trying to cash in on the scandal:

> Our verdict is that S&B are guilty of gross intellectual negligence in-so-far as they systematically misunderstand and distort the research programme of Jacques Lacan and its relation to mathematical science. No serious effort is made to give Lacan the benefit of the doubt or to engage in scholarly fashion with the literature on this topic, openly admitting that they know next to nothing about psychoanalysis. Had it not been for S&B's link to the scientific establishment—an institution whose authority one tends to accept without question—*Intellectual Impostures* would not have seen the light of day. (Glynos and Stavrakakis 2002, p. 224)

If they are correct, then science as a social institution, credited with the authority of the 'subject who is supposed to know,' is inherently in conflict with its aim of unswervingly confronting the truth. As Edward Tverdek observes in his review of *The Sokal Hoax*: 'Had Sokal written a sincere, straightforward essay titled "What's Wrong with 'Science Studies' and How it Threatens to Undermine the Left," it would have been long forgotten, even had the editors of *Social Text* decided to publish it at all' (Tverdek 2003, p. 91). Tverdek is correct to say that the Sokal hoax and *Fashionable Nonsense* were never meant to be a reasoned critique of Lacan and his contemporaries. This event was primarily an act of power, a flexing of the muscles of science as a social institution and, as such, an imperious gesture designed to strip away the intellectual authority of an enemy that could only ever be positioned rhetorically as a pretender, a charlatan.

Enjoy Your Enlightenment!

In order to understand the bigger picture of what is at stake in *Fashionable Nonsense*, it is necessary to look beyond the specific treatment of Lacan to examine the broader arguments that Sokal and Bricmont make in their book. Writing a decade after the hoax in *Rhetorical Occasions* (2006), for instance, Michael Bérubé takes a more considered view of what they were setting out to achieve. In contrast to Tallis, whose criticisms were motivated primarily by what he saw as the takeover of the humanities by post-Saussurean theory, Bérubé explains that Sokal, in particular, was heavily influenced by the publication of Paul Gross and Norman Levitt's *Higher Superstition: The Academic Left and Its Quarrels with Science* (1994), a book that provided the basic template for *Fashionable Nonsense*. Gross and Levitt are also scientists, with both Levitt and Sokal claiming to be 'old-fashioned' adherents of the left who were concerned by the political direction of French theory.

Rather than openly taking a side in this conflict, Bérubé portrays the confrontation between science and the humanities as riddled with mutual misunderstandings. 'Sokal's explanation of his hoax demonstrated that he didn't know very much about theories of rhetoric and language, none of which requires a suspension of belief in the "real," or phenomenal, world,' he explains. 'To many humanists, Sokal's cry, "If everything is language, then everything is permitted" sounded as strange as the cry, "If everything is atoms and chemicals, then everything is meaningless" might sound to a scientist' (Bérubé 2006, p. 17). Bérubé takes seriously Sokal's claim that his real concern is with a more traditional debate about politics. At its center is a conflict over scientific foundationalism versus postmodern anti-foundationalism (or, to put it in more familiar terms, universalism v. relativism). 'The Sokal fallout is so critical, I think, precisely because it has forced a confrontation between these two theories of justification for political belief and action,' contends Bérubé (2006, p. 36). The deeper question that the hoax opened up was whether 'anti-foundationalist theoretical commitments undermine progressive politics' (Bérubé 2006, p. 35). For Sokal and Bricmont, the answer to that question lies in the affirmative, a perspective that casts French theory as a new irrationalism that is incompatible with their narrow understanding of rational, Enlightenment-based politics and thought.

Whereas critics of Sokal and Bricmont tend to acknowledge the scientific and mathematical mistakes identified in *Fashionable Nonsense* as being the strongest part of their case, Bérubé takes the alternative view that this part of the book is actually the least consequential. After all, 'even if Lacan was a charlatan toward the end of his life, twiddling with knots and holding five-minute sham therapy sessions, who cares?' (Bérubé 2006, p. 56).

Instead, he suggests that readers of *Fashionable Nonsense* consider it as a book of two parts, the second half of which has too often been neglected:

> At the very least, Sokal and Bricmont have made the case that there was something very odd about the French psychoanalytic left in the 1960s and 1970s, and that oddness varied directly with the influence of Jacques Lacan (who, in his senescence, became unfathomably odd himself). But this half of the book, though it gives the book its title, isn't the half worth learning from. The book's other half consists of a handful of essays on the status of knowledge in the sciences and humanities; it's here that the book offers something edifying and useful and here that its argument is really worth debating. (Bérubé 2006, p. 55)

While I disagree with Bérubé's reformulation of the book's central theme in terms of a political debate over the foundations of progressivism, an error that comes from taking Sokal's left-wing credentials at face value, his recommendation that readers consider the importance of these overlooked chapters of *Fashionable Nonsense* is nonetheless solid. After all, the problem with even the best and most insightful Lacanian defenses is that they are too narrowly focused on the chapter that deals with Lacan. This approach prevents critics from seeing that chapter in the context of the bigger intellectual picture that Sokal and Bricmont are painting.

The painstaking work that critics have put into countering Sokal and Bricmont's charges against Lacan has provided some small, technical victories, but they do not change the fact that *Fashionable Nonsense*, for all its many faults, has achieved a significant public relations triumph that such refutations do little to overturn. The attention created first by the original Sokal hoax, and then by the clamor surrounding the book, achieved the ultimate aim of its authors, which was to consolidate the prestige and authority of science in the minds of both its practitioners and the general public. Any effective response to Sokal and Bricmont cannot focus solely on deconstructing the minutiae of their arguments or the weakness of their methodology while missing this key point. A genuine critique of *Fashionable Nonsense* must counter its effects at this broader level, and to do so it is necessary to understand exactly how they achieved such a victory. There is a marked difference between Sokal and Bricmont's calm and measured style and the verbal pyrotechnics of reviewers like Dawkins and Tallis. Indeed, there is admirable skill and restraint in the way they present their arguments (as opposed to the poverty of the arguments themselves) that gives new energy to some very old rhetorical maneuvers. In contrast to the controversy surrounding *Fashionable Nonsense*, for instance, Sokal and Bricmont strategically emphasize their purported 'neutrality' on two important fronts. The first is the charge that, as scientists and mathematicians, they are opposed to the humanities and the social sciences, thus perpetuating the hostility of the division between these two areas of inquiry. To nullify this accusation, Sokal and Bricmont address the issue in the introduction to their book:

> We are not attacking philosophy, the humanities or the social sciences *in general*; on the contrary, we feel that these fields are of the utmost importance and we want to warn those who work in them (especially students) against some manifest cases of charlatanism. In particular, we want to 'deconstruct' the reputation that certain texts have of being difficult because the ideas in them are so profound. In many cases we shall demonstrate that if the texts seem incomprehensible, it is for the excellent reason that they mean precisely nothing. (Sokal and Bricmont 1998, p. 5)

This position is restated in a preface added to later editions of *Fashionable Nonsense*, in which Sokal and Bricmont distance themselves from some of their reviewers. 'Similarly, to view this book as a generalized criticism of the humanities or the social sciences—as some French reviewers did—not only misunderstands our intentions, but is a curious assimilation, revealing a contemptuous attitude toward those fields in the minds of those reviewers' (Sokal and Bricmont 1998, p. xi). The putatively 'neutral' position which Sokal and Bricmont occupy leads them to promise that they will only make judgments about their particular areas of expertise. '[W]e do not purport to judge Lacan's psychoanalysis, Deleuze's philosophy, or Latour's concrete work in sociology,' they insist, 'We limit ourselves to their statements about the mathematical and physical sciences or about elementary problems in the philosophy of science' (Sokal and Bricmont 1998, p. 4).

For similar reasons, secondly, they reject any accusations that they are agents of political conservatism, or that they are opposed to the (mostly) left-wing thinkers they criticize due to ideological reasons. Sokal and Bricmont insist that they themselves are left-wing humanists who, far from being conservatives, are simply concerned about the intellectual and political direction of their own side. 'But our book is not against political radicalism, it is against intellectual confusion,' they write. 'Our aim is not to criticize the left, but to help defend it from a trendy segment of itself' (Sokal and Bricmont 1998, p. xiii). Sokal and Bricmont may claim that such statements about their intellectual and political positions are a practical consequence of their insistence on theoretical clarity, but there is an underlying rhetorical point to all this positioning. To situate oneself as both a political moderate and a thinker who respects the boundaries of expertise is to project oneself as a model of 'reasonableness.' Whether or not that is an accurate characterization hardly matters: *Fashionable Nonsense* is a performance intended to create a division, by the power of rhetoric rather than reason, into the opposing camps of measured rationality, represented by the forces of Enlightenment and science, and the 'dangerous' radicalism of the postmodernists, a dichotomy that Sokal and Bricmont play for all it is worth.

This scenario is enacted whenever Sokal and Bricmont deal with the challenge of postmodernism: first, they set themselves up as the agents of truth and rationality, then they charge postmodern thinkers with misleading their disciples through the seductive power of their words, an accusation that is repeated in passages again and again:

> Displaying a superficial erudition by shamelessly throwing around technical terms in a context where they are completely irrelevant. The goal is, no doubt, to impress and, above all, to intimidate the non-scientist reader. [...] Manipulating phrases and sentences that are, in fact, meaningless. Some of these authors exhibit a veritable intoxication with words, combined with a superb indifference to their meaning. (Sokal and Bricmont 1998, p. 5)

> They imagine, perhaps, that they can exploit the prestige of the natural sciences in order to give their own discourse a veneer of rigor. And they seem

> confident that no one will notice their misuse of scientific concepts. No one is going to cry out that the king is naked. (Sokal and Bricmont 1998, p. 5)

> But if these writers have become international stars primarily for sociological rather than intellectual reasons, and in part because they are masters of language and can impress their audience with a clever abuse of sophisticated terminology—nonscientific as well as scientific—then the revelations contained in this essay may indeed have significant repercussions. (Sokal and Bricmont 1998, p. 8)

Positioning themselves as the models of sincerity and reasonableness, and their postmodern opponents as cynical manipulators who abuse their mastery of language in order to mislead their audiences, Sokal and Bricmont score a victory by this clever use of rhetorical tricks (even as, like Socrates against the Sophists, they denounce them in their opponents).

Looking beyond the Lacan chapter to examine the broader critique of postmodernism put forward in Chaps. 4 and 7 of *Fashionable Nonsense* reveals how, from the very beginning, Sokal and Bricmont characterize postmodernism as a perverse and irrational challenge to the legacy of the Enlightenment:

> '[P]ostmodernism': an intellectual current characterized by the more-or-less explicit rejection of the rationalist tradition of the Enlightenment, by theoretical discourses disconnected from any empirical test, and by a cognitive and cultural relativism that regards science as nothing more than a 'narration', a 'myth' or a social construction among many others. (Sokal and Bricmont 1998, p. 1)

Sokal and Bricmont situate themselves, by contrast, as the defenders of the Enlightenment tradition of rationality. In Chap. 4, they launch an assault on what they call 'epistemic relativism,' beginning with the dismissal of two key philosophical methods: solipsism and radical skepticism. Although Sokal and Bricmont acknowledge there may be some technical validity to these approaches, they argue that the importance of these concepts is nonetheless only of marginal practical value. Such 'radical' logic is too focused on the extremes, on the exceptions, to the detriment of understanding how the world in general works. As such, these 'outlying' philosophical concerns can more profitably be marginalized in order to focus pragmatically on the larger benefits of scientific reason.

> Once the general problems of solipsism and radical skepticism have been set aside, we can get down to work. Let us suppose that we are able to obtain some more-or-less reliable knowledge of the world, at least in everyday life. We can then ask: *To what extent* are our senses reliable or not? To answer this question, we can compare sense impressions among themselves and vary certain parameters of our everyday experience. We can map out in this way, step by step, a practical rationality. When this is done systematically and with sufficient precision, science can begin. (Sokal and Bricmont 1998, p. 56)

However 'reasonable' this proposal may sound, this approach can hardly be characterized as following in the footsteps of the Enlightenment. Solipsism and radical skepticism are the very foundation of the Enlightenment tradition, the keys to understanding its greatest thinkers. Francis Bacon, René Descartes, Baruch Spinoza, Blaise Pascal, David Hume, and Immanuel Kant all built their ideas on a foundation of radical doubt and solipsistic inquiry, without which the Enlightenment could not exist. Sokal and Bricmont's version of the Enlightenment thus excludes the key defining features of its most important thinkers. Indeed, according to this definition, which historical Enlightenment figures actually *can* be included? Sokal and Bricmont, characteristically, do not say.

Sokal and Bricmont are also unable to link this so-called 'anti-Enlightenment' critique of postmodern relativism to any of the theorists they claim to examine in the course of *Fashionable Nonsense*. Instead, they set up a generalized 'radical skeptic' as their target:

> [T]he radical skeptic or relativist will ask what distinguishes science from other types of discourse about reality [...] and, above all, what *criteria* are used to make such a distinction. [...] First of all, there are some general (but basically negative) epistemological principles, which go back at least to the seventeenth century: to be skeptical of *a priori* arguments, revelation, sacred texts, and arguments from authority. Moreover, the experience

> accumulated during three centuries of scientific practice has given us a series of more-or-less general methodological principles [...] that can be justified by rational arguments. However, we do not claim that these principles can be codified in a definitive way, nor that the list is exhaustive. [...] Nevertheless—and this is the main difference between us and the radical skeptics—we think that well-developed scientific theories are in general supported by good arguments, but the rationality of those arguments must be analyzed case-by-case. (Sokal and Bricmont 1998, p. 58)

Again, without producing actual examples, this 'radical skeptic' can never be anything but a straw man. In fact, none of the thinkers referred to in *Fashionable Nonsense* are straightforwardly opposed to the Enlightenment, but instead represent different responses to the problem of how meaning and value are to be determined in a world where authority has been radically destabilized by Enlightenment rationality.

Every aspect of modernity ultimately turns on this instability, which upsets previous ideas about religious belief, political power and, with the discovery of the unconscious, who we think we are. As Saul Newman writes in *The Politics of Postanarchism* (2010):

> The problem is [...] that aspects of the Enlightenment paradigm have broken down and are no longer sustainable[.] [...] It is not so much that ideas of emancipation and rational enlightenment have been relinquished, but there is a certain scepticism regarding their universality[.] [...] [T]he Enlightenment paradigm must be reconsidered; its discursive limits must be interrogated. That is precisely what poststructuralist thinkers like Derrida, Lacan, Lyotard and Foucault have tried to do. It is entirely incorrect to say that poststructuralist thought is anti-Enlightenment. Rather, it sees the attempt to transcend the limitations of Enlightenment thought as being part of the very project of the Enlightenment. Central to the Enlightenment, in other words, is a critical reflection on its own limits. (Newman 2010, pp. 46–47)

Sokal and Bricmont, by contrast, describe a world in which these anxieties only exist as the obsessions of extremists and illusionists, who try to distract us from the 'real' task of allowing the transparent instruments of rationality to get on with the job of revealing the secrets of the universe.

All this postmodern doubt seems to them so neurotic, so paranoid—and yet the instruments of reason and science are only possible (and indeed, only necessary) because of a compulsive, radical skepticism that pushes us to doubt and verify in an endless cycle of uncertainty that has engulfed even our subjectivity. Sokal and Bricmont take the thinkers in *Fashionable Nonsense* to task for their abuse of scientific and mathematical discourse, when it is they who are guilty of stripping the Enlightenment of the radical forces of skepticism that make modern science possible. They thereby reduce science to a form of bourgeois 'reasonableness' that refuses to see the value and purpose of any other kind of rationality. While claiming to support the Enlightenment, therefore, they actually distort and betray its core values and ideas.

Sokal and Bricmont's rejection of the more 'radical' elements of Enlightenment thought has a long and oppressive genealogy. In the introduction to *Enjoy Your Symptom!* (1992), Žižek notes how, despite the Enlightenment's apparent challenge to traditional authority, it has a track record of placing limitations on the amount of actual subversion it will tolerate. Žižek points to the example of Kant's essay 'Answering the Question: What is Enlightenment?' (1784), in which Kant

> provides the famous definition of Enlightenment as 'man's release from his self-incurred tutelage,' i.e., his courage to make use of his understanding without direction from another, he supplements the motto 'Argue freely!' by 'Argue as much as you will, and about what you will, but obey!' This and not 'Do not obey but argue!' is, according to Kant, the Enlightenment's answer to the demand of traditional authority. 'Do not argue but obey!' We must be careful here not to miss what Kant is aiming at—he is not simply restating the common motto of conformism, 'In private, think whatever you want, but in public, obey the authorities!' but rather its opposite: in public, 'as a scholar before the reading public,' use your reason freely, yet in private (at your post, in your family, i.e. as a cog in the social machine) obey authority! (Žižek 2008, pp. xxi–xxii)

Kant is not alone in championing this division, remarks Žižek, noting that the 'same split occurs already in Descartes,' so that from the beginning to the end of the Enlightenment period, from Descartes to Kant, this division between public questioning and private obedience constitutes the prevailing attitude (Žižek 2008, p. xxii). The title of *Enjoy Your Symptom!* captures perfectly the paradoxical logic at work here. Lurking beneath it is the contradiction that so confounded Spinoza: if something is designated as 'good,' why must we be commanded to enjoy it? Shouldn't we naturally experience something that is good as enjoyable and desirable, therefore making such a command redundant? The existence of such an apparently unnecessary imperative alerts us to its underlying ideological purpose, a repression designed to close off critical questioning for the sake of conformity. Žižek thus argues that the result of the public/private division outlined by both Kant and Descartes leads to a functional form of cynicism.

> The ideological attitude opened up by this split [...] is that of cynicism, of cynical distance which pertains to the very notion of Enlightenment and which today seems to have reached its apogee: although officially undermined, devalorized, authority returns through the sidedoor—'we know there is no truth in authority, yet we continue to play its game and to obey it in order not to disturb the usual run of things...' Truth is suspended in the name of efficiency: the ultimate legitimization of the system is that it works. (Žižek 2008, p. xxii)

With these words, Žižek puts his finger on the mindset that underpins *Fashionable Nonsense*. Look at how well everything done by modern science and mathematics works, is the real message of Sokal and Bricmont's ideology, and then consider how ungrateful your criticism of the Enlightenment really is! How dare you show your lack of respect by having the temerity to question its limitations and contradictions, like that charlatan Lacan! Stop this nonsense and enjoy your Enlightenment!

Mathematics and Mastery

The version of the Enlightenment that Sokal and Bricmont assemble in *Fashionable Nonsense* is thus an ideological construct that insidiously rewrites the Enlightenment's genealogy in order to justify their own authority. In his essay 'What is Enlightenment?' (1984), Foucault observes how this kind of strategy is often used as a kind of intellectual 'blackmail,' painting even the most reasonable criticisms of the Enlightenment as 'irrational' and 'anti-Enlightenment.' That is why Foucault tries to articulate a position that aligns with the ethos of the Enlightenment while retaining the freedom to be critical of its shortcomings:

> But that does not mean that one has to be 'for' or 'against' the Enlightenment. It even means precisely that one has to refuse everything that might present itself in the form of a simplistic and authoritarian alternative: you either accept the Enlightenment and remain within the tradition of its rationalism (this is considered a positive term by some and used by others, on the contrary, as a reproach); or else you criticize the Enlightenment and then try to escape from its principles of rationality (which may be seen once again as good or bad). (Foucault 1984, p. 43)

Lacan's work is located in a similar critical space, one that builds on the Enlightenment while remaining critical of its limitations. 'As for me,' states Lacan in *Seminar XIX*, 'as I wrote on the back cover of my *Écrits*, I take the side of the Enlightenment thinkers' (Lacan 2018, p. 22). Miller reiterates this position in his introduction to *Television*: 'My reference was and still is the Enlightenment. That was Lacan's reference as well, but in his own way' (Lacan 1990, p. xxv). Contrary to what Sokal and Bricmont claim, at no stage does Lacan ever reject the Enlightenment tradition.

Indeed, when in *Seminar XI* Lacan sketches his own genealogy of the conditions that made psychoanalysis possible, the key point of origin he highlights, one that long predates the advent of Freud, is the Enlightenment figure of Descartes. The importance of Descartes lies in the 'split' he creates in modern thought, which divides the subject between certainty and doubt. Lacan highlights in particular how certainty, not truth, is the focus of Descartes's search. Certainty is important because it can only come from something that appears to possess genuine authority. Descartes's philosophical quest is to use his method to discover an authority that stands up to the scrutiny of absolute doubt. In the same manner, Lacan argues, 'Freud's method is Cartesian—in the sense that he sets out from the basis of the subject of certainty' (Lacan 1994, p. 35). What

Lacan is saying, in his idiosyncratic way, is that Freud was a Cartesian in a specific and unconventional sense. Freud takes the principle of rational doubt and reapplies it, more radically, to the sovereignty of the human subject, to the 'I' that announces itself in Descartes's famous formula. 'I think,' says Descartes—but what Freud then does is to doubt, systematically, that it is the 'I' that is actually doing the thinking. Lacan then makes a shrewd comparison of the disruptive function of Cartesian doubt to the discovery of displacement by the ancient Greek mathematician, Archimedes:

> It seems something of a new departure—and it is—that I should have referred to the subject when speaking of the unconscious. I thought I had succeeded in making you feel that all this happens in the same place, in the place of the subject, which—from the Cartesian experience reducing to a single point the ground of inaugural certainty—has taken on an Archimedic value, if indeed that really was the point of application that made possible the quite different direction that science has taken, namely, that initiated by Newton. (Lacan 1994, p. 43)

Descartes's method of systematic doubt created a rational system for challenging all forms of authority, a philosophical gesture that displaced, for instance, the Scholasticism that dominated intellectual thought during the late medieval period. At the same time, Lacan argues, Descartes created the tools that would, in turn, displace the authority of his own philosophy. This rational doubt is the true heart of the Enlightenment project.

In spite of Descartes's stated intention of placing no limits on doubt, he retreated from this position when it began to threaten his religious beliefs. In *Meditations on First Philosophy* (1641), in particular, Descartes expresses his concern that atheists might use his method to doubt the existence of God. This maneuver is repeated in *Fashionable Nonsense* when Sokal and Bricmont declare that the tools of Enlightenment rationality may be used to examine the world, but if a thinker strays beyond a certain limit they are suddenly designated a 'radical skeptic or relativist' (Sokal and Bricmont 1998, p. 58). Yet there is nothing demonstrably 'reasonable' about this limit, since it is a wholly arbitrary line between rational doubt and radical skepticism that Sokal and Bricmont are drawing, one that they do not (and cannot) define clearly and distinctly.

Descartes's attempt to prove the existence of God is an instructive example of how, even in a system that radically challenges authority, it remains possible to re-establish the master's authority by using a logical loophole. For Descartes, God functions as the ultimate guarantor of logical consistency, a non-deceptive Other. Descartes is so convinced that God and logic overlap that he deploys their convergence as a decisive argument against atheism:

> Besides, an atheist knows clearly and distinctly that the three angles of a triangle are equal to two right angles. However, they are so far from supposing God's existence that they openly deny it because, they argue, if God existed he would be the supreme being, the supreme good, that is, he would be infinite. But in every class, the infinite excludes every other perfection, that is, every entity and good and, even more, every non-entity and evil; since there are many things, beings, goods, non-beings and evils, we think you should answer this objection properly so that the impious have nothing left to rely on. (Descartes 2003, p. 78)

Yet making God the guarantor of the rules of logical thought is a dangerous step, Lacan points out, because having taken truth into his own hands with his method, Descartes now gives it back 'into the hands of the Other, in this instance the perfect God' (Lacan 1994, p. 36). Because this God is supposed to be sovereign 'whatever he might have meant, would always be *the* truth—even if he had said that two and two make five, it would have been true' (Lacan 1994, p. 36). Far from being the guarantor of logic, Descartes gives God the authority to be arbitrary to the point where even basic mathematical logic can be regarded as certain, not because it is irrefutably correct, but purely *because God says it is so.*

For Lacan, this logical twist is nonetheless a crucial moment, for while Descartes's attempt to establish the sovereignty of God by refracting it through the weight of mathematical certainty is a failure, it does nonetheless establish that there is a form of authority that is impervious to rational doubt: mathematical logic. Descartes is right to say that neither he, nor his atheist opponents, can dispute the formal properties of a triangle, but this is not because God (the Other) guarantees this state of affairs. Whether it is a triangle or a mathematical equation, the authority of its irrefutability lies within itself—quite simply, logic does not need a divine guarantor to confirm that it is correct:

> In effect, Descartes inaugurates the initial bases of a science in which God has nothing to do. For the characteristic of our science, and its difference with ancient sciences, is that nobody even dares, without incurring ridicule, to wonder whether God knows anything about it, whether God leafs through modern treatises on mathematics to keep up to date. (Lacan 1994, p. 226)

Lacan's reading of Descartes in *Seminar XI* is thus essential for understanding his recurrent avowal that mathematics is connected to the real. This insistence does not come from the idea that mathematical formalization can describe *reality* more accurately, but rather because equations carry the weight of an authority that can be neither refuted nor explained.

As Badiou demonstrates in his essay 'Lacan and the Pre-Socratics' (2006) this notion of authority is the cornerstone of thought even at the dawn of Greek philosophy, before the foundations of mathematics had been laid. 'The question reaches far beyond the point where, with Descartes, we enter the modern epoch of the subject, or what Lacan calls the subject of science,' argues Badiou. 'Of course, psychoanalysis could appear only within the element of this modernity' (Badiou 2006, p. 7). How, then, can the Pre-Socratics play the important role that Badiou assigns to them if 'Lacan holds mathematization to be the key to any thinkable relation to the Real' and 'never varied on this point' (Badiou 2006, p. 8)? Because, contends Badiou, like Descartes, the Pre-Socratic philosophers applied rational doubt to Greek mythical thought, creating a new discourse that grounded its authority in the power of logic:

> [T]heir writings prefigure mathematization, although the latter is not present in its literal form. The premonition appears in its paradoxical inversion, the use of poetic form. Far from opposing, as Heidegger did, the Pre-

> Socratic poem to Plato's matheme, Lacan has the powerful idea that poetry was the closest thing to mathematization available to the Pre-Socratics. […] [T]he poetic form contains a grandiose anticipation of the matheme. (Badiou 2006, p. 9)

The Pre-Socratics did not have access to mathematics, argues Badiou, but their philosophy rests not on the capricious will of the divine, but on the newfound power of logic to explain the world. The authority of logic and mathematics, similarly, is the foundation of Lacanian thought, which always opposes itself to the arbitrary power of both master and divinity.

Among the Pre-Socratic thinkers, Badiou notes that there is a 'canonical opposition between Parmenides and Heraclitus,' with Lacan opting, 'quite explicitly, for the latter' (Badiou 2006, p. 8). Parmenides is the founder of the philosophical tradition, a thinker who 'attests to the fact that the grasp of thought upon the Real can be established only by the regulated power of the letter' (Badiou 2006, p. 9). He uses the organizing structure of the philosophical poem to think about the world. Badiou argues that Heraclitus and Lacan, by contrast, are 'anti-philosophers' who seek to push the limits of thought toward the real of the unconscious:

> Lacan is an anti-philosopher. This anti-philosophy, however, is already manifested, in a certain sense, by Heraclitus. The philosophical idea is that being thinks, for want of a Real. Against this idea, Heraclitus immediately puts forward the diagonal dimension of signification, which is neither revelation nor dissimulation, but an act. In the same way, the heart of the psychoanalytic procedure lies in the act itself. Heraclitus thus puts in its place the pretension of the master, of the oracle at Delphi, but also the pretension of the philosopher to be the one who listens to the voice of the being who is supposed to think. (Badiou 2006, p. 15)

Heraclitus is also the great thinker of becoming, of the ungraspable nature of existence that so resembles the notion of the unconscious. He does not have the same modern tools as Lacan to articulate these ideas, but he nonetheless puts his finger on the problem of authority. In such a world, the one who claims to be a master can only be a fraud and a charlatan.

Lacan's interest in mathematics is intimately related to this theme of mastery. In the best Cartesian tradition, he sets out to doubt systematically, to allow nothing to stand on authority. Mathematics is fascinating to him precisely because it is authoritative. Its equations have an irrefutable power, a power that is grounded in rational logic—and yet the power of that rationality cannot itself be explained. Why do two plus two equal four, and not five? Why do the interior angles of a triangle always add up to the sum of two right angles? Why the world is structured in conformity with this logic remains as inexplicable as the mystery that it exists in the first place. Like Heraclitus, Lacan discovers the irrational authority that lies even at the heart of rationality. Bérubé's earlier observation that the Sokal and Bricmont controversy is ultimately about foundationalism versus anti-foundationalism, and his question as to which of these two modes leads to a progressive politics, thus finds its answer: the master's discourse is always ultimately on the side of foundationalism. Whether it is the defense of theism in Descartes, or of an idealized Enlightenment in Sokal and Bricmont, what we are really witnessing are examples of reactive thinkers who are re-asserting their masterly authority in order to retreat from the more disturbing implications of their thought. For these ideological reasons, Lacan is cast as a 'radical' in whose thought Sokal and Bricmont claim we not only *cannot* find anything of value, but also, in that eternal irony of the paternal 'no,' we *must* not.

References

Badiou, A., 2006. Lacan and the Pre-Socratics. In: S. Žižek, ed. *Lacan: The Silent Partners*. London and New York: Verso, pp. 7–16.

Bérubé, M., 2006. *Rhetorical Occasions: Essays on Humans and the Humanities*. Chapel Hill: University of North Carolina Press.

Bowie, M., 1991. *Lacan*. London: Fontana.

Clément, C., 1983. *The Lives and Legends of Jacques Lacan*. New York: Columbia University Press.

Dawkins, R., 1998. Postmodernism Disrobed. *Nature*, 9 July, Volume 394, p. 141.

Derrida, J., 2005. 'Sokal and Bricmont Aren't Serious'. In: *Paper Machine*. Stanford: Stanford University Press, pp. 70–72.
Descartes, R., 2003. *Meditations and Other Metaphysical Writings*. London: Penguin.
Dor, J., 1996. The Epistemological Status of Lacan's Mathematical Paradigms. In: D. Pettigrew & F. Raffoul, eds. *Disseminating Lacan*. Albany(NY): State University of New York Press, pp. 109–121.
Fink, B., 2004. *Lacan to the Letter: Reading Écrits Closely*. Minneapolis: University of Minnesota Press.
Foucault, M., 1984. What is Enlightenment? In: P. Rabinow, ed. *The Foucault Reader*. New York: Pantheon, pp. 32–50.
Gallop, J., 1985. *Reading Lacan*. Ithaca(NY) and London: Cornell University Press.
Glynos, J. & Stavrakakis, Y., 2002. Postures and Impostures: On Lacan's Style and Use of Mathematical Science. In: J. Glynos & Y. Stavrakakis, eds. *Lacan and Science*. London and New York: Karnac, pp. 207–229.
Goshgarian, G., 1999. Review of *Impostures Intellectuelles*. *Rethinking Marxism*, 11(1), pp. 120–131.
Lacan, J., 1988. *The Seminar of Jacques Lacan, Book II: The Ego in Freud's Theory and in the Techniques of Psychoanalysis, 1954–1955*. Cambridge: Cambridge University Press.
Lacan, J., 1990. *Television: A Challenge to the Psychoanalytic Establishment*. New York and London: W.W. Norton & Company.
Lacan, J., 1994. *The Four Fundamental Concepts of Psycho-Analysis*. Harmondsworth: Penguin.
Lacan, J., 2018. *The Seminar of Jacques Lacan, Book XIX: …or Worse*. Cambridge UK and Malden MA: Polity.
Macey, D., 1988. *Lacan in Contexts*. London and New York: Verso.
Melville, S., 1987. Psychoanalysis and the Place of 'Jouissance'. *Critical Inquiry*, 13(2), pp. 349–370.
Newman, S., 2010. *The Politics of Postanarchism*. Edinburgh: Edinburgh University Press.
Roudinesco, É., 1997. *Jacques Lacan: Outline of a Life, History of a System of Thought*. New York: Columbia University Press.
Roustang, F., 1990. *The Lacanian Delusion*. Oxford: Oxford University Press.
Sokal, A. & Bricmont, J., 1998. *Fashionable Nonsense: Postmodern Intellectuals' Abuse of Science*. New York: Picador.

Tallis, R., 1988. *Not Saussure: A Critique of Post-Saussurean Literary Theory*. Basingstoke and London: Macmillan.
Tallis, R., 1999. Sokal and Bricmont: Is this the beginning of the end of the dark ages in the humanities? *PN Review*, Volume 128, pp. 35–42.
Tverdek, E., 2003. Review: Fool Me Once. *Science and Society*, 67(1), pp. 87–99.
Žižek, S., 2008. *Enjoy Your Symptom! Jacques Lacan in Hollywood and Out*. New York: Routledge.

4

Lacan the Scientific Charlatan

A Confession of Faith

In 2005, Jonathan Gottschall and David Sloan Wilson published a collection of essays titled *The Literary Animal: Evolution and the Nature of Narrative*, which formed part of an ambitious project to establish a Darwinian model of literary studies in the first decade of the twenty-first century. While the book featured many familiar names from the field of 'literary Darwinism,' it also included several authors whose support for the project might have come as a surprise to some readers. The first chapter in the collection, for instance, 'Literature, Science, and Human Nature,' by the novelist Ian McEwan, is a beautifully-written meditation that illustrates just how little human nature has changed in the three thousand years since Homer. McEwan's reflections on Odysseus's homecoming, especially the reader's ability to identify with a character who seems so distant in time and yet whose emotions still resonate with our own, are a powerful reminder of how biology plays a crucial role in determining who we are as human beings. Another of the more surprising chapters in the book is a piece titled 'From Lacan to Darwin' by Dylan Evans, a secular confession of faith in which Evans traces the path that led

P. D. Mathews, *Lacan the Charlatan*, The Palgrave Lacan Series,
https://doi.org/10.1007/978-3-030-45204-9_4

him to renounce psychoanalysis in order to become an evolutionary psychologist.

This feeling of surprise derives from the fact that, only a few years before, Evans was best known to scholars in the humanities as an emerging expert on Lacanian theory. His first book, *An Introductory Dictionary of Lacanian Psychoanalysis* (1996), is a glossary of terms and concepts that is still widely used and cited by critics. Two years after that book, Evans also contributed the essay 'From Kantian Ethics to Mystical Experience: An Exploration of Jouissance' to Nobus's *Key Concepts of Lacanian Psychoanalysis*, its position as the opening chapter signaling to readers that Evans was a rising star in the field. The personal story outlined in 'From Lacan to Darwin,' therefore, is a tale of 'apostasy,' a rupture with Lacan in favor of evolutionary psychology (Evans 2005, p. 38). In reality, this break had already been signaled by a flurry of books that Evans published in the years leading up to *The Literary Animal*, including *Introducing Evolutionary Psychology* (1999), *Emotion: The Science of Sentiment* (2001), *Introducing Evolution* (2001), and *Emotion, Evolution and Rationality* (2004), all of which were written using the ideas and methods of evolutionary psychology rather than Lacanian psychoanalysis.

As with *Fashionable Nonsense*, the importance of 'From Lacan to Darwin' lies less in the substance of what it says than its rhetorical performance, its public affirmation of the author's adherence to a particular set of ideas and beliefs. 'This is the story of an intellectual journey,' writes Evans, following, without seeming to be aware that he is doing so, the long-established formula of the confession of faith. 'It starts with my enthusiastic embrace of the ideas of the French psychoanalyst Jacques Lacan and ends with my eventual rejection of those ideas some five years later' (Evans 2005, p. 38). Dylan Evans once was a blind Lacanian sinner but now, thanks to the grace of science, he sees. This performance is not only an affirmation of the scientific community he wishes to embrace but also a public renunciation of the Lacanian community he has left behind:

> Nowadays, […] I occasionally receive e-mails from puzzled Lacanians[.] […] The most interesting thing about these e-mails is not so much their

> content as their tone, which tends to be one of shock, dismay, or anger that a former disciple should have betrayed the faith so completely. They may not use religious references explicitly, but it is clear from their vexation that it is more than just an intellectual matter for these correspondents. They do not see my change of mind as the result of an honest and sincere search for truth but as a betrayal, an apostasy, a fall from grace. (Evans 2005, p. 38)

Evans uses these religious terms to frame his break with Lacanian thought, which he characterizes as a kind of false belief. There is no obvious reason to doubt Evans when he says that his intellectual shift is 'the result of an honest and sincere search for truth,' yet his example nonetheless provides a fascinating case study of how scientific rationality can subvert its own claims to being reasonable.

What distinguishes Evans from the critics examined so far is that he is extremely well-qualified to carry out a meaningful critique of Lacan's work. Evans recalls that he first encountered Lacan's theories while working as an English teacher in Argentina in 1992. Upon returning to England in 1993, he did a master's degree in psychoanalytic studies at the University of Kent at Canterbury while also training to become a psychoanalyst, a process that saw him regularly travel for short periods to Paris to undertake sessions with a French mentor. As this process neared its completion, Evans recounts that he began to have doubts although, in a continuation of the chapter's religious echoes, there was 'no blind flash of insight, no awful moment when it suddenly dawned on me' unlike St. Paul's vision on the road to Damascus (Evans 2005, p. 42). Instead, it was his immersion in Lacan's ideas while writing his dictionary that Evans credits for initiating the break:

> As far as the theory was concerned, it was the process of writing the dictionary that was most responsible for my growing skepticism. As I became more familiar with Lacan's teachings, the internal contradictions and lack of external confirmation became ever more apparent. And as I tried to make sense of Lacan's bizarre rhetoric, it became clearer to me that the obfuscatory language did not hide a deeper meaning but was in fact a direct manifestation of the confusion inherent in Lacan's own thought. But whereas most of Lacan's commentators preferred to ape the master's style

> and perpetuate the obscurity, I wanted to dissipate the haze and expose whatever was underneath—even if it meant seeing that the emperor was naked. […] Ironically, it was this attempt to open Lacanian theory up to criticism that played a major role in leading me to reject Lacanian theory myself. (Evans 2005, p. 42)

Evans thus repeats the now-familiar charge that Lacan was nothing more than a clever stylist who used the brilliance of his rhetoric to delude his followers into believing in him, that underneath this flashy exterior there is nothing but a void, that he is an emperor with no clothes, a charlatan.

This feeling grew, recounts Evans, when he decided to pursue further academic studies in Lacanian theory. Finding that his clinical options were limited in Great Britain, he enrolled in a doctoral program in literary theory at Buffalo, an American university famous for its Lacanian focus. He was disappointed to discover that the students and academics there were only interested in Lacan from a literary perspective, an approach that, for Evans, was too detached from the world of clinical analysis. 'No wonder they were so unconcerned about the consistency of Lacan's ideas,' he concludes. 'They had completely misunderstood the whole of Lacan's project' (Evans 2005, p. 45). Evans left Buffalo shortly after, instead undertaking a doctorate in philosophy at the London School of Economics, where his suspicions that Lacan was just a master stylist with no substance continued to deepen:

> That's when I began to realize, with growing alarm and shame, that I had never really asked myself what the evidence for psychoanalysis was! I had simply been carried along by the panache and stylistic flourishes of two great wordsmiths—Freud and Lacan—without pausing to ask the most important question of all: On what evidence did they base their far-reaching claims? And was that evidence sufficiently solid to support those claims? (Evans 2005, p. 45)

Evans claims that he grew increasingly concerned that Lacan's disciples never questioned his theories or put them to the test. They treated his work 'as if it were holy writ,' complains Evans, and acted as though 'Lacan was supposed to be immune from criticism' (Evans 2005, pp. 45–46). The rigid orthodoxy of the Lacanians contrasted poorly with the intellectual energy of the Darwin Seminars held at the London School of Economics, which featured speakers like Steven Pinker and Daniel Dennett. It was their influence, in particular, that helped to transform Evans from a Lacanian into an evolutionary psychologist.

Evans follows this personal tale of his intellectual journey with his chief critical objections to Lacanian thought. Drawing mainly on Lacan's work on the 'mirror stage,' Evans's first point of criticism is the systematic way that Lacan purges Freudian thought of its biological basis, and so turns psychoanalysis into a cultural or philosophical project. 'These developments in Lacan's concept of the mirror stage are a microcosm of changes in his work as a whole,' claims Evans. 'Other strands in his work show the same shift away from the empirical world of biology to the metaphysical world of "structures"' (Evans 2005, p. 48). Evans charges Lacan with retreating from reality into a kind of structuralist idealism in order to insulate psychoanalysis from empirical criticism:

> This strategy was doomed, however. It appeared to save Freud's work from refutation by modern biology, but it did so at the price of removing all empirical import. The biological Freud was wrong, but at least he advanced clear, testable claims. The cultural-linguistic Freud that Lacan invented, on the other hand, was completely untestable. He was not merely impervious to contradictory evidence in biology; he was impervious to any evidence at all. Lacan rescued Freud from a fatal encounter with modern biology by removing him from the world of science altogether. (Evans 2005, p. 49)

Just as Sokal and Bricmont tie Lacan to postmodernism, so too Evans associates Lacan with the Standard Social Science Model, a constructivist approach that appears as a recurring theoretical bogeyman in *The Literary Animal*, even though Lacan, as established in the last chapter, had no connection to either postmodernism or the SSSM.

Evans's second point of criticism is Lacan's perceived failure to follow through on the promise of cybernetics and artificial intelligence. This topic is a particular area of interest for Evans, who has worked on robotic intelligence for many years, including at his current job as a Senior Research Scientist at University College Cork. Evans observes that, in the early seminars, Lacan was groundbreaking in his reflections on cybernetics and computational theory—these topics are covered in *Seminar II*, for instance—but claims that Lacan later retreated 'toward a hydraulic model of the mind [...] in the guise of the term "jouissance"' (Evans 2005, p. 53). Outwardly, this compromised version of Lacan borrowed ideas from mathematics and science, but Evans insists that really he 'was a closet Romantic all along' (Evans 2005, p. 53).

> Some support for this view can be found [...] in Lacan's attempts to develop a mathematical notation for psychoanalytic theory. His formulas and his diagrams give an initial impression of scientific rigor, at least to a nonscientifically trained eye, but on closer examination it becomes evident that they break even the most elementary rules of mathematics. These equations are supposedly there to give substance to Lacan's avowed desire to formalize psychoanalysis. The fact that they are mathematically meaningless gives the lie to that claim. If Lacan was really concerned with formalizing his discipline, he would surely have taken more care to get his math right. The fact that he didn't suggests that he was more interested in the rhetoric of formalization than the reality. For Lacan, 'formalization' and 'mathematization' were just metaphors, mere sound bites for his neosurrealist technopoetry. (Evans 2005, pp. 53–54)

The resemblance of this argument to Sokal and Bricmont's is no accident: Evans's footnote for this paragraph attributes these ideas directly back to them. For all the idiosyncrasies of his intellectual journey, the two central points in Evans's critique of Lacan in 'From Lacan to Darwin' are familiar retreads of the arguments already encountered in the previous two chapters. Yet there is more—much more—to the story of Dylan Evans than this confession of faith, taken on its own, can reveal. Hidden between the lines of this text is an extraordinary pattern of hysterical behavior that can only be understood by considering the broader perspective of his life and writings.

The Sticky Branch

It should be understood from the outset that the word 'hysteric' is being used in this chapter in a specific sense. Despite its negative history, hysteria continues to be an important term in Lacanian theory—the title of Žižek's 1982 doctoral thesis, for instance, was *The Most Sublime Hysteric: Hegel with Lacan*. The modified sense in which I am using the term 'hysteric' borrows from this Žižekian derivation: it has no clinical meaning, nor does it attempt to describe any kind of mental illness or similar condition. Instead, hysteria, in this revised context, refers to one of Lacan's four discourses from *Seminar XVII*, in which the subject seeks repeatedly to contest the authority of the master. In her essay 'When Surplus Enjoyment Meets Surplus Value' (2006), Alenka Zupančič observes that, in particular,

> the hysteric likes to point out that the emperor is naked. The master, this respected S_1, admired and obeyed by everyone, is in reality a poor, rather impotent chap, who in no way lives up to his symbolic function. He is weak, he often doesn't even know what is going on around him, and he indulges in 'disgusting' secret enjoyment; he (as a person) is unable to control himself or anybody else. (Zupančič 2006, p. 165)

In his discussion of anxiety in *Seminar X*, Lacan calls this process 'acting-out' (Lacan 2014, p. 116), observing how the hysterical subject, while appearing to challenge the authority of the master, is in reality enacting a covert test of the master's authenticity. The hysteric does not actually want to *become* a master, they simply wish to know whether the master they serve has genuine authority, or if that master is merely a charlatan.

The difficulty of understanding a hysteric, as Freud discovers in the Dora case, is that the internal conflict between wanting to serve the authority of a master, on the one hand, and the compulsion to question it, on the other, leads to a lot of confusing, mixed signals. In particular, the hysterical subject tends to acknowledge only the visible process of 'acting-out' against the master's authority, while repressing their ulterior desire to conform to that authority. That is why the ultimate disappointment for the hysteric is to learn that their suspicions were right, that the master was a charlatan all along:

> In this sense, the hysteric is much more revolted by the weakness of power than by power itself, and the truth of her or his basic complaint about the master is usually that the master is not master enough. In the person of the master, the hysteric thus attacks precisely those rights she is otherwise so eager to protect, namely what remains or exists of the master besides the master signifier. In other words, the target of the attack on the master is his surplus enjoyment, *a*. This is what is superfluous, what should not be there, and what, on the obverse side of the same coin, represents the point where the master is accused of enjoying at the subject's expense. (Zupančič 2006, p. 165)

There is little cause for triumph in such a revelation, because this act of unmasking the master's impotence leaves the hysteric without a cause to serve. The hysteric is thus always driven by a hidden, ulterior motive, one that has a very different relationship to the master's power than what appears in their outward behavior. Indeed, this denial of power relations is one of the hysteric's most powerful modes of contestation: the 'neutrality' of science and mathematics, with their claims to methodological objectivity, are a challenge to the irrational and arbitrary aspects of the master's discourse.

Lacanian theory thus regards the hysterical discourse as a decisive step in the establishment of modern science. The hysteric's challenge is meant to test the authority of the master, based on the conviction that only a master who is not ignorant is truly worthy of being a leader. Colette Soler argues that this inherent tension between master and hysteric over the question of knowledge has been crucial to the development of science:

> Lacan introduced something different: hysteria as a cause that is not without responsibility for the evolution of civilizations. He thus attributes to the hysterical position—upon which psychoanalysis, at the private level, throws light—a major social role, particularly in the emergence

> of science and of its unstoppable passion for knowledge. He recognizes the emblematic figure of this operation in Socrates, the Socrates of Plato (there is no other), who in questioning the ancient master, enjoins him to display his knowledge as master. Modern science, as founded by Galileo, could well be a long-term repercussion of this challenge. We see how Lacan locates the hysterical subject: she is the one who, as a vocation, makes the other produce knowledge. The hysteric and the man of science are an attractive couple, one of whom stimulates while the other, who is not hysterical at all, works on knowledge. (Soler 2006, pp. 287–288)

The anti-authoritarian attitude of the hysteric, far from being purely negative, is seen here by Soler as crucial to the ongoing possibility not only of science, but also of psychoanalysis. The hysteric's disruptive questions, whether directed at Lacanian theory or the precepts of the Enlightenment, are an essential part of both discourses. To accede to the discourse of the master is to adhere to an authority grounded in tyranny and arbitrariness, the very opposite of the scientific (and hopefully, the psychoanalytic) spirit.

'From Lacan to Darwin' provides initial evidence of a hysterical resistance to a master discourse, beginning with Evans's enthusiastic discovery of Lacanian thought while teaching in Argentina, his growing doubts about the field while training to be a psychoanalyst, and finally, a dramatic reversal, in which he 'acts up' by turning vehemently against the authority of his former interest in psychoanalysis by becoming an evolutionary psychologist. This pattern of behavior is not an isolated incident, however, but a repeated cycle that Evans has replicated in different forms since his adolescence.

Consider, for example, an episode from his youth that he relates in his book *Atheism: All That Matters* (2014). In the preface, Evans recalls how, even as a young boy, he was naturally skeptical about religion—he briefly believed in Father Christmas, he says, but never in the supernatural realm of the divine. The atheism of his youth only deepened when he went to school and learned some basic scientific facts. Sure in his lack of faith, Evans remembers that he would tease his Catholic grandmother with what he had learned in school, and how this knowledge flatly contradicted the beliefs of the church. In an event that foreshadows his later conversion to Lacan, Evans recollects a dramatic change that occurred in his late teens:

> Like many children, I found church extremely boring, and on those rare occasions when I was forced to go (by my school), I found the stories about Jesus and his disciples bizarre and nonsensical. When I was a teenager, I became interested in Zen Buddhism, and part of what attracted me about it was that it didn't require me to believe in gods. But then, at the age of 17, I had an intense conversion experience. I was sitting at my desk in my bedroom one evening, trying to do my homework, when all of a sudden I felt my body bathed in waves of cosmic love, and I felt forgiven. Tears came to my eyes, and for the first time in my life I thought to myself: 'There is a god!' (Evans 2014, p. ix)

Evans went from despising his grandmother's religion to becoming a devout Catholic, all in a brief period. Inspired by his new faith, he enrolled at the local university to pursue a degree in religious studies, but by this time his fervor had become so great that he dropped out and instead went to Ireland to train as a priest.

The youth who would later immerse himself so deeply in Lacanian theory that he wrote a well-regarded dictionary of its concepts similarly threw himself into the rigors of training for the priesthood. Nor was this just any path to the priesthood. Evans chose for himself one of the most grueling and difficult institutions in which to carry out his training.

> It was a very strict missionary order with the fierce-sounding name of the Legionaries of Christ, but I loved the military discipline and the austere spirituality. After a few months, we went through a week of spiritual exercises. Based on a sequence of meditations and prayers devised by St Ignatius of Loyola in the 16th century, these exercises are designed to lead you to a point of intense personal conviction and commitment. […] Everything was designed to lead up to the final meditation on the last day of the retreat, when we would practice 'seeing god in nature.' […] And you know what I saw? A beautiful sunset. And that was it. (Evans 2014, pp. x–xi)

Evans's abrupt conversion to Catholicism involves the ecstatic acceptance of a divine master discourse that he initially embraces, submitting himself to its teachings and practices until, in classic hysterical style, his critical side awakens and he begins to 'act out.' The master discourse that had once seemed so liberating suddenly starts to feel like a prison. The hysteric's shifting relationship to authority that emerges at this point is particularly telling. 'I knew immediately that my spiritual director wouldn't like this,' recounts Evans. 'So I didn't tell him at first, and tried to continue as I had before' (Evans 2014, p. xi). When he finally does break down and tell his spiritual director, the symbolic representative of authority, about his doubts, the director agrees that Evans should return immediately to England. 'And after my few years holidaying in the land of religion, I went back to being the atheist I always was' (Evans 2014, p. xi). None of these details are mentioned in 'From Lacan to Darwin,' even though they establish the exact pattern of behavior that Evans follows in his conversion to (and apostasy from) Lacan.

Evans's intellectual interests in the period following his shift away from psychoanalysis in favor of evolutionary psychology continue to show a hysterical fascination with the different forms of authority that separate belief from science. This theme is particularly evident in his 2003 book *Placebo: Mind Over Matter in Modern Medicine*, in which Evans analyzes the history of the placebo and how medical science has tried to account for its effects. The authority figure this time is Henry K. Beecher, whose article 'The Powerful Placebo,' published in *JAMA: The Journal of the American Medical Association* in 1955, established the orthodox view of the placebo that Evans sets out to examine in this work:

> The rise to dominance of the clinical trial has not been an unambiguous victory for rational medicine. Beecher saw it as a way of overcoming centuries of blind appeal to authority and intuition. Ironically, however, the final acceptance of placebo controls owed more to Beecher's own authority and intuition than to proper scientific evidence. Beecher was a respected researcher, so nobody paused to question the accuracy of his 1955 paper. Nobody suspected that he had reshaped the data so that they

> would support his prior intuitions about the power of the placebo effect. The result is that, fifty years later, many medical researchers accept without question that placebo effects are ubiquitous and powerful. (Evans 2004, p. 12)

Evans repeatedly finds himself drawn to the emotional power of apparently irrational belief that people like Beecher have been able to instill. Indeed, he dedicates a whole chapter of *Placebo* to what he calls 'the belief effect' underlying the effectiveness of placebos, while acknowledging that there 'is, at present, no scientific consensus as to exactly what this secret ingredient is, beyond the simple observation that it must be some process or event in the brain' (Evans 2004, p. 71). Evans's youthful conversion to Catholicism and subsequent loss of faith, his embrace of Lacanian theory followed by a dramatic turn toward evolutionary psychology, together with this fascinated but critical attitude toward belief, all form a pattern of which Evans himself appears largely unaware. Perhaps there is a good reason for this lack of insight into his own behavioral loops, for at this point in his life he was about to embark on the most extraordinary iteration of them all.

Evans published 'From Lacan to Darwin' in 2005, a confession of faith that effectively declared that, after many twists and turns, his intellectual journey had finally made it onto the straight and narrow path of science and rationality. In spite of these experiences, Evans again became infatuated with a new, much crazier idea. A trip to Mexico in 2005 led him to contemplate the collapse of the Mayan civilization. This thought quickly translated into an obsessive meditation on the possibility that modern civilization might soon collapse. In 2006, Nick Bostrom, a friend from Evans's days as a doctoral student at the London School of Economics, introduced him to the writings of Ted Kaczynski, better known to the world as the Unabomber. Evans's behavior began to follow a familiar pattern:

> The Unabomber gave me a convenient scapegoat for my ills. My angst had nothing to do with me; it was all society's fault. More specifically, it was the fault of the industrial-technological system, which robbed us of

> our autonomy, diminished our rapport with nature, and forced us 'to behave in ways that are increasingly remote from the natural pattern of human behavior.' It was hardly an original idea, and not one that had held any attraction for me before, but now the simple, stark language of the manifesto hypnotized me, and within a few days I was spouting Kaczynski's strange gospel as fervently as a religious convert. (Evans 2015, p. 46)

This latest conversion led Evans to plunge into the literature of societal collapse, a period in which he devoured such books as Martin Rees's *Our Final Century* (2003), James Lovelock's *The Revenge of Gaia* (2006), and Jared Diamond's *Collapse* (2005), all works 'by new doomsayers with impeccable scientific credentials' (Evans 2015, p. 65). His most drastic move came in mid-2006 when he quit his academic job, sold his house, and used the proceeds to set up 'The Utopia Experiment,' a self-sufficient community in Scotland that would test the possibility of surviving the imminent collapse of civilization. By May 2007, Evans had been involuntarily committed to a mental hospital, suffering from severe depression and deeply disillusioned by the failure of his project.

It took Evans nearly a decade to confront this painful episode from his life, which he recounts in his 2015 memoir of that period, *The Utopia Experiment*. This fascinating document reveals the limited extent to which Evans has come to grips with his behavior. Late in the book, for instance, the reader witnesses some glimpses of insight, especially into the hysterical aspects of Evans's character. 'Just when I had ensnared them all [his followers] in my delusion, I found I no longer believed in it myself,' he observes toward the end of *The Utopia Experiment*. 'And it had slipped away as mysteriously as it had first taken root. But this liberation was not pleasant. On the contrary, it left me feeling deflated and broken' (Evans 2015, p. 203). Evans jokes that his stubborn personality is a peculiar manifestation of the 'difficult bastard effect,' for whereas most people have a tendency to follow the crowd, in such situations his doubts only grow, so that the 'more those around me came to believe in the experiment, the more sceptical I became' (Evans 2015, p. 237). Only in the final thirty pages does Evans finally begin to join the dots that reveal what to others must be an obvious pattern:

> This had happened on several previous occasions in my life. When I was nineteen I spent a year training to be a priest, only to discover that, unlike my fellow seminarians, I didn't really believe in God. Ten years later I thought I had discovered the ultimate truth in the writings of Jacques Lacan, only to recoil in horror when I had surrounded myself with his most ardent disciples. I was like a foolish bird that kept alighting on sticky twigs, all coated in birdlime to trap him. [...] I never seemed to learn that each branch was as sticky as the last. Try as I might, I just could not find the perfect disappointment[.] (Evans 2015, pp. 237–238)

This paradoxical search for the 'perfect disappointment,' this simultaneous longing for an authority that wields an illusion of mastery that, when it appears, will undergo an initial period of idealization, before being violently overthrown by a critical scrutiny that can only end in disillusionment. Hysterics are inherently dissatisfied because they are at odds with their own desire: they react against every form of authority, even as they secretly long for an authority that masters them.

Repressed Power

Žižek points out in 'The Limits of the Semiotic Approach to Psychoanalysis' that the desire for mastery may be repressed, but it cannot be abolished; as such, it will always resurface in unconscious ways. The more forcefully the desire for mastery is repressed, the more ferociously it returns:

> When knowledge itself takes on itself the moment of 'authority,' summons, command, imperative, a short circuit between the 'neutral' field of knowledge and the 'performative' dimension is produced. Far from limiting itself to a kind of 'neutral' declaration of the given objectivity, the discourse 'becomes mad' and starts to behave itself in a 'performative' way towards the given of the facts themselves. More precisely, it masks its own 'performative force' under the shape of 'objective knowledge,' of the neutral 'declaration' of the 'facts.' (Žižek 1990, p. 103)

Although Žižek's words are aimed at what Lacan calls the 'university discourse,' they apply equally to the discourse of the hysteric—what, after all, is the hysteric's 'acting out' if not a kind of performative madness in the face of their own loss of mastery? Evans's life and writings are punctuated by such moments: firstly, by his joyous embrace of a new master discourse, and secondly, by his hysterical disruption of that discourse's authority. Recall, for instance, his new devotion to Catholicism, his appreciation of its rigorous asceticism and spiritual exercises. For Evans, what most people would consider the most difficult and unpleasant aspects of religious training were the parts he enjoyed the most. This same pattern is replicated in his later obsessions, in which he enthusiastically throws himself into reading difficult Lacanian texts, or builds an experimental survivalist community in the harsh environment of the Scottish Highlands. Evans feels a joy, a passion, during this initial stage, at being the useful instrument of a master discourse.

Just when this hard work is about to pay off, however, at the very moment when he is about to enjoy the fruits of his labor, he begins to 'act up.' Evans comes so close to accomplishing his various aims of becoming a priest, a psychoanalyst, even a cult-style guru, yet on the threshold of realizing each goal he finds, strangely, that he is unable to enjoy his achievements. Žižek elaborates: 'By becoming "mad," it [knowledge] begins to directly command enjoyment: the turning point where freedom-to-enjoy [is] permitted is reversed into an obligatory enjoyment which is, one must add, the most effective way to block the access of the subject to enjoyment' (Žižek 1990, p. 104). Evans thus finds himself stuck in an impossible paradox: in order to get what he wants, he happily gives himself up to a master discourse (religion, Lacan, survivalism); but when he gets what he wants, he comprehends that he has sacrificed his own sense of mastery in order to realize his desire, rendering him incapable of enjoying it. The hysteric's grasp of the truth comes at the cost of disempowerment.

Equally unsatisfactory among Lacan's four discourses is the analyst's discourse, which Evans, in his rejection of psychoanalysis, misinterprets as just another variant of the master's discourse. Given the repeated cycle of enthusiasm and disappointment that marks Evans's life, with each turn bringing a deeper sense of depression and disempowerment, it is hardly surprising that he eventually turns to the university discourse, the only option left to him among the four discourses. The university discourse of the scientist appears to be the perfect fit for the fugitive hysteric, a natural ally in their mutual opposition to the master's discourse. The authenticity of this resistance is open to question, however, for while the hysteric *appears* to challenge the master, this antagonism does not reject the master's discourse as such. The real meaning of the hysteric's performance, as Fink explains in 'The Master Signifier and the Four Discourses' (1998), is to test the authority of the master's discourse in order to find out whether it is grounded in actual knowledge, or just a superficial effect of symbolic power:

> [W]hat Lacan says of the hysteric: the hysteric pushes the master—incarnated in a partner, teacher, or whomever—to the point where he or she can find the master's knowledge lacking. Either the master does not have an explanation for everything, or his or her reasoning does not hold water. In addressing the master, the hysteric demands that he or she produce knowledge and then goes on to disprove his or her theories. Historically speaking, hysterics have been a true motor force behind the medical, psychiatric, and psychoanalytic elaboration of theories concerning hysteria. (Fink 2018, p. 36)

The hysteric and the master routinely profit from this mutual antagonism, Fink shows, with the resistance of one pushing the other to greater heights. What the hysteric objects to in the master discourse is not the exercise of authority and power. After all, it is the desire to *adhere* to an authentic system of masterly authority that brings Evans such joy in the initial forays into his various enthusiasms. Instead, what the hysteric cannot abide is the anxiety of arbitrariness: the imagined reliability and consistency of the Other is always the hysteric's emotional priority. This includes the arbitrariness of reality which, since it cannot be adequately explained by priests or psychoanalysts, causes the hysteric to turn to the university discourse of science, which rationalizes reality while claiming that its method serves no master.

The university discourse's assertion that it has renounced all claims to mastery is not taken seriously in Lacan's formula, which he writes so that knowledge (S_2) speaks in the place of the master signifier (S_1). Instead of the latter disappearing altogether, however, it moves below the bar—that is to say, the master's authority is repressed, shifted out of sight. The university discourse's claim to objectivity is thus an act of power, one that paradoxically *demands* to be regarded as neutral. In this respect, the university discourse is a revamped version of the master discourse that has been cosmetically modified to conceal its true authority in order to appear objective:

> What Lacan recognizes in the university discourse is a new and reformed discourse of the master. In its elementary form, it is a discourse that is pronounced from the place of supposedly neutral knowledge, the truth of which (hidden below the bar) is Power, that is, the master signifier. The constitutive lie of this discourse is that it disavows its performative dimension: it always presents, for example, that which leads to a political decision, founded on power, as a simple insight into the factual state of things (or public polls, objective reports, and so on). (Zupančič 2006, p. 168)

This critique of the university discourse's hidden will to power does not apply only to science. In fact, the same issue of power extends to all four of the discourses, which are unanimously compromised by the problem of authority. That includes the analyst's discourse, which is why in *Seminar XI* Lacan interrogates the 'desire of the analyst' (Lacan 1994, p. 156) by posing some difficult questions about the power dynamic of the analytic setting.

Lacan tries to solve this dilemma in *Seminar XI* by showing how the analyst occupies the symbolic place of the master in an ironic, even fraudulent manner, while the analysand makes the mistake of placing the analyst in the position of the 'subject who is supposed to know.' The analyst thus enters the analytic situation knowing themselves to be a charlatan who is simply playing the part of the master. The task of the patient, by contrast, is to come to the realization that the analyst-master is an empty signifier, an epiphany that hopefully extends to their comprehending, in turn, the emptiness of *all* master signifiers. The psychoanalytic situation, in this respect, is an exercise in refuting the master discourse, in rejecting the arbitrariness of power. The patient's role in seeing through the fraudulence of the 'subject who is supposed to know' is crucial to the effectiveness of this technique, since making the patient work to dispel their own illusions is regarded as more effective, more empowering than having the analyst do it for them. Indeed, that is why Lacan is so critical of the reversal of this dynamic in ego psychology, in which power is placed firmly in the hands of the master analyst.

What this scenario does not account for, however, is the potential disappointment of the patient at discovering the impotence of the Other. The hysteric, in particular, does not feel at all empowered by the analyst's game. For while the hysteric feels the need to contest the authority of the master, the true point of this contestation is to establish whether or not this authority is authentic. As such, the discovery that the analyst is a self-aware charlatan who never took the position of master seriously can only create a profound sense of disillusionment in the hysteric. Evans expresses such disappointment in 'From Lacan to Darwin,' for instance, in his comments about the 'subject who is supposed to know':

> In the course of the treatment, the patient would come to 'de-suppose' the analyst of this knowledge—that is, to lose his faith in the analyst. That, in fact, was the whole point of psychoanalytic treatment. Why, then, did the analyst collude in the original gullibility of the patient rather than simply telling the patient up front that there was no secret knowledge to be had? Because it was only by learning the hard way, so to speak, that the patient could experience the painful process of disillusionment and thereby realize that *nobody* held the key to his life except him. (Evans 2005, p. 41)

Whereas Lacan regards the analytical process as a process of rational disillusionment that, ethically, must be driven by the desire of the patient, Evans instead interprets the psychoanalytic scenario as a sadistic exercise in which the analyst cruelly withholds the truth from the patient in order to torture them.

Despite the ethical terms in which he frames them, Evans's rebellions against the tyranny of the master discourse are hardly selfless in their motivations. When standing up to perceived abuses of power, he rarely expresses ethical concerns for others. In the account of his conversion to Catholicism, for instance, Evans does not speak of his compassion for those who are suffering from the burden of sin, nor of a yearning to save the souls of the anguished and lost. The spiritual journey he undertakes is only ever a stage in *his* individual quest for meaning. In the unraveling of his Lacanian phase, similarly, Evans expresses a few vague concerns about his patients, but the true focus is his own intellectual crisis. The paradoxes of Evans's ostensible altruism can be seen most clearly in *The Utopia Experiment*, a task he undertakes in order to save the world, but which devolves into a symbol of his own inner conflict.

The sources that inform Evans's view of this project—he initially imagines his community will be 'a cross between Plato's Academy and *The Beach*' (Evans 2015, p. 33)—are telling for the way they avoid the questions of power and inequality. Evans prefers to regard the problems of society and its survival in terms that are stripped of all historical and structural idiosyncrasies. He instead makes sweeping pronouncements like: 'The eco-villages of today, and the hippy communes of the sixties, are just the latest in a long line of utopian experiments, stretching back thousands of years' (Evans 2015, p. 75). This claim overlooks the fact that what differentiates the eco-villages and the hippy communes from their ancient counterparts is a shared desire to escape the conditions of capitalism. Evans thus avoids examining the crucial role that capitalist logic plays not only in shaping contemporary thinking about the future of human survival, but also the way that it conceals power relations that permeate modern society through the ideological fiction of social equality.

These two factors haunt, in particular, the examples of Evans's paradoxical attitude toward power as recorded in *The Utopia Experiment*. The most important dynamic that Evans fails to account for in his utopian community is the fact that he is financing the whole endeavor. Evans thus finds himself torn between an egalitarian fiction and the reality that it is his capital that makes the existence of this community possible:

> In swarm robotics, all the robots are exactly the same. There is no leader. And in my experiment there would be no leader either, no authoritarian figure to impose values from on high. The values would just *emerge*—right?—from interactions between equal individuals. But of course that was to overlook the peculiar nature of my own role in the experiment. I was

> to be simultaneously the founder and just another one of the volunteers. I wanted to join in the daily work with everyone else, to participate while I observed, and let things take their own course. But at the same time, it would be me who set the parameters. I had conceived of the whole idea in the first place and written the basic scenario that would govern our narrative. It was my experiment, after all. (Evans 2015, pp. 80–81)

The theoretical equality of the participants in the experiment is inherently at odds with Evans's position as the financial master of the project. 'Of course I would inevitably play some kind of leading role,' he writes, then immediately adds his own counterpoint. 'But I didn't want to be a charismatic figure, let alone a dictator. [...] Or did I? Was there perhaps some secret desire to be a kind of guru or cult leader, some unacknowledged form of megalomania?' (Evans 2015, pp. 81–82). Evans leaves this question hanging at the end of the chapter, but the ghost of its unspoken, implied affirmative is the perverse contradiction that haunts the rest of his book.

The benevolent fantasy of leadership that Evans imagines for himself re-enacts the contradictions of capitalism's ideological claim that all subjects are free and equal. The theoretical conjunction between Lacan and Marx has produced some fertile ideas on this topic in recent Lacanian criticism. A. Kiarina Kordela reminds us in 'Marx and Psychoanalysis,' for instance, that the most important homology between these two thinkers comes from the overlap between Marx's 'surplus-value' and Lacan's 'surplus-enjoyment' (Kordela 2018, pp. 160–163). Žižek, who opens his first book *The Sublime Object of Ideology* (1989) with an analysis of this convergence, summarizes its consequences for the discourse of mastery:

> With the establishment of bourgeois society, the relations of domination and servitude are *repressed*: formally, we are apparently concerned with free subjects whose interpersonal relations are discharged of all fetishism; the repressed truth—that of the persistence of domination and servitude—emerges in a symptom which subverts the ideological appearance of equality, freedom, and so on. (Žižek 1989, p. 26)

The Utopia Experiment is both fascinating and grotesque for the way it reproduces this contradiction, with Evans fantasizing how 'at the centre of it all, unassuming but indisputably wise, would be me, the founder, loved and revered by my fellow utopians,' whereas reality often sees him in bitter conflict with his fellow residents over the direction of 'his' project (Evans 2015, p. 91). Evans never acknowledges how his position as the provider of the project's capital introduces a problematic hierarchy into the community, instead displacing its effects either with fantasies of benign leadership or, later in the narrative, a sullen withdrawal into anxiety and depression.

Twice in *The Utopia Experiment*, Evans refers to the work of Thomas Malthus as a crucial influence on his increasing panic about global collapse. In his *Essay on the Principle of Population* (1798), Malthus famously points out the dangers of overpopulation and how nature, through disasters like war, disease, and famine, brings society back into balance. Evans's reaction to Malthus is to regard the problems he describes as a universal dilemma, one that connects the Mayans, who first triggered Evans's anxiety, to the present day. 'The parallels between the Maya collapse and our current global predicament are clear,' he writes. 'Just as the Maya grew too numerous for the carrying capacity of their environment, so the global population was threatening to grow beyond the carrying capacity of the earth itself' (Evans 2015, p. 23). Yet the historical moment at which Malthus formulates these ideas is also highly influenced by its capitalist context. Capitalism, in particular, provides a social configuration where inequality is repressed to the point where it becomes possible to look upon disasters with dispassion, to speak of the death of thousands, even millions, as an objective 'correction,' in 'neutral' language that is the signature of the university discourse.

The other major factor to which Evans attributes his interest in the imminent collapse of civilization is his fascination with the effects of technology. In *The Utopia Experiment*, he cites the influence of Ray Kurzweil's *The Age of Spiritual Machines* (1999) on his thinking, a book that predicts artificial intelligence will soon overtake human intelligence, with both positive and negative consequences. The most powerful influence on Evans's rising panic about society's collapse is Ted Kaczynski, whose paranoid manifesto depicts a world destroyed by technology. Evans again follows his usual pattern of enthusiastic devotion, only this time it is not the obscurantism of Lacan that weaves its opaque magic, but Kaczynski's 'simple, stark language' that seduces him (Evans 2015, p. 46). Language, it seems, does not have to be difficult or hermetic to mislead effectively after all. Again, this fascination with technology is regarded as an independent, historically-detached phenomenon, somehow disconnected from the capitalist development that made these advanced machines possible in the first place.

This repression of capitalist logic occurs because there are unconscious class and status assumptions built into Evans's image of his survivalist future. The exceptional status he imagines for himself is again evident, for instance, in Evans's democratic fantasy of regarding himself as simply one of the laborers, an aristocratic figure who benevolently joins the peasants in the field. This picture is egalitarian in imagination only for Evans clearly sees himself as set apart subjectively from the rest, as he expresses in passages like these:

> But I had no idea about farming. [...] The idea of me tilling the land, and planting seedlings, and harvesting the crops, would have seemed ludicrous to my friends and family. But at that time I had heroic visions of becoming a horny-handed son of toil, labouring away like some diligent yeoman in a Thomas Hardy novel. I was blissfully unaware of how ill-suited I was to that way of life. (Evans 2015, p. 32)

Indeed, throughout *The Utopia Experiment* Evans assumes that he should inhabit a superior position, characterized by a complacent sense that, while everyone is theoretically equal, he has always been destined for a place among those who rule. When Evans is committed to the mental hospital, even the doctor tells him that life among the poor is not a fate for which he has been socially conditioned:

> I see a lot of people from pretty poor backgrounds. I know that they will probably stay poor for the rest of their lives. When they are old, they will

> spend what little money they have playing bingo or drinking in their local pub. They don't have a problem with that. That vision doesn't hold any fear for them. But you would hate that. That's not the world you come from. (Evans 2015, p. 13)

Evans cannot help but agree with him. 'The image of my older self eking out his last days in some cockney boozer, rubbing shoulders with badly spoken drunks and geriatric bingo players,' writes Evans, 'put the fear of god in me. I would do anything to avoid that fate' (Evans 2015, p. 13). Throughout *The Utopia Experiment*, therefore, there is an ongoing split between the theoretical equality of human beings, and Evans's practical that his money and education authorize his position of mastery.

The most disturbing outcome of this way of thinking is how Evans then uses this logic of privilege to justify an undemocratic social system ruled by a technocratic authority figure. While recovering in hospital, Evans rereads Steven Pinker's *The Blank Slate: The Modern Denial of Human Nature* (2002). Evans focuses in particular on the contrast that Pinker makes between Hobbes and Rousseau, arguing that these political philosophers represent the two basic views of human nature: good (Rousseau) and evil (Hobbes). 'In a nutshell,' Pinker writes, 'Hobbes was right, Rousseau was wrong' (Pinker in Evans 2015, p. 143). The conclusion that Evans draws from this example, as *The Utopia Experiment* unfolds, is that societies need a strong, authoritarian figure to keep them in order. This idea is presented in the context of Evans's exchange with a journalist, who claims that the 'lack of any singular organizing figurehead played the biggest role' in the community's failure—if only Evans had run the project with the strong hand of a master, things would have turned out differently (Evans 2015, p. 263). A few pages later, Evans extends this conclusion to society in general:

> Pinker is right to say that Hobbes was a better anthropologist than Rousseau [...] By submitting to a strong sovereign, we can at least live in relative peace. It won't be a Utopia, but it will be better than the continual war of all against all. (Evans 2015, p. 269)

This political capitulation is a typical outcome for the hysteric, whose 'acting up' is never a true questioning of authority. 'Lacan links (hysterical) revolt with the call for a master: "What the hysteric wants is a master,"' writes Peter Klepec. 'It is exactly this new form of master, the new, perverted form of the master that is present in the discourse of the university. […] Such positioning signifies that behind all knowledge there is power, mastery, the mastery of knowledge, and the domination of the other to whom this knowledge is imparted' (Klepec 2016, p. 127). The hysteric is a charlatan who only plays at being a revolutionary. Evans does not want a real revolution, he wants a master, and, as Lacan predicts, he will get one, even though he disavows his enjoyment of that result by claiming that his position is grounded in 'the objective facts, the external, rational justifications' (Evans 2015, p. 154).

Knowledge and Enjoyment

Evans also has a recurrent tendency to ignore how enjoyment affects the human relationship to knowledge. Consider, for instance, his confessional narrative of how he switched from psychoanalysis to evolutionary psychology. This journey is set up in 'From Lacan to Darwin' by a forceful contrast between the miserable intellectual conformity he encountered at Buffalo and the academic vitality he experienced at the London School of Economics. After comparing these two different phases of his studies, Evans reflects:

> I had a terrible time shedding my Lacanian skin and many agonizing moments when I wondered if my doubts about psychoanalysis were motivated by some repressed wish or other or whether this was not just some kind of 'negative therapeutic reaction' or resistance against the process of analysis. […] [I]t was, in the end, the intellectual arguments and empirical evidence, and not any repressed wishes, that finally convinced me to jettison Lacan completely and become an evolutionary psychologist[.] (Evans 2005, pp. 46–47)

Evans talks extensively about how his time among the Buffalo Lacanians was marked by a growing sense of agitation about the fact that their enjoyment of Lacan's work trumped their critical abilities. 'They based their beliefs on their wishes rather than on proper evidence,' he recalls. 'I was appalled, disgusted by this abnegation of curiosity, by this waste of human intelligence, by this shameless embrace of illusion for illusion's sake' (Evans 2005, p. 46). In *The Utopia Experiment*, Evans reveals that he suffered his first bout of clinical depression while studying in Buffalo, in which 'the gloom was deeper and darker than anything I had experienced before, and I began to suffer from horrible panic attacks' (Evans 2015, p. 61). Things improved after his return to England, but within a year he had another episode and sought professional help, with the depression reappearing whenever he stopped taking his medication. Academic life at the London School of Economics, by contrast, especially the monthly Darwin Lectures, was 'marked by an intellectual frisson the likes of which I had never witnessed' (Evans 2005, p. 46). In the emotional context just described, Evans's insistence that he made a completely impartial decision to choose one field over the other *purely* because of 'intellectual arguments and empirical evidence' is simply not credible (Evans 2005, p. 47). What he overlooks in this account is the part played in his choice by enjoyment, by what gave him an emotional sense of mastery over his life and ideas.

That is not to say that Evans was *not* ultimately persuaded or influenced by the superior rationality or empirical evidence of evolutionary psychology: the entanglement of logic and emotion is not a zero-sum game. Nonetheless, it is strange that a man who has published three books on the topic of emotion is so unwilling to acknowledge that enjoyment could have played *any* part in his decision. The emotional state of human beings is the malleable frame through which they are persuaded about the validity of science and logic, the proof of which can be seen in Evans's own personal history. In the initial phase of his various enthusiasms, he readily submits himself to the new master signifier to an extraordinary degree until, in the next phase, he suddenly begins to regard this same discourse as oppressive. In the initial stage, there is nothing that can change Evans's mind about how insightful and life-changing Lacan's theories are, for instance, while in the next phase he can only see them as manipulative and wrong. This phenomenon recurs in *The Utopia Experiment* when Evans calls his sister Charlotte to tell her his plans for the survivalist community, and she responds with shocked silence. 'I was amazed by her failure to grasp the importance of the project, and worried that she would be stranded in London when the crash came' (Evans 2015, p. 67). Just before leaving for Scotland, Evans has an argument over the phone with another friend, Caroline, who finally exclaims: 'Listen to yourself Dylan! [...] You've got a fucking god complex!' (Evans 2015, p. 64). It is not until he has been committed to a mental hospital that Evans begins to acknowledge that his obsession with the collapse of society might be flawed:

> In hospital, [...] I began to probe for the first time my ulterior motives for embarking on my bizarre project. From conception in Mexico, through the months of preparation, and right up to those terrible days in May 2007, I never paused to ask myself what psychological forces or personal issues might be propelling me along this strange path. I was completely focused on what I saw as the objective facts, the external, rational justifications. (Evans 2015, p. 54)

This revelation makes Evans's affirmation of his own rationality and lack of unconscious motives in 'From Lacan to Darwin,' published just two years before this mental collapse, seem all the more hollow. 'For someone who claimed to know so much about the theory of human nature, I sure didn't seem to understand it very well in practice,' he observes (Evans 2015, p. 79). Caught up in his enthusiasm for a new idea, Evans repeatedly shows himself to be unreceptive to even the most logical and factual objections.

The Utopia Experiment, in particular, is punctuated by reflections in which Evans wonders how he could have 'forgotten' about facts, books, arguments, examples, and other contradictory evidence that might have reined in the more extreme aspects of his folly. What Evans confronts in these moments is the unsettling reality that no truth is ever received on neutral ground, through a coolly impartial framework, but always operates in the context of a subject's emotional constitution. That is why, argues Lacan in *Seminar VII*, the analyst cannot simply tell the patient what is wrong:

> One of my friends and patients had a dream [...] in which someone cried out concerning me, 'But why doesn't he tell us the truth about truth?' I quote this, since it is an impatience that I have heard expressed by a great many in other forms than dreams. The formula is true to some extent—I perhaps don't tell the truth about truth. But haven't you noticed that in wanting to tell it—something that is the chief preoccupation of those who are called metaphysicians—it often happens that not much truth is left? (Lacan 1992, p. 184)

The game of truth that Lacan examines in the analytical situation is one in which *neither* participant is sincere. On one side of this Lacanian farce, the analys and disingenuously demands a truth that, because of its very structure as a demand, makes its fulfillment inauthentic: that is what happens in Evans's quests to become, by turn, a priest, a psychoanalyst, and a survivalist leader. On the other side is the role of the empty symbolic authority, the master charlatan, who neither acknowledges nor refuses the subject's demand. The analyst instead allows the drama of the analysand's false desire to play out in the void: this is what happens when Evans becomes disillusioned and rails against the empty figure of masterly authority. When Lacan claims in *Seminar VII* that 'every truth has the structure of fiction' (Lacan 1992, p. 12) he is referring to this farcical double game.

Evans's renunciation of psychoanalysis thus follows *exactly* the analytical scenario described by Lacan. This resemblance is particularly striking in Evans's discussion of the 'subject who is supposed to know' in 'From Lacan to Darwin,' a passage in which he accuses the analyst of being cruel for not simply telling the patient that they do not possess a special knowledge that will result in a cure. A few pages later, Evans writes:

> Why was Lacan supposed to be immune from criticism? Was he supposed to have some kind of infallibility like the pope? From where did this infallibility derive? Was it, in fact, merely a projection of his disciples, who put Lacan in the position of the subject-supposed-to-know, Lacan's term for

> the position of the analyst via-à-vis the patient? In which case, did a successful 'cure' mean discovering that Lacan was a fraud, an impostor, who really had no more access to the truth than anyone else, and probably less? (Evans 2005, p. 46)

Evans means this last question sarcastically, but the honest answer is surely a resounding 'yes.' To fall out of love with Lacan, as Clément puts it in *Lives and Legends of Jacques Lacan*, to end the hold that the illusions of transference wield over the subject, that is surely the ultimate, paradoxical goal of psychoanalysis. This death drive at the heart of psychoanalysis is exactly what is meant by a 'cure.'

References

Evans, D., 2004. *Placebo: Mind Over Matter in Modern Medicine.* Oxford: Oxford University Press.

Evans, D., 2005. From Lacan to Darwin. In: J. Gottschall & D. S. Wilson, eds. *The Literary Animal: Evolution and the Nature of Narrative.* Evanston(IL): Northwestern University Press, pp. 38–55.

Evans, D., 2014. *Atheism: All That Matters.* London: Hodder & Stoughton.

Evans, D., 2015. *The Utopia Experiment.* London: Picador.

Fink, B., 2018. The Master Signifier and the Four Discourses. In: D. Nobus, ed. *Key Concepts of Lacanian Psychoanalysis.* New York: Routledge, pp. 29–47.

Klepec, P., 2016. On the Master in the Four 'Discourses'. In: S. Tomšič & A. Zevnik, eds. *Jacques Lacan: Between Psychoanalysis and Politics.* London and New York: Routledge.

Kordela, A. K., 2018. Marx and Psychoanalysis. In: *Epistemontology in Spinoza-Marx-Freud-Lacan.* New York and London: Routledge, pp. 151–165.

Lacan, J., 1992. *The Seminar of Jacques Lacan, Book VII: The Ethics of Psychoanalysis, 1959–1960.* New York and London: W.W. Norton & Company.

Lacan, J., 1994. *The Four Fundamental Concepts of Psycho-Analysis.* Harmondsworth: Penguin.

Lacan, J., 2014. *The Seminar of Jacques Lacan, Book X: Anxiety.* Cambridge(UK) and Malden(MA): Polity.

Soler, C., 2006. *What Lacan Said About Women: A Psychoanalytic Study.* New York: Other Press.

Žižek, S., 1989. *The Sublime Object of Ideology*. London and New York: Verso.
Žižek, S., 1990. The Limits of the Semiotic Approach to Psychoanalysis. In: R. Feldstein & H. Sussman, eds. *Psychoanalysis And....* London and New York: Routledge, pp. 89–110.
Zupančič, A., 2006. When Surplus Enjoyment Meets Surplus Value. In: J. Clemens & R. Grigg, eds. *Jacques Lacan and the Other Side of Psychoanalysis: Reflections on Seminar XVII*. Durham NC and London: Duke University Press, pp. 155–178.

5

Lacan the Ethical Charlatan

A Tale of Two Books

In the second session of *Seminar XXIII*, a tired and grumpy Lacan demands that his audience ask him a question (Lacan 2016, p. 28). The question he receives comes from a young American named Stuart Schneiderman, who queries Lacan about the usefulness of Chomsky to psychoanalytic thought. When Schneiderman seeks further clarification about Lacan's hermetic reply, Lacan cuts him off with a tangential rant about how only Americans ask him real questions anymore. Schneiderman tries to repeat his question, only to find himself cut off again by an irrelevant exclamation from Lacan. The seminar then moves on and Schneiderman's question remains forever unanswered. Despite Lacan's bluster about only getting genuine questions from Americans, he is characteristically oblivious to the fact he has just rudely shut down one of the few actual Americans attending his seminar. Lacan was known for his blunt lack of etiquette, and this example is far from the only instance of his notorious impoliteness.

Schneiderman came to Paris in 1973 with the aim of becoming a disciple of Lacan. Over the next few years, he produced some influential

P. D. Mathews, *Lacan the Charlatan*, The Palgrave Lacan Series,
https://doi.org/10.1007/978-3-030-45204-9_5

introductory texts on Lacanian psychoanalysis, the most notable being an edited collection titled *Returning to Freud* (1980). In his best-known book, *Jacques Lacan: The Death of an Intellectual Hero* (1983), Schneiderman devotes the first chapter to a reflection on Lacan's moral character. Presenting Lacan to the public was difficult because as 'Philippe Soller, critic, novelist, and a friend of Lacan's, said [...] Lacan had bad manners—no, not bad, execrable,' reflects Schneiderman. 'Now why would I want to introduce you to someone who had execrable manners?' (Schneiderman 1983, p. 2). Schneiderman presents the reader with an extensive justification of Lacan's behavior, arguing by turns that his master is a rebel, a brilliant critic, and a tragic figure in the mold of King Lear. For all his faults, Lacan is lauded throughout as 'an extremely generous man' who 'often showed a degree of hospitality quite out of character in his city,' and 'his devotion and dedication to his patients had few limits' (Schneiderman 1983, p. 12). Schneiderman also repeats Lacan's observation about Americans asking him the best questions—minus, of course, the humiliation he received while trying to ask his question about Chomsky (Schneiderman 1983, p. 87). In short, Schneiderman tries to rationalize Lacan's actions to the reader (and to himself) at every opportunity.

As a book, *Jacques Lacan: The Death of an Intellectual Hero* suffers from a lack of direction and purpose. In some parts, Schneiderman attempts to provide a lukewarm introduction to some of Lacan's basic theories, while other sections represent one of the earliest attempts at a biographical overview of Lacan's life. Schneiderman's real purpose in writing this book, though, is intimately connected to its historical context. Published in 1983, the book was written in the immediate aftermath of Lacan's death in 1981. As such, *Jacques Lacan: The Death of an Intellectual Hero* is a love letter from an adoring disciple to his recently-deceased master. Like a neurotic with an unresolved transference, Schneiderman does not really want to undertake the academic task of coldly outlining psychoanalytic theories or biographical details: what he actually wants is to talk obsessively about the lost object of his love.

This unrequited love can be read between every line of Schneiderman's book. His description in Chaps. 4 and 5 about 'the pass,' for instance, the controversial process by which students in the EFP were certified as fully-fledged psychoanalysts, is given a positive spin that is glaringly at odds with the negative testimonies recorded by Turkle. Schneiderman insists that the pass worked because Lacan's method is grounded in a way of thinking that resists the dogmatism of conviction:

> Lacan, for one, stated clearly that psychoanalysis should have nothing to do with states of conviction. In his experience conviction was always associated with the unshakable attitude of psychotics when confronted with any doubt about their beliefs. [...] Thus it is false to say that psychoanalysts are engaged in an activity that will lead their patients to the conviction of their interpretations. Lacan rejected the idea that, when patients refuse or disagree with an analyst's interpretation, they are resisting and that the resistance should be analyzed. He also never tried to convince anyone to undertake psychoanalysis. That desire must come from the prospective analysand; the most the analyst can do is to offer a treatment. (Schneiderman 1983, p. 94)

Yet this supposed openness is put to the test when Schneiderman himself undergoes analysis with Lacan. In Chap. 7, for instance, Schneiderman defends the effectiveness of Lacan's 'short sessions,' in which the standard fifty-minute session was jettisoned in favor of allowing the analyst to judge when a session was over. Schneiderman describes how his initial meetings with Lacan were warm and pleasant, as the two men chatted and drank Jack Daniels together. 'He was convivial, friendly, acting to put his guest at ease, not a very easy task,' he recalls. 'As a listener he was patient and attentive, exhibiting what seemed to be total concentration through an air of puzzlement' (Schneiderman 1983, p. 131). This first period of his analysis ended dramatically, however, with Lacan suddenly becoming cold and distant, the very opposite of the kind listener he was before. Schneiderman explains in some detail how this process was a beneficial strategic maneuver designed to jolt him back to reality, but there is a wounded tone to this account, one that reveals his own unresolved feelings about Lacan's abrupt emotional withdrawal.

What is obvious, both from the incident in *Seminar XXIII* and *Jacques Lacan: The Death of an Intellectual Hero*, is that while Schneiderman loved Lacan, Lacan certainly did not love him in return. According to

Schneiderman's own testimony, Lacan was routinely rude and emotionally cold toward him, functioning as an impossible object of love that fits exactly Schneiderman's neurotic justifications of Lacan's behavior. This state of denial is what leads him to proclaim in the introduction to his book:

> In the mid-sixties general Parisian opinion had it that Lacan was 'le seul génie du moment' ['the only genius of the moment']. At the time few took this too seriously; it was only another intellectual fad. The years would prove them wrong. The importance and influence of Lacan deepened, and, within an environment studded with brilliant intellectual stars, his word gained an authority reserved only for the very great. And within the world of psychoanalysis only Freud had the same kind of personal following and respect, to say nothing of the same hostility. (Schneiderman 1983, p. vi)

If Schneiderman's love for Lacan was a hopeless case when he was alive, the latter's death confirmed this impossibility. Unrequited love can very easily turn into resentment and hatred, and that is exactly what happened in this instance. After returning to the United States and practicing as a psychoanalyst in New York City for a number of years, Schneiderman started to declare his disaffection with Lacanian ideas, and psychoanalysis in general.

Schneiderman relates in his online profile that his ideas began to shift with the publication of his book *Saving Face: America and the Politics of Shame* (1996), a work that contrasts Japan and the United States, a shame culture and a guilt culture. Schneiderman, who has no academic expertise in Japanese culture, relies heavily on Ruth Benedict's influential but much-critiqued study *The Chrysanthemum and the Sword* (1946). More explicit indications of a shift in Schneiderman's thinking arrived in the form of a personal essay titled 'That Night at Elaine's,' published in the journal *The Reading Room* in 2002. In that piece, Schneiderman recounts a dinner-party conversation about Woody Allen, virtue, and psychoanalysis, in which a very different attitude toward Lacan starts to emerge. From this point on Lacan is no longer an 'intellectual hero.' Instead, he is described as an 'eccentric' figure who 'spawned personality cults in France, Argentina, Venezuela, and Brazil' (Schneiderman 2002).

Schneiderman looks back with sudden bitterness on his experiences as one of Lacan's disciples:

> Bedecked in a maroon velvet cape, chomping on a twisted cigar, Lacan drew masses of intellectuals to his public lectures from the late 1960's to the late 1970's. From 1973 to 1977 I was among them—a young man who had forsaken a career teaching literature to fly off to Paris and sit at the Great Man's feet. Lacan was idolized by people like myself who saw in his radicalism a chance to test the limits, both of thought and behavior. In his public performances he served up a cornucopia of tantalizing oracular pronouncements, never bothering to explain himself, never really caring whether his assembled acolytes could grasp his meaning. [...] It mattered little that we did not understand; Lacan had implicitly promised that once we were well-enough analyzed we would. (Schneiderman 2002)

This passage is the exact opposite of the sentiments expressed in *Jacques Lacan: The Death of an Intellectual Hero*. Schneiderman no longer jumps to Lacan's defense at every turn to rationalize the latter's bad behavior or theoretical shortcomings. From this point on he sees himself as a once-faithful disciple whose love and devotion have been exploited and betrayed. The dinner-party conversation also prompts Schneiderman to think about a patient he was treating, a case in which the usual Lacanian methods had proven unsatisfying, a failure that seems to epitomize his problems with psychoanalysis. The unrequited love for Lacan that Schneiderman manifests in the earlier phase of his life has fermented into undisguised hatred.

The consequences of this change become clearer in the online blog that Schneiderman created in 2008, which bears the provocative title *Had Enough Therapy?*. This blog is the main outlet for Schneiderman's occasional writings on diverse topics. There is also a discernible political shift to the right in Schneiderman's views, opinions that carry the distinctive stamp of American neo-conservatism. Schneiderman has renounced not only Lacan, but the entire discourse of psychoanalysis, instead marketing himself as an 'executive life coach' who helps people to solve problems related to relationships, business, and life in general. In his online profile, for instance, Schneiderman begins by outlining his time as a follower of Lacan:

> Stuart Schneiderman spent most of his career practicing psychoanalysis and psychotherapy in New York City. After earning academic degrees in literature he trained in psychoanalysis in Paris with Jacques Lacan. While he was there he worked in a psychiatric clinic and hospital and taught at the University of Paris. He wrote about his training in an acclaimed book, *Jacques Lacan: The Death of an Intellectual Hero*, published by Harvard University Press. While he was an analyst he wrote and edited other books about the field and lectured on four continents. For nearly three decades he practiced psychoanalysis and psychotherapy in New York City. (Schneiderman n.d.)

He then provides a brief outline as to why he turned away from psychoanalysis toward life coaching—in short, 'people wanted guidance, not interpretations' (Schneiderman n.d.)—and then launches into an advertisement for the various services he provides. Despite his rejection of Lacan and psychoanalysis, he continues to foreground that history, knowing that his earlier activities carry a patina of success and respectability that reflect well on him.

A perusal of Schneiderman's more recent writing nonetheless reveals a tendency to distort and obscure his past as a follower of Lacan. Consider, for example, a blog entry from June 7, 2015 bearing, in an echo of the Apostle Peter's denial of Christ, the title 'Who Was Jacques Lacan?':

> Once upon a time I wrote a book about French psychoanalyst Jacques Lacan. In it I discussed my own experience as Lacan's analysand and presented his theories alongside some aspects of his biography. It was well-reviewed and well-received in America. Not so in France. The powers-that-be in French Lacanian circles were horrified that I had broken protocol by mentioning, for example, that Lacan was a notorious womanizer. They were even more appalled by the fact that Lacan was being introduced to his widest American audience by someone other than themselves. They told their cult followers in France not to read the book and never to mention it. Like good lemmings their followers complied. (Schneiderman 2015)

It is important to pay attention to the language that Schneiderman uses in this opening passage. Gone are the temporal specifics he uses in 'That Night at Elaine's,' for instance, which are replaced by the fairytale-like opening 'once upon a time.' Schneiderman's repression of his book's title is also striking, as it strategically hides the fact that the thinker he is now attacking was once his 'intellectual hero.' The most notable part of this discourse, however, is Schneiderman's paranoid fantasy of a Lacanian conspiracy against him. His earlier book was indeed a success in English-speaking circles when it was first published, at a time Lacan's ideas were just gaining traction in the Anglophone academy. Like Tallis, Schneiderman does not cite any sources for the purported smear campaign by the French Lacanians against him. The most grievous charge I could find comes from Roudinesco, ten years after the publication of *Jacques Lacan: The Death of an Intellectual Hero*, who argues that Schneiderman had a propensity to give too much credence to personal stories and second-hand information, with the result that his book 'gaily mingled fantasy with rumor, hagiography with anecdotes from private life' (Roudinesco 1997, p. 388). Like any book about a controversial thinker, Schneiderman's text has received some criticism, but his claim that there was a concerted campaign by French Lacanians to blacklist his book simply does not bear scrutiny.

After this introduction, Schneiderman turns to his most recent book, *The Last Psychoanalyst*, in which he 'presented a history of psychoanalysis, from the first unanalyzed analyst, Sigmund Freud, to the last analyst, Jacques Lacan' (Schneiderman 2015). There is again an implicit dishonesty to the way Schneiderman moves from one book to the next, the concealment of the earlier title giving the reader the erroneous impression that the two books occupy similar territory in terms of both tone and content, when in reality they could not be more different. Schneiderman enhances this appearance by arguing that Lacanians reacted to *The Last Psychoanalyst* with the same 'vehemence' as his earlier book:

> I suggested that Lacan wanted to end psychoanalysis as a clinical practice and allow it to fulfill its destiny as a force for cultural revolution. Since I did not limit myself to theories but placed some emphasis on Lacan the man, Lacanian cult followers in this country were told not to read the

> book. If you want to control minds, you must be able to control what people read and discuss. Moreover, it is always much easier to control an ignorant and uneducated mind. (Schneiderman 2015)

Schneiderman thus gives his readers the false impression that, in both books, he upset the Lacanian establishment by daring to criticize Lacan, and that in both cases his publications were met with spiteful, ideologically-motivated reprisals that saw him blacklisted as a dangerous enemy.

For anyone who has read *Jacques Lacan: The Death of an Intellectual Hero*, this account is clearly disingenuous. Few books about any public figure, let alone Lacan, have been more sycophantic than Schneiderman's. If this text has fallen out of favor in critical circles, its descent has everything to do with having been eclipsed by more rigorous scholarly works, and nothing to do with Lacanian 'cults' declaring it to be off-limits. The conspiratorial tone with which Schneiderman envelops the supposed ill-treatment of *The Last Psychoanalyst* is equally misleading. The entry of these two books into the public sphere could hardly have been more different, with *Jacques Lacan: The Death of an Intellectual Hero* published by the prestigious Harvard University Press, whereas *The Last Psychoanalyst* was self-published on Amazon. Far from rising up in anger against *The Last Psychoanalyst*, most Lacanians probably have no idea of the existence of this obscure, self-published book, a text that burns with a hatred that mirrors Schneiderman's earlier love for Lacan.

The End of Shame

In 'Who Was Jacques Lacan?', Schneiderman recalls Chomsky's famous remark that Lacan was an 'amusing and perfectly self-conscious charlatan' (Chomsky in Schneiderman 2015). He does so in order to strip Lacan's discourse of its authority, while himself committing the logical fallacy of appealing to authority:

> Since Lacan claimed to be a theorist of language and linguistics, the fact that Noam Chomsky—not a man of the extreme right, by the way—considered him to be a charlatan argues against the notion that Lacan was

> a great thinker. Calling someone a charlatan does not merely suggest that he was wrong. It means that his work is not worth considering. (Schneiderman 2015)

The passing allusion to Chomsky's politics is important, for politics now represents the primary frame through which Schneiderman views the practice of psychoanalysis. His conservative political agenda similarly underpins the central arguments of *The Last Psychoanalyst*. Posing as the moral guardian of modern society, Schneiderman's central thesis is that psychoanalysis constitutes a pernicious attack on traditional social and sexual values, removing these ethical safeguards in order to bring victims of psychoanalytic brainwashing under the insidious control of their manipulative therapists.

Far from being a measured reflection on the history of psychoanalysis, as Schneiderman claims, *The Last Psychoanalyst* is a meandering, unstructured text that reads more like an extended rant than a carefully-argued thesis. From this mixture of wild accusations and angry swipes, it is nonetheless possible to discern a line of argument that is grounded, in particular, in Schneiderman's arguments about sexuality and social order. Schneiderman presents the surprising contention that the Austria in which Freud grew up was not a repressed society at all, but a hotbed of sexual license:

> As a Jew in libertine Vienna, Freud was like the poor boy whose face was pressed against the window of the candy store. Unable to enter, he could only yearn for delights that were available to others. Perhaps that's why his theory emphasized desire more than gratification. (Schneiderman 2014, p. 76)

Although Schneiderman acknowledges that Freud himself did not live a sexually adventurous life, he nonetheless insists that Freud 'was using sex as a lure to attract people into his cult' (Schneiderman 2014, p. 18). Sex was just a front for a system of control that, by getting people 'in closer touch with their inner libertines' would cause them to lose all shame (Schneiderman 2014, p. 18). This 'full frontal attack on feminine modesty' so deeply enslaves the psychoanalytic patient to their lust for pleasure that they fall hopelessly under the authoritarian control of the psychoanalyst (Schneiderman 2014, p. 18).

While the brunt of the attack on psychoanalysis in *The Last Psychoanalyst* is focused on Freud, Schneiderman also casts his former master in a very different light to his earlier book. In *The Last Psychoanalyst*, Lacan is little more than a variation on Freud's war on shame, enlivening the latter's grim vision by injecting it with a French *joie de vivre*. Lacan is portrayed by Schneiderman as someone who lived the hedonistic philosophy of psychoanalysis more deeply than Freud, throwing aside all customs and mores in his single-minded pursuit of pleasure:

> When Jacques Lacan arrived on the scene, he added some joy to Freud's theory of sexuality. By giving a special place to what he called *jouissance*, or enjoyment, Lacan redeemed Freudian sexuality. The French word *jouissance* has a decidedly positive connotation. Its lilting cadence even sounds joyous. It's easier to sell enjoyment than to peddle Freud's stoically tragic vision. Good Freudian that he was Lacan also had to insist that *jouissance* was ultimately destructive. (Schneiderman 2014, p. 17)

These wholly inaccurate depictions of Freud and Lacan and their respective ideas are unrecognizable to anyone who has actually read their work. Is not the central idea of Freud's *Civilization and Its Discontents* (1930) that we need to repress and sublimate our most violent, erotically-charged instincts for the sake of preserving society? Is not Lacan's *Seminar VII: The Ethics of Psychoanalysis* a critical discussion of the paradox that unbridled pleasure turns out to be the *least* effective path to gratification? Whatever Schneiderman may claim, he is not describing Freud or Lacan honestly—the philosophy shown here more closely resembles that of the Marquis de Sade than psychoanalysis. Schneiderman deceptively uses these cartoonish versions of Freud and Lacan to mislead and manipulate his unsuspecting readers.

Schneiderman chooses to attack them in this way, it seems, because they are easy targets for the conservative political agenda that is central to his new persona, which rests on two broad pillars. The first pillar is a defense of 'Judeo-Christianity':

> Obviously, the Freudian pseudo-religion differs radically from Judeo-Christianity. Psychoanalysis promotes permissiveness and devalues character. It glorifies histrionic displays of emotion over more temperate expressions. It produces people who are more prone to indulge their appetites than to discipline them. It prefers empty assertions of self-esteem to earned self-confidence. It has never encouraged humility and has always been at war with modesty. (Schneiderman 2014, pp. 56–57)

This easy juxtaposition between psychoanalysis and traditional religion is highly questionable—Marcia Ian, for instance, has an insightful article on how psychoanalysis would have been impossible without the influence of Judaism on Freud and Catholicism on Lacan—but such inaccuracies are simply ignored in Schneiderman's text (Ian 1997). The second pillar of Schneiderman's politics is an elevation of Anglo-American culture over a decadent and immoral European tradition, with the latter represented in the book by France and Austria. At the end of Chap. 9 of *The Last Psychoanalyst*, for instance, Schneiderman asks the reader to imagine, through the eyes of Freud, who fled from the Nazis to London in 1938, the difference between a powerful (and thus sexually potent) nation like Great Britain, and the impotence (in both senses of the word) of his homeland, Austria:

> When Great Britain and America became hegemonic powers their people felt more optimistic, more accomplished, more confident and more proud. If their citizens did not advertise their sexuality, perhaps they did not need to manufacture and sustain desire artificially. In a declining nation like Austria the psycho-cultural forces were aligned differently. It makes sense that Freud, coming of age in the midst of a Long Depression and a military defeat, should have felt demoralized. More so since, as a Jew, he did not feel like a full member of Viennese society. (Schneiderman 2014, p. 99)

This overflowing praise for the 'hegemonic powers' of the United States and Great Britain does not, of course, acknowledge the ethical (or indeed, sexual) shortcomings of those two countries. The collective histories of colonization, genocide, slavery, racism, misogyny, and economic exploitation they have carried out are simply omitted from the heroic political narrative that Schneiderman wants to fabricate.

Lacan's personal promiscuity is also interpreted by Schneiderman as a reflection of the chaotic decadence of French culture, in contrast to the sober rationality he attributes to Anglo-Americans:

> Lacan was defying Anglo-American cultural norms. British culture, in particular, requires consistency and regularity, punctuality and decorum. It does not respect people who follow their whims. A culture where everyone queues up does not abide deviants gladly. (Schneiderman 2014, p. 146)

Schneiderman admires regimented displays of social order, be it the British stereotype of the 'stiff upper lip,' the biblical ten commandments, Confucian filial piety, or the patriarchal family structure, all of which are lavishly praised in the course of *The Last Psychoanalyst*. By contrast, ideas and movements seen as disruptive to tradition (the French Surrealists, the Bloomsbury Group, and Freudian psychoanalysts are all singled out for Schneiderman's contempt) are regarded with hatred and fear. This respect for an imaginary ideal of social order is regarded as the necessary foundation for the 'great successes' of Anglo-American civilization, 'especially the modern Industrial Revolution and liberal democracy,' with psychoanalysis's attempts to 'liberate people from this civilization' demonized as both irrational and anti-democratic (Schneiderman 2014, p. 251).

The centerpiece of this political vision is Schneiderman's nostalgia for the patriarchal family. The figure of the father, he argues, ought to be 'revered, respected and honored' since, far from being 'an incipient or repressed tyrant,' the father, without exception, 'is the model of benevolence' (Schneiderman 2014, pp. 238–239). One of the greatest sins of psychoanalysis was that 'Freud rejected the ethic of paternal benevolence,' an attack on the head of the family that, in turn, brought the rest of the family structure crashing down (Schneiderman 2014, p. 239). The father is the traditional religious and moral center of the family, and before 'modern minds were gender-bent out of shape everyone knew that mothers nurtured children and that fathers protected and provided for them' (Schneiderman 2014, p. 239). The most refined examples of this patriarchal family structure developed out of the rationality and sense of justice that supposedly underpins British culture:

> Among the reasons for French (and Continental) enmity toward Albion must have been a single, strange British custom. The […] Anglosphere led the charge in replacing traditional arranged marriages with what is commonly called love marriage. For most of human history marriage has been an arrangement, an alliance between families. Most human cultures have been loath to allow callow young people a free choice in such an important matter. Thus, they have refused to grant young women the freedom to choose their husbands. Great Britain changed all that. By giving a woman an important say in her choice of a husband, it expanded the practice of human freedom. For reasons that are probably not too mysterious, this new custom made romantic love an essential component of marriage. It is no exaggeration to say that the change was revolutionary. (Schneiderman 2014, p. 82)

This system was further perfected in America where, because that country had 'dispensed with all vestiges of aristocracy, it practiced a purer form of love marriage than even the British,' allowing 'women to choose their husbands and also to take responsibility for their actions' (Schneiderman 2014, pp. 82–83). Schneiderman's argument in *The Last Psychoanalyst* depends on accepting this narrative about the inherent benevolence of the patriarchal family.

Schneiderman argues that the 'revolutionary' notion of marrying for love gave rise to a new social mechanism, that of shame. Shame became a necessary concept because, he argues, unlike in the old system of arranged marriages, adultery loomed as a potential threat to the love match, especially for women, and so moral and legal laws were supplemented by a new kind of moral conscience:

> Since guilt for having transgressed the Seventh Commandment had proven to be relatively powerless in stopping adultery, people lit on a stronger sanction: shame. […] In a community that practiced love marriage more people knew with a higher degree of certainty who their parents were and what their place in society was. Thus, the new Anglo-American custom sustained social order better than the decadent pleasure principle. (Schneiderman 2014, pp. 83–85)

Shame is the central principle of the mythological social contract that Schneiderman describes in *The Last Psychoanalyst*. It is presented to the reader as not only a moral emotion but also a rational one, insofar as the individual living in a thriving society benefits more from conforming to the collective than pursuing their personal self-interest.

Understanding this logic of shame is also crucial to identifying why Schneiderman regards psychoanalysis as such a threat in *The Last Psychoanalyst*. The possibilities for personal freedom that come with the advent of psychoanalysis supposedly encourage the patient to indulge in behaviors that are 'destructively' individualistic. It does not matter that neither Freud nor Lacan never actually advocated such things: Schneiderman has already cast them in his mythical drama as the antisocial villains who prescribe rampant and dangerous forms of hedonism:

> In one of his earlier seminars Lacan declared that people who wanted to live Freudian lives should follow one basic rule: they should bring their actions into accord with their desire. In everyday language this translates: Do what you want! Unfortunately, when someone tells you to do what you want—in English or in French—he is really saying that you should stop pestering him. 'Do what you want' means: Get out of my face! The principle is either very obvious or very obscure. Lacan called it an ethical principle, but it was more amoral than moral. (Schneiderman 2014, pp. 162–163)

This distorted example is presented by Schneiderman as damning evidence that Lacan is an ethical charlatan who manipulated his audiences with promises of selfish depravity. Weaving together this heady mixture of fantasies, distortions, and inaccuracies in *The Last Psychoanalyst*, Schneiderman concludes that it is Lacan who has no shame.

The Man of Pleasure

In his personal life, Lacan was indeed a man of pleasure who enjoyed expensive food and wine, collected rare books and art, dressed in tailored suits made from luxurious materials, and had numerous dalliances with women. In her memoir *Life With Lacan* (2016), Catherine Millot, Lacan's mistress during the last decade of his life, describes how Lacan had an uncanny ability to bulldoze his way through any obstacle to get what he wanted, a trait that was particularly terrifying when it came to his reckless driving. 'He didn't like closed doors any more than he liked red traffic lights,' recalls Millot after a special visit to the convent of Santa Trinità dei Monti, to which Lacan somehow obtained his own key. 'Enclosure was a challenge he had accepted, maliciously suggesting that he could have violated the building's privacy under cover of night if he had wanted to' (Millot 2018, p. 16). In his theoretical work, though, Lacan's interest in hedonism is focused on the paradox that, while moral prohibitions have become more relaxed in modern society, so too has the ability to enjoy their once-forbidden objects. Contrary to what Schneiderman claims, Lacan's critique of the 'man of pleasure' (Lacan 1992, p. 4), of the kind of person who shamelessly breaks prohibitions in order to seek after pleasure, is the main target of his ethical theory.

Lacan focuses on this question in two main texts: the early sessions of *Seminar VII*, and the essay 'Kant with Sade' (1963) from *Écrits*. Lacan's critique of the 'man of pleasure' is a historical one, rooted in the late eighteenth-century figures of Immanuel Kant and the Marquis de Sade. At first glance, these two thinkers could not be more dissimilar, since Kant's categorical imperative, with its emphasis on rational and unemotional judgment, appears to be the moral culmination of Enlightenment thought, standing in direct contrast to the perversity and apparent lawlessness of Sade's libertines. Yet Lacan makes the startling argument that Sade, far from being the opposite of Kantian philosophy, would not have been possible without the logical shift that Kant introduced:

> Sade represents here the first step of a subversion of which Kant, as piquant as this may seem in light of the coldness of the man himself, represents the turning point—something that has never been pointed out as such, to the best of my knowledge. *Philosophy in the Bedroom* came eight years after the *Critique of Practical Reason*. If, after showing that the former is consistent with the latter, I can demonstrate that the former completes the latter, I

> shall be able to claim that it yields the truth of the *Critique*. (Lacan 2006, pp. 645–646)

Lacan's argument is that Sade's hedonistic logic, far from being in opposition to Kant's, is actually its logical outcome, the key difference between the two thinkers being that Sade was more honest about the consequences of the shift that Kant initiated.

As Miller explains in an insightful discussion of 'Kant with Sade,' the western philosophical tradition had long understood ethics in terms of what is considered to be good. As such, ethics was, much like hygienics, rooted in the practical experience of our bodies and the world, and because of that it was possible to formulate specific rules that would ensure maximum health (not drinking too much alcohol, for instance) or social cohesion (such as respecting one's mother and father). In the *Critique of Practical Reason* (1788), by contrast, Kant discards the notion of the good, replacing it instead with an ethics that is grounded in what is rational. Miller elucidates the dramatic consequences of this shift:

> Kant's fundamental law [...] doesn't mention any specific act that you have to carry out. It's not the ten commandments: it [...] doesn't specify anything you should or should not do. [...] All of that is eliminated. Kant's fundamental law is a true bulldozer in the field of ethics. [...] Kant's ethics is thus a kind of Terror-radical and destructive—because in it the world disappears[.] [...] You have a formal law and that's it. A formal law is a law which does not specify an object. All content of the law disappears, and we have but a formal criterion of morality. (Miller 1996, p. 226)

Kant's philosophy thus disrupts the complacent assumption that goodness is rooted in rationality, with the categorical imperative insisting instead that a rational course of action is true regardless of whether it brings pleasure or pain. This potential co-existence of cruelty and rational action leads directly to Sade, who ingeniously grasps the disjunction between goodness and rationality. Such clarity allows Sade to perceive that the categorical imperative can be used to transform rape, murder, incest, deceit, and other forms of traditional immorality into rational virtues that can be practiced without shame: the contrasting fates of the honorable Justine and the rational Juliette in his fiction attest to the power of this perverse logic.

Sade's path toward hedonism is nonetheless thwarted in an unexpected way. In finding a justification for pleasure in the mechanisms of rational logic, the libertine walks into a trap that turns enjoyment into a compulsion. Sade, like Kant, bans all 'pathology'—that is to say, all feelings of pain or pleasure—from the ethical decision, which means that the libertine is compelled to do their rational 'duty,' regardless of whether they actually feel like raping, murdering, cheating, and so on. Kordela highlights in *$urplus: Spinoza, Lacan* (2007) how the Sadian libertine, who speaks and acts like a master, is unmasked by Lacan as an instrument (or slave) of a compulsory enjoyment:

> In [...] 'Kant avec Sade,' Lacan argued that, appearances to the contrary, the sadist—as the subject capable of also performing the monstrosities that mark our history—is not the master but 'no more than the instrument of *jouissance*,' the object of the Other's enjoyment. What sadism, therefore, shows us is that the so-called dialectic between master and slave, in which the slave turns out to be the true master, is a mirage. In sadism, the positions of the master (Other) and the slave (subject), far from being magically convertible, remain rigid, with the Other always in mastery. Monstrosities do not occur out of the subjects' will to power, but out of their will to offer themselves to the Other as its object of enjoyment, which they do by projecting a will to it. (Kordela 2007, p. 20)

As Kordela points out, however, the libertine quickly finds out that this path to freedom is really a trap. The libertine cannot really do whatever they want and, in this respect, they only *appear* to be a master, an illusion achieved by enslaving themselves to the mechanism of *jouissance*. Within the Sadian libertine dwells a secret shame—not a moral shame, of course, but an irresolvable perplexity that their brazenness has produced something so utterly lacking in enjoyment. The tedium of reading Sade's lists of endless transgressions against conventional morality is a testament to this paradox.

Much of Lacan's *Seminar VII* is devoted to exploring how the outward advance of human freedom that arises from the philosophy of the eighteenth-century Enlightenment has resulted in an inverse decrease in the modern capacity for enjoyment. The more shameless we become, the more we do away with the prohibitions on behaviors considered morally taboo, the less we seem to enjoy those behaviors. The 'naturalist liberation of desire' (Lacan 1992, p. 3) promised by the Enlightenment appears to have achieved the very opposite of its goal:

> Now the naturalist liberation of desire has failed. The more the theory, the more the work of social criticism, the more the sieve of that experience, which tended to limit obligation to certain precise functions in the social order, have raised in us the hope of relativizing the imperative, the contrary, or, in a word, conflictual character of moral experience, the more we have, in fact, witnessed a growth in the instance of genuine pathologies. The naturalist liberation of desire has failed historically. We do not find ourselves in the presence of a man less weighed down with laws and desires than before the great critical experience of so-called libertine thought. (Lacan 1992, pp. 3–4)

Lacan's project is framed by the Enlightenment dilemma of having to choose between rationality and enjoyment. '[W]e analysts know full well that if God doesn't exist, then nothing at all is permitted any longer,' Lacan says in *Seminar II*. 'Neurotics prove that to us every day' (Lacan 1988, p. 128). Kant's ruthless abandonment of the good in favor of a narrowly-defined vision of the rational places these terms in an irresolvable dichotomy that not even a shameless hedonist like Sade, the ultimate 'man of pleasure,' can resolve.

Utilitarian Fictions

This question of freedom and pleasure does not, of course, end with Kant and Sade and the eighteenth century. The most important transformation of this ongoing debate begins in the early nineteenth century with the rise of utilitarian thought, a development that Lacan recognizes in *Seminar VII* in his discussion of Jeremy Bentham, and again ten years later when, in *Seminar XVII*, he traces the metamorphosis of utilitarianism into the university discourse. In a lecture titled 'Discourse to Catholics,' delivered by Lacan in 1960, right in the middle of *Seminar VII*, Lacan contemplates Freud's lack of enthusiasm for utilitarian ideas. 'Everyone knows that Freud was a crude materialist,' observes Lacan. 'Why then wasn't he able to resolve the problem, which is nevertheless so easy, of moral agency (*instance*) by resorting, as is classic, to utilitarianism?' (Lacan 2013, p. 20). The answer to Lacan's question can be found in the sessions from *Seminar VII* that immediately follow this lecture, which Miller places under the shared rubric of 'the paradox of *jouissance*' (Lacan 1992, p. 165). There, Lacan articulates his thoughts on the death of God and contemplates an earlier pairing of Kant with Sade that precedes his famous essay.

The paradox of *jouissance* derives from the conflict between the good and the rational that arises from Kant's attempt to redefine the former in terms of the latter. Kant's removal of the 'pathological' domain of pleasure and pain from the ethical creates a split between right action and enjoyment. Kant calls his ethics a 'practical philosophy,' but the great irony of the categorical imperative, and one of the reasons why Lacan says that '*The Critique of Practical Reason* is manifestly a book of eroticism that is extraordinarily more amusing than what Éric Losfeld has published' (Lacan 2007, p. 169), is that it is so utterly *impractical* when it comes to making actual ethical decisions. Nonetheless, as Marc De Kesel notes in *Eros and Ethics* (2009), the philosophical questions that Kant and Sade are posing are given their impetus by the political context of the French and American revolutions:

> In a society where everyone is treated as equal, an ethics of the master as presented in Aristotle becomes an anomaly. Henceforth, no one can seize their happiness at the expense of others, at least theoretically. Happiness must be for everyone, if not, it is unjust. 'There is no satisfaction for the individual outside of the satisfaction of all.' It is not surprising, then, that the first postrevolutionary ethics is utilitarian. There, for the first time, morality is based on a happiness that is exclusively 'democratically' founded. (De Kesel 2009, p. 142)

In the wake of these eighteenth-century political and social upheavals, therefore, utilitarianism is an attempt to recast utility as the 'democratic' measure of the rational, papering over the Kantian split by insisting that utility can be the basis for both ethics *and* enjoyment. In this way, utilitarianism claims to put the 'practical' back into 'practical reason.'

Utilitarianism has naturalized the idea that utility is the basis of the rational, a rationality that in turn lights the path toward happiness and enjoyment. Yet, as Kordela observes, the modern lack of enjoyment seems only to have increased under the auspices of utilitarian principles:

> Through the introduction of utilitarianism, all forms of enjoyment are subsumed under the yoke of utility and need, and should therefore be remunerated. [...] One exists only in the service of capital and need/necessity, without any room for 'useless' enjoyment. [...] The ultimate consequence of utilitarianism is the subjection of all life to the totalitarianism of need and necessity. (Kordela 2013, p. 160)

The utilitarian falls into the same error as Sade's libertines, in which the logical path that supposedly leads to enjoyment turns out to be a trap. Now enjoyment can *only* be defined as that which is productive and useful. To desire something else, something perversely 'useless,' is prohibited not only because it is unproductive, but also because it is defined as 'irrational.' In this perverse way, an ethics grounded in pure rationality separates enjoyment from the definition of the good.

In Chap. 4 of *Read My Desire*, Copjec traces the origins and implications of utilitarian thought in Lacanian terms. Her starting point is a series of more than twenty thousand photographs taken by G. G. de Clérambault, Lacan's former teacher, while recovering from a wound in Morocco during World War I. These photographs, which depict local people dressed in traditional Moroccan garb, were the basis for a series of lectures on drapery that Clérambault gave at the École des Beaux-Arts in the 1920s, in which he contemplated the differences between practical and decorative changes in the evolution of clothing. Copjec observes how Clérambault's reflections about clothing converge with the language of Le Corbusier's functionalist classic *Towards a New Architecture* (1923). The usual dichotomy between the classicism of the Beaux-Arts tradition and the modernism of Le Corbusier is complicated, argues Copjec, by their shared adherence to a break that occurred at the dawn of the nineteenth century, in which architects stopped thinking about a building in terms of 'its character or physiognomy,' or according to 'some primitive or ideal form' or 'symbolic function,' and instead began using 'nouns designating a building's *use*' (Copjec 1994, p. 75).

This transition had a significant impact on the way architects think about buildings, notes Copjec, a shift that culminates in Le Corbusier's functionalist style. She observes that the rise of this utilitarian approach to architecture creates a conceptual division between a building's essential functions and the decorative effects in which those functions are, as it were, 'draped':

> The isolation of utility as the essential parameter of a building's definition resulted not only in the assigning to style and ornament the task of *expressing* this essential definition, of linking themselves to use, it resulted as well in the underlying assumption that obliged this task: namely, that style and ornament were separate from and secondary to function. It is at this point that style and ornament began to be considered precisely as *clothing*; their connection to the building, in other words, was taken as arbitrary rather than necessary, and they were thus viewed, for the first time, as the wrapping or covering of an otherwise nude building. (Copjec 1994, pp. 75–77)

The conceptual point at which architecture and clothing thus converge, exemplified by the congruent language of Clérambault and Le Corbusier, is in the complementary metaphors of nudity and clothing. The 'naked' human being is stripped down to the essentials of their most basic needs, the biological primacy of existence making it appear rational to pursue those desires first.

This hierarchy of priorities is the founding myth of utilitarian thought. Artificially pushing the instinct for survival into the foreground of human desire, utilitarianism implies that a passion for 'superfluous' pleasures beyond bare life can never be a motivating force as powerful as the survival instinct. Yet as Lacan points out in *Seminar VII*, the authority on which this philosophy is grounded does not come from empirical reality or experience, but from a series of *a priori*, theoretical 'fictions.' Lacan's criticism is particularly aimed at Bentham, as De Kesel explains:

> For Lacan, the importance of Bentham's utilitarian ethics […] is the fact that Bentham attributed an independent status to what, in contrast to the real, he called 'fiction'[.] […] Things we talk about in language are not exclusively the direct, perceptible 'real entities'[.] […] [T]here are also things that exist solely thanks to language. Abstract things such as quality, quantity, potency, soul, duty, the good, and so forth are what Bentham called 'fictitious entities.' […] This is not to say that Bentham already claims we must approach the *whole* of reality as fiction, that is, as a signifier (as Lacan will do more than a century later), but he does at least display an unmistakable sensitivity toward the autonomous operation of language in our […] relation to reality, and toward language's capacity to generate its own fictitious 'reality.' (De Kesel 2009, p. 60)

The Benthamite fiction insists that its authority derives from the force of a logic that describes the world as it really is. 'Bentham's derivation of ethics from a descriptive psychology is often described as the derivation of *ought* from *is*,' counters Copjec. 'It now seems more fitting to say that, in utilitarianism, *ought* is derived from *ought*' (Copjec 1994, p. 87). In the utilitarian mindset, if someone were perversely to seek enjoyment in something that is not grounded in utility yet brings them joy, they are targeted by a double sanction: not only is their 'useless' pleasure regarded as 'irrational,' it is also logically, as a result, *not* enjoyable. The 'irrational' enjoyment of such pleasures thus finds itself under a strange prohibition in which the perverse enjoyment of useless things, despite being theoretically 'impossible,' is also not allowed.

We can see, then, why it is that Lacan calls Bentham's theory of utilitarianism a fiction. By defining how a human being *ought* to act according to a series of *a priori* principles, utilitarianism creates a predictive narrative that is meant, theoretically, to apply to any given situation. This ideology has remained influential, argues Copjec, mainly because it is a powerful tool for concealing narratives of social hierarchy. In the French colonial period, for example, utilitarianism was used to construct a narrative of benevolence, in which the brutality of the imperial endeavor was overlaid with the paternalistic idea that French colonization is actually a benefit to the colonized people because it teaches them how to 'rationalize' their desires:

> The imperative to extend benevolence infinitely stems from the notion that man can be counted as zero. Defined as essentially pleasure seeking, he becomes total compliance. For, once his motive is established, his manipulability is assured. The ambitious imperialism of functionalism does not expect to encounter resistance. Since it arrives bearing what man wants—happiness—it expects its subjects to submit to its embrace. For this reason, French colonialism adopted a policy of 'assimilation.' (Copjec 1994, p. 87)

The self-justifying logic of utilitarianism creates a fiction of desire that is then projected onto the subject in order to predict what, rationally, they should want and desire. This fiction displaces what the subject *actually* wants in favor of what, according to the Other, they rationally *ought* to desire.

Much has been written by Lacanian theorists about the consequences of the shameless free-for-all that has resulted from this utilitarian overthrow of traditional moral prohibitions. Far from celebrating this collapse, as Schneiderman contends, this body of criticism is replete with concerns that the rampant pursuit of enjoyment in modernity has produced an unprecedented level of human dissatisfaction. The participants in the modern hedonistic system have become slaves to their own desires, a subordination that is paid for by an endless demand for more frustrating and unsatisfying pleasure. 'What the society of enjoyment thus makes manifest is the impossibility of any direct experience of enjoyment,' explains Todd McGowan in *The End of Dissatisfaction?* (2004). 'This is because the barrier to enjoyment is essential to the experience of it. In fact, what we enjoy is the barrier itself' (McGowan 2004, p. 7). McGowan's thesis, that the amount of enjoyment we get from indulging in pleasure is inversely proportional to how easy that pleasure is to obtain, explains why the cheap pleasures of modern society are so profoundly unsatisfying. In a perverse, Sadian twist, the utilitarian incitement to maximize one's pleasure without shame has become the new categorical imperative.

Clearly, then, the answer to the modern problem of dissatisfaction cannot lie in becoming more 'rational' in the prescribed utilitarian sense. The pursuit of greater pleasure does not bring greater enjoyment, as was naively expected, but instead a deadening of enjoyment, an excess that culminates in an 'unpleasure' that Lacan, after Freud, calls the death drive. Rather than being a retreat into the irrational, however, the death drive is interpreted by Lacan as rationality turning on itself. 'The death drive (in its strict Freudian sense) is not the subject's willing surrender to the abyss, his acceptance of being swallowed by the deadly vortex, but the very repetitive circulation on the edge of the abyss,' explains Žižek. 'In other words, death drive is on the side of reason, not on the side of irrationality as often thought' (Žižek 2016, p. 257). Far from being the self-serving advocate of shameless pleasure that Schneiderman portrays in *The Last Psychoanalyst*, therefore, in his work Lacan develops a rigorous ethical critique of the limitations of the unbridled hedonism that derives from the eighteenth-century 'man of pleasure.' Much of the focus among Lacanians on this topic draws from the ideas presented in such middle-period works as *Seminar VII* and 'Kant with Sade,' in which Lacan develops his analyses of Kant, Sade, and utilitarianism. It is not until the beginning of the late period of Lacan's work, however, that he makes the surprising diagnosis that the society of enjoyment, if it is to escape its enslavement to this new form of mastery, must embrace shame.

Sham *Jouissance*

Lacan's discussion of shame occurs in the final session of *Seminar XVII*, in which he proposes examining its centrality to human existence through the creation of an '(h)ontology' (the 'h' in French is silent, making this word phonologically indistinguishable from 'ontology') (Lacan 2007, p. 180). Although this particular session was held on June 17, 1970, Lacan's discussion of shame properly begins on December 3, 1969, during his meeting with the revolutionary students at Vincennes. The anti-authoritarian fervor of the students is on full display at their meeting with Lacan, whom they mock and heckle to such an extent that he cuts his presentation short. Lacan expresses skepticism about how genuinely revolutionary the new university at Vincennes is really going to be for, as Tomšič explains, its greatest 'actual novelty was the credit-point system, which adopted the Anglo-American model of the valorisation of knowledge' (Tomšič 2015, p. 212). While this innovation 'signals the commodification of knowledge' that Lacan connects to the university discourse, Tomšič notes that Lacan's greater concern is with 'the production of capitalist subjectivity' in the university's students, along the utilitarian lines described in the previous section (Tomšič 2015, pp. 212–213).

In 'May '68, The Emotional Month' (2006), Copjec focuses more deeply on the effects of May 1968 on *Seminar XVII* and how they influenced Lacan's new formulation of shame. In the grip of the prevailing revolutionary spirit, the students who attended the meeting at Vincennes repeatedly accuse Lacan of being a reactionary and a tool of the capitalist system. After Lacan tries unsuccessfully to explain the four discourses to this hostile audience, the meeting descends into a mixture of denunciations from the students and Lacan's increasingly sardonic attempts to respond. The culmination of this exchange occurs when Lacan states that 'the revolutionary aspiration has only a single possible outcome—of ending up as the master's discourse. This is what experience has proved. What you aspire to as revolutionaries is a master. You will get one' (Lacan 2007, p. 207). Lacan's comments contradict the common view, perpetuated by Schneiderman, that he was a thinker of the radical left. Many critics have tried to correct and qualify this misperception: Macey, for instance, takes Turkle to task for her 'evident nostalgia for May '68 and [...] her apparent belief that Lacan is in some sense an anti-authoritarian figure' (Macey 1988, p. 14), while Tomšič points to a 'wealth of biographical trivia and more or less trustworthy anecdotes regarding Lacan's political preferences, which, it is said, inclined towards Charles de Gaulle's conservatism' (Tomšič 2015, p. 1). For Copjec, though, the confrontation between Lacan and the Vincennes students goes beyond the usual political divisions of right and left, revolutionary and conservative.

Copjec detects something more in Lacan's prediction that the students are secretly longing for a master. Beyond any conventional politics, she recognizes that what Lacan has identified is a contradiction within revolutionary discourse, a secret desire for a form of authority that is also reflected, for instance, in the hysteric's discourse. The hysteric's notion of revolution results, as we saw in the last chapter, in the production of the university discourse, a form of knowledge that pretends to objectivity even as it tacitly replicates the inequalities of the existing hierarchy. That is why Lacan repeatedly warns the students that, for all their efforts to get outside the system, the form of discursive authority to which they subscribe ensures that they are inevitably drawn back into it. 'In this seminar Lacan maintained that although the students wanted to believe they were abandoning the university for the streets, the university was not so easily abandoned; it had already begun to take them over—as well as the streets,' writes Copjec. 'Which is why even certain elements of their revolt reflected academic business as usual' (Copjec 2006, p. 90). Lacan sees what the Vincennes students cannot, which is that the 'naturalness' of the utilitarian logic that underpins the university discourse is an ideological construct.

The success of this ideology is nonetheless the cornerstone, for Copjec, of the implementation of the university discourse as a disavowed form of mastery. Building on the insights developed in *Read My Desire*, in this essay she focuses in particular on how the university discourse proceeds from its concept of humanity as a blank slate, detached from any pre-existing forms of authority, a cipher that can then be shaped by the master discourse of the Other:

> Man came to be viewed as a being without foundation, without roots, or as so intertwined with the Other as to be infinitely mouldable. This is the heart of the conception of the cosmopolitical subject, nomadic, homeless man of the world. Capitalism drives and profits from this conception of the malleability of man[.] […] [I]f the subject becomes conceivable as completely intertwined with the Other, this is because modern science comes to be conceived as universal, as having triumphed over and supplanted every other realm and every other form of truth. Man is totally taken up, then, *without exception*, into the Other of the scientific world. (Copjec 2006, p. 98)

The strategy of the university discourse is to present itself as the only *rational* universal, allowing it to become, by default, the universal master signifier. The scientific rationality of the university discourse presents itself as an objective mirror that reflects reality, whereas in truth it is a strategy for implanting in the subject the desire of the Other. The result, says Copjec, is a 'sham *jouissance*,' a pleasure that cannot be satisfying because it is never what we actually want (Copjec 2006, p. 110).

For Lacan, the problem with the revolutionary students lies not in their political aims, but in the fact that they fail to recognize what authorizes their desire. As such, they remain ignorant of the master signifier that defines and restricts the very parameters of what is considered enjoyable. Unlike the naked power of mastery wielded by kings or popes, the master signifier of the university discourse has to conceal its authority by an act of disavowal that presents what is being done as being in *your* interest, not theirs. Consider the discourse of advertising, for instance, in which companies market their goods to the public through a rhetoric of enjoyment. In the process, the advertiser disavows their own benefits in the transaction, focusing entirely on that of the consumer—*you* enjoy, *you* save, *you* benefit, exclusively, without a thought for anyone else. Yet we know that advertising does not really exist for our benefit, but for the ultimate enjoyment of the Other, whose gains from any transaction far outweigh any 'sham *jouissance*' received by the consumer. According to Copjec, it is the slavish willingness of humanity to settle for these counterfeit enjoyments that is the source of Lacan's call for a return to shame:

> It is only against this background that Lacan's call to shame makes any sense. His is a recommendation not for a renewed prudishness but, on the contrary, for relinquishing our satisfaction with a sham *jouissance* in favour of the real thing. The real thing—*jouissance*—can never be 'dutified,' controlled, regimented; rather, it catches us by surprise, like a sudden, uncontrollable blush on the cheek. (Copjec 2006, p. 110)

The truly subversive thing about psychoanalysis, according to Copjec, is precisely that it does not seek to bring pleasure or enjoyment, instead creating a space in which the subject is, for once, left undefined by the Other. 'True *jouissance* never reveals itself to us, it remains ever veiled,' writes Copjec in her conclusion. 'But instead of inhibiting us, this opacity now gives us that distance from ourselves and our world that allows us creatively to alter both; it gives us, in other words, a privacy, an interiority unbreachable even by ourselves' (Copjec 2006, p. 111). Helping the subject to find relief from the constant, self-serving incitement of the Other is a key part of Lacan's ethics.

In *Seminar VII*, Lacan provides the following warning: 'Whoever he might be, the traditional moralist always falls back into the rut of persuading us that pleasure is a good, that the path leading to good is blazed by pleasure' (Lacan 1992, p. 185). Looking at Schneiderman's writings with this warning in mind allows us to comprehend what he is doing, especially in *The Last Psychoanalyst*, in a new light. The central tactic of that book is to denounce the 'hedonism' of psychoanalysis as a path to false enjoyment in order to outline a rational and moral path to enjoyment in Schneiderman's own terms:

> People with a sense of shame do the right thing because they enjoy doing the right thing. As Aristotle put it, they act virtuously for the sake of acting virtuously. Inhabitants of a shame culture enjoy following community standards and living according to the rules. They enjoy getting along with their friends and neighbors. They do not believe that 'hell is other people.' (Schneiderman 2014, p. 84)

Schneiderman's path to moral enjoyment is defined by its conservative parameters: Judeo-Christian in its religious morality, Anglo-American in its culture, and patriarchal in its social structure. It just so happens that, in a repetition of the pattern described by Copjec, this prescription for happiness only ever points in one direction: to the figure of Schneiderman the master. *The Last Psychoanalyst* is not, and never has been, a serious academic refutation of psychoanalysis; in reality, it was only ever a veiled advertisement for Schneiderman's services. The book, in short, is an unabashed commercial, one in which the Other pretends that, by defining enjoyment in the terms that suit him, he is really doing *you* a favor. Yet it is Lacan that Schneiderman, without a hint of irony at his own hypocrisy, repeatedly accuses of being an ethical charlatan who shamelessly promotes a cult of personality for his own profit.

References

Copjec, J., 1994. *Read My Desire: Lacan Against the Historicists*. Cambridge MA and London: The MIT Press.

Copjec, J., 2006. May '68, The Emotional Month. In: S. Žižek, ed. *Lacan: The Silent Partners*. London and New York: Verso, pp. 90–114.

De Kesel, M., 2009. *Eros and Ethics: Reading Jacques Lacan's Seminar VII*. Albany(NY): State University of New York Press.

Ian, M., 1997. Freud, Lacan, and Imaginary Secularity. *American Imago*, 54(2), pp. 123–147.

Kordela, A. K., 2007. *$urplus: Spinoza, Lacan*. Albany(NY): State University of New York Press.

Kordela, A. K., 2013. *Being, Time, Bios: Capitalism and Ontology*. Albany(NY): State University of New York Press.

Lacan, J., 1988. *The Seminar of Jacques Lacan, Book II: The Ego in Freud's Theory and in the Techniques of Psychoanalysis, 1954–1955*. Cambridge: Cambridge University Press.

Lacan, J., 1992. *The Seminar of Jacques Lacan, Book VII: The Ethics of Psychoanalysis, 1959–1960*. New York and London: W.W. Norton & Company.

Lacan, J., 2006. *Écrits: The First Complete Edition in English*. New York and London: W.W. Norton & Company.

Lacan, J., 2007. *The Seminar of Jacques Lacan, Book XVII: The Other Side of Psychoanalysis*. New York and London: W.W. Norton & Company.

Lacan, J., 2013. *The Triumph of Religion, Preceded by Discourse to Catholics*. Cambridge UK and Malden MA: Polity.

Lacan, J., 2016. *The Seminar of Jacques Lacan, Book XXIII: The Sinthome*. Cambridge UK and Malden MA: Polity.

Macey, D., 1988. *Lacan in Contexts*. London and New York: Verso.

McGowan, T., 2004. *The End of Dissatisfaction?: Jacques Lacan and the Emerging Society of Enjoyment*. Albany(NY): State University of New York Press.

Miller, J.-A., 1996. A Discussion of Lacan's 'Kant with Sade'. In: R. Feldstein, B. Fink & M. Jaanus, eds. *Reading Seminars I and II: Lacan's Return to Freud*. Albany(NY): State University of New York Press, pp. 212–237.

Millot, C., 2018. *Life With Lacan*. Cambridge UK and Medford MA: Polity.

Roudinesco, É., 1997. *Jacques Lacan: Outline of a Life, History of a System of Thought*. New York: Columbia University Press.

Schneiderman, S., 1983. *Jacques Lacan: The Death of an Intellectual Hero*. Cambridge MA and London: Harvard University Press.
Schneiderman, S., 2002. That Night At Elaine's. *The Reading Room*, 4, pp. 205–222.
Schneiderman, S., 2014. *The Last Psychoanalyst*. self-pub: CreateSpace.
Schneiderman, S., 2015. *Who Was Jacques Lacan?*. [Online] Available at: http://stuartschneiderman.blogspot.com/2015/06/who-was-jacques-lacan.html [Accessed 2 December 2019].
Schneiderman, S., n.d. *About Stuart Schneiderman*. [Online] Available at: http://www.stuartschneiderman.com/about-stuart-schneiderman/ [Accessed 2 December 2019].
Tomšič, S., 2015. *The Capitalist Unconscious: Marx and Lacan*. London and New York: Verso.
Žižek, S., 2016. Divine Ex-sistence: Theology Between Politics and Psychoanalysis. In: S. Tomšič & A. Zevnik, eds. *Jacques Lacan: Between Psychoanalysis and Politics*. London and New York: Routledge, pp. 253–267.

6

Lacan the Absolute Charlatan

The Unwitting Puppet

The main role in which we have encountered Mikkel Borch-Jacobsen so far in this book is as one of the contributors to *Le livre noir de la psychanalyse*. Born in France to Danish parents, Borch-Jacobsen did his formal training in the Department of Psychoanalysis at Vincennes, a 'stronghold of Lacanian orthodoxy' (Borch-Jacobsen 1997, p. 214) as he calls it in a 1993 interview with Chris Oakley—and no wonder, since that department was founded in 1969 by Serge Leclaire, Roustang's analyst and one of Lacan's earliest followers. Borch-Jacobsen reflects that he was fortunate that his supervisors at Vincennes were Lacoue-Labarthe and Nancy, who provided him with the critical tools he needed to avoid becoming a Lacanian disciple. Roustang has also been another crucial influence on Borch-Jacobsen's career. The two thinkers share a professional interest in hypnosis as an alternative to psychoanalysis, for instance, with both men presenting papers on that topic at a conference in 1983. The following year, Borch-Jacobsen also published a book titled *Hypnoses*, in collaboration with Nancy and Éric Michaud, while Roustang followed suit with his own exploration, *Qu'est-ce que l'hypnose?*, in 1994. In 1992, when

P. D. Mathews, *Lacan the Charlatan*, The Palgrave Lacan Series,
https://doi.org/10.1007/978-3-030-45204-9_6

Borch-Jacobsen's 1982 doctoral dissertation was revised and translated into English as *The Freudian Subject*, Roustang wrote the preface. Borch-Jacobsen is now Professor of Comparative Literature and French at the University of Washington, having migrated to the United States in 1986.

Borch-Jacobsen has often articulated his concerns about the rigid orthodoxy of many Lacanians, particularly their refusal to confront some of the more profound problems and contradictions that arise from psychoanalytic theory. He describes how his initial approach to this resistance was to apply deconstruction to psychoanalysis, after the manner of Nancy and Lacoue-Labarthe, identifying its paradoxes and logical flaws in the hope of bringing some intellectual honesty to the Lacanian sphere:

> At the beginning, my project was to 'infiltrate' psychoanalysis, like a double agent, and change it from within. Remember, I was a trained 'deconstructionist,' and this is what the strategy of deconstruction is all about: you take a theory and use its own conceptuality to highlight its internal contradictions, aporias, etc. But when you engage in this kind of parasitic activity, you obviously run the risk of becoming yourself a victim of the conceptuality you feed upon. And this is the trouble with so many deconstructionist readings, whether they be of Hegel, Heidegger, or Freud: they simply cannot escape the problematic they claim to deconstruct. This has certainly been my feeling after a while. (Borch-Jacobsen 1997, p. 216)

The failure of this approach foreshadows the jaded response that Borch-Jacobsen later expresses in the face of the negative reactions to *Le livre noir*. 'I grew tired of pointing out to psychoanalysts the inconsistencies in Freud or Lacan—especially since the psychoanalytic community as a whole is so incredibly immune to logical argument,' he says in the same interview. 'I mean, psychoanalysts are like Teflon—nothing sticks' (Borch-Jacobsen 1997, p. 216). No theoretical inconsistency, however great, seems to disturb the adherents of psychoanalysis, according to Borch-Jacobsen, and he admits to having lost any hope of changing or reforming the field.

Also like Nancy and Lacoue-Labarthe, Borch-Jacobsen is interested in the problematic way that Lacan engages with his influences, weaving together various texts and ideas in order to create his own peculiar blend of ideas. Borch-Jacobsen is less impressed by this performance than his mentors, however, regarding Lacan's rhetoric as an ultimately superficial display of erudition:

> Lacan was an inspired autodidact—that is, a prodigious *assimilator*, open to every influence, quick to grasp resemblances and analogies among the most diverse fields. [...] [I]t is the basis of the famous Lacanian 'style,' so consistently citational and allusional. [...] 'Jacques Lacan' (who enjoyed speaking of himself in the third person) was thus deliberately, openly, *honestly* a plagiarist. (Borch-Jacobsen 1991, pp. 1–2)

The impression that Lacan gives of being an accomplished ringmaster who can bring heterogeneous ideas into the circle of his seminar is, as far as Borch-Jacobsen is concerned, an illusion. Lacan may *appear* to be the master of this show, but he is actually the unwitting puppet of a number of discourses assimilated from other thinkers, chief among them Heidegger, Lévi-Strauss and, most important of all, Kojève. Lacan is thus charged with being a charlatan who, while playing the part of a master, is blithely unaware of the puppet strings that are manipulating him.

Before launching into the complexities of the critique presented in Borch-Jacobsen's key work *Lacan: The Absolute Master*, it is worth stepping back for a moment to consider more broadly the influence of Kojève on Lacan. A lifelong friend and correspondent of Leo Strauss, Kojève is best known for delivering a series of influential lectures from 1933 to 1939 on the topic of Hegel's *Phenomenology of Spirit* (1807), which were attended by a small but highly influential group of intellectuals, including Georges Bataille, Maurice Blanchot, Maurice-Merleau-Ponty, Michel Leiris, André Breton, and of course, Lacan. These lectures were compiled by Raymond Queneau into an important book, *Introduction to the Reading of Hegel: Lectures on the* Phenomenology of Spirit, in 1947. The master/slave dialectic forms the conceptual center of this unconventional reading of Hegel. Kojève contemplates the process by which, rather than destroying (negating) each other, the two participants in this struggle for prestige enter into a complex social relationship founded on inequality. The apparent winner, the master, ultimately turns out to be the loser, for what he really desires is recognition from an equal, something a lowly slave is unable to provide. The slave, by contrast, may start off in a worse position, but through the process of work he is able to transcend his status and gain the self-consciousness required to become a true master. Jeff Love's intellectual biography, *The Black Circle: The Life of Alexandre Kojève* (2018), gives a substantive overview of Kojève's life and influence, including the fact that he was an important architect of the European Union. Although Kojève is important to many left-wing thinkers, he is seen by conservative intellectuals, by contrast, as an implacable enemy—Roger Scruton calls him a 'dangerous psychopath' in a 2006 piece in *Open Democracy* (Scruton 2006).

In 'L'Étourdit' (1972), Lacan takes the rare step of admitting his debt to 'Kojève, whom I hold to be my master for having initiated me into Hegel' (Lacan in Harris 2017, p. 37). Like other French thinkers of his generation—Blanchot and Bataille share this habit, for instance—when Lacan refers to Hegel, what he really means is Kojève's interpretation of Hegel, whose philosophy is interpreted through the prism of later thinkers like Marx and Heidegger. The effect of this displacement has been to obscure Kojève's real influence on French thought, which can indeed give the impression that he is an invisible puppet master. Consider, for example, the way that Lacan reformulates the psychoanalytic process in Hegelian terms in his early lecture 'The Symbolic, the Imaginary, and the Real':

> [E]very two-term relationship is already more or less marked as imaginary in style. In order for a relationship to take on its symbolic value, the mediation of a third personage is necessary who, in relation to the subject, realizes the transcendent element thanks to which his relation to the object can be sustained at a certain distance. [...] As soon as a third party is introduced, as soon as it enters into the narcissistic relationship, the possibility of a real mediation opens up essentially by means of the personage who, in relation to the subject, represents a transcendent personage—in other words, an image of mastery by means of which the subject's desire and fulfillment can be symbolically realized. (Lacan 2013, pp. 28–29)

This passage provides strong evidence of the extent to which Hegelian (Kojèvian) logic has invaded the Freudian discourse. The centrality of Hegel to Lacan continues to persist in Lacanian circles, due in large part to Žižek, whose fascination with both thinkers is one of the cornerstones of his intellectual project.

When Borch-Jacobsen published *Lacan: The Absolute Master* in 1991, this influence was rather less well-known. Macey's *Lacan in Contexts*, published three years earlier, shows how the reception of Lacan was so intensely focused on the structuralist aspects of his work that it effectively obscured many of his other crucial touchstones: 'Predictably, the structuralist references in Lacan come to dominate everything else: the debts to surrealism, to phenomenology, to Bataille, Kojève and Queneau simply disappear beneath the waves on which the signifier floats. [...] Knowledge of the past is forgotten or repressed' (Macey 1988, p. 5). The problem goes deeper than this historical flattening of Lacan's thought, however, as Macey explains in an illuminating chapter titled 'Philosophy and Post-Philosophy.' One of the main misconceptions about Lacan is that his work operates at an established intersection of philosophy and psychoanalysis. 'Lacan's foregrounding of philosophy and his willingness to enter into theoretical-epistemological controversy,' writes Macey, 'are very much the exception to the rule' (Macey 1988, p. 75). What is more, Macey warns against the assumption that Lacan's interest in philosophy comes by virtue of his French education. Macey reminds his readers of the true state of academic philosophy during the Third Republic, which was mired in a neo-Kantian orthodoxy so stifling that it drove Lacan's contemporaries, including Sartre, Lévi-Strauss, and Paul Nizan (the subject of Macey's doctoral thesis), to revolt against its restrictions in new and creative ways.

For Macey, then, Lacan is unusual in his willingness to engage with philosophy in the context of psychoanalysis, but he is even more unusual in his choice of philosophical interests. The prejudices of the French academic system were driven by a mixture of nationalism and anti-German sentiment that excluded both Freud and Hegel from the prescribed curriculum. Lacan's growing fascination with these two thinkers thus comes not from the mainstream of the French education system, but from the marginal, avant-garde groups with which Lacan associated in the 1930s. Chief among these were the College of Sociology, founded by Bataille in 1937, and Kojève's lectures, which Macey claims were of such 'incalculable importance' that 'it is difficult not to see the lectures as a precursor of Lacan's Seminar' (Macey 1988, p. 96). Macey's nuanced genealogy reveals the extent to which Kojève really is the key channel for Lacan's appropriation of Hegelian logic into psychoanalysis:

> To return to Kojève after reading Lacan is to experience the shock of recognition, a truly uncanny sensation of *déjà vu*. A return to Hegel induces the feeling that there is a kinship between the philosopher and the psychoanalyst, but not the same overwhelming shock. This is perhaps less surprising if one recalls that there are relatively few indications of Lacan having any extensive knowledge of Hegel himself; virtually everything is filtered through the words of Kojève, the 'master' who initiated him into matters Hegelian, so much so that it might be more accurate to say that Lacan is Kojèvian rather than to suggest that he is a Hegelian. (Macey 1988, p. 98)

Macey provides the context necessary to understand Borch-Jacobsen's claim that Lacan is, to all intents and purposes, the puppet of Kojève. Such a reading clearly goes against the prevailing tendency at the time to read Lacan in terms of structuralist linguistics, which is why *Lacan: The Absolute Master* is such an important moment in the history of Lacanian thought.

Three Puppet Masters

The title of Borch-Jacobsen's book contains a double point of reference—to Lacan's status as a French '*Maître*,' on the one hand, and the dialectic of the master/slave that Kojève places at the forefront of his reading of Hegel on the other. Despite appearances, the title of 'master,' in this context, is not a desirable one for, in Kojève's interpretation of this dynamic, the master fails to get what he wants: recognition from a source that he respects and acknowledges. As a result, Timothy Huson explains in his essay 'Truth and Contradiction: Reading Hegel with Lacan' (2006), the slave occupies the more important position in the dialectic:

> The situation of this slave—the subject in the process—is precisely that of a self-relation in the Hegelian sense (the relation of slave to master) and in the Freudian sense (the relation of ego to ego-ideal). The social theatre is being performed for an Other who exists only as the 'presupposed' (posited as not-posited) ruler of the actors' actions. The recognition by the Other should be a liberating recognition, ultimately a self-recognition—the slave's recognition that the Other is herself. Yet this self-recognition will not suffice. Since the Other names desire, one must leap without support—the ultimate leap, the other desire: death. This is the final enigma in Lacan's seminar. Adding the ending, the last quoted sentence above continues: '…there is no master except the absolute master, death.' (Huson 2006, pp. 76–77)

The quotation to which Huson is referring in this passage comes from *Seminar I*, and provides a further twist on the term 'master' in Borch-Jacobsen's critique (Lacan 1991, p. 287). As though descending along a metaphorical sliding scale, Borch-Jacobsen shrewdly shifts Lacan's position ever downward, from the respected authority of a French *Maître*, to the dissatisfied charlatanry of the Hegelian master, until he finally reaches the nihilism of the Absolute Master, which is death.

In *Lacan: The Absolute Master*, Borch-Jacobsen identifies Kojève, Heidegger, and Lévi-Strauss as the three puppet masters who, having infected Lacan with their ideas, surreptitiously control the direction of his thought. The reason Lacan was an effective puppet, argues Borch-Jacobsen, was because he played his role as a charlatan with such genuine enthusiasm that even those who knew him well believed in his veracity:

> And this personage, naturally, masked no one: self-display (*Selbstdarstellung*) without a self (*Selbst*). Lacan, whose exhibitionism was immense (it verged on the ridiculous), exhibited nothing after all but his own histrionics—that is, his own absence of 'self.' This fascinating personage, who so obligingly took the stage in his seminars and in private life, was a terrific actor (or 'clown,' as he himself said), capable of all roles to the same extent that he was incapable of any one in particular. […] Thus developed, over the years,

> the myth of a discourse all the more sovereign and all-encompassing for belonging to no one. [...] The impeccably removed place from which Lacan spoke was the place (always the Other Place) from which *all* knowledge, including 'absolute knowledge,' was derided and its relativity proclaimed. (Borch-Jacobsen 1991, p. 3)

According to Borch-Jacobsen, the Lacanian performance was just an exhibition, the work of an intellectual cipher that year after year turned out its prodigious roll-call of names and ideas in order to conceal the reality of its own emptiness. Where did Lacan learn such an extraordinary trick? From Kojève, of course, for 'Lacan was the faithful disciple of his "master,"' learning from him the pantomime of bringing 'Hegel's Wise Man onstage the better to scoff at absolute knowledge' (Borch-Jacobsen 1991, pp. 4–5).

Borch-Jacobsen detects a lurking nihilism in Lacan's three puppet masters that leads toward the absolute master that is death. In Kojève this nihilism presents itself in the form of the twin Hegelian concepts of Absolute Knowledge and the End of History, ideas that leave the subject with the ultimate dissatisfaction of having reached the conclusion of everything.

> Did Kojève, too, the Wise Man, know that absolute knowledge, in the end, opens only on a dissatisfaction that is itself absolute? Could this master, who fascinated a whole generation of French intellectuals, have known what desire is about—the very definition, according to Lacan, of the 'subject supposed to know' who arouses the transference? [...] In short, Lacan could accept as master only one who was limited, unsatisfied (or sworn to excesses of finitude—Clérambault, the other 'master,' killed himself in front of a mirror). This really would have made Kojève laugh: he who had taught full satisfaction, transformed here into a doctor of desire, a master of ignorance—a Lacanian analyst! (Borch-Jacobsen 1991, p. 8)

In short, Kojève is Lacan's 'master,' an idealized object of transference by whom Lacan not only remains transfixed, but also the precursor from whom Lacan learns how to produce a charismatic glamor for his own disciples. Borch-Jacobsen goes so far as to accuse Lacan of effectively abandoning Freud for Kojève, arguing that 'Lacan was searching through Freud only for what would serve to confirm "facts" that he had already interpreted in para-Hegelian terms,' discarding everything that was genuinely Freudian except for the 'analysis of the ego' (Borch-Jacobsen 1991, p. 28). Psychoanalysis was a clever front for Lacan's covert enactment of Kojève's interpretation of Hegel.

The Hegelian reinterpretation of the analytical situation imposes the impasse of the master/slave dialectic on Freudian thought. As a result, instead of seeking to free the patient from alienation, the Lacanian analyst (master) can only frustrate the analysand (slave) with the impossibility of ever aligning with their own self-image:

> Thus, in Lacan's eyes, to return the subject's own image to him is no longer to de-alienate him; rather, it is exactly the opposite: it is (as Lacan had already said in his famous 'Discourse of Rome' of 1953) to trap him once again in 'an objectification—no less imaginary than before—of his static state or of his "statue," in a renewed status of his alienation,' for the 'ego' in which he recognizes himself, 'even if it were his (spit and) image, can never become one with the assumption of his desire.' On the contrary, it only frustrates him more, locking him into an endless aggressivity. (Borch-Jacobsen 1991, p. 85)

Instead of providing a cure, therefore, Lacanian theory presents the patient with the conclusion that there is no escape from alienation: even to be oneself, to contemplate the image of oneself, is experienced as a misrecognition. In such a context, asks Borch-Jacobsen, what is the point of psychoanalysis, which does nothing more than taunt the patient with an endless cycle of alienation and aggression? 'In other words, the analytic mirror no longer works—and neither does dialectic,' he contends. 'Or, if it does work, it is with no goal, as if it has gone mad, with neither resolution nor reconciliation possible' (Borch-Jacobsen 1991, pp. 85–86). Lacanian theory collapses from its corruption by Kojève's interpretation of Hegel, a logical phantom that has perversely turned against its own therapeutic precepts.

The second of the puppet masters, Martin Heidegger, enters Lacan's discourse in a still more subtle way. In Chap. 3 of *Lacan: The Absolute*

Master, Borch-Jacobsen points to the 'Rome Discourse' as compelling evidence of the way Lacanian theory seeks to blend together Freudian psychoanalysis with a philosophical form of dialectical thinking that, according to Lacan, represents a tradition that stretches from Socrates to Hegel. What, ponders Borch-Jacobsen, are the conditions for such a dialectic, which is neither strictly Hegelian nor Freudian? A clue is to be found, he asserts, in the unusual jargon that Lacan deploys, a modified form of Hegelian terminology, such as 'dialectic of recognition,' 'dialectic of desire,' and 'desire to have one's desire recognized':

> Now, these terms, which are obviously not Freudian, are also not, appearances to the contrary, strictly Hegelian. They are actually linked to the anthropologizing and para-Heideggerian *interpretation* of Hegel that Kojève proposed in his course on the *Phenomenology of Spirit*. And so haven't we also found the solution to our problem? Isn't Lacan's 'other' dialectic simply Kojève's dialectic—that is, the dialectic of master and slave, interpreted from over Heidegger's shoulder in terms of a 'philosophy of death' and finitude? (Borch-Jacobsen 1991, p. 87)

For Borch-Jacobsen, this philosophy is a cruel kind of theater, in which the Heideggerian notion of being-towards-death shapes not only our sense of time but also of enjoyment. 'The truth of desire—the truth of the subject—from now on is "*beyond*" the mirror, *behind* the reflections that claim to present it' (Borch-Jacobsen 1991, p. 96). Once again, instead of psychoanalysis providing therapeutic relief, the analysand is tortured by having the possible escape from alienation placed forever out of reach.

The effects of Lacanian ideas on speech and veracity are even more troubling for Borch-Jacobsen. The inherent alienation of the human subject in Lacanian theory means that words are not able to articulate the truth of being, since they can never capture or reflect the state of inner truth. 'Thus, for Lacan, desire "reveals" itself always and only through *Verneinung*, through the negation that makes a thing present by its absence' (Borch-Jacobsen 1991, pp. 103–104). In a perverse reversal, then, it is only through *repression* that subjects can articulate their desire:

> It follows, in the strange 'logic' established here, that there is only a lying truth, only repressed desire. […] [T]his 'Freudian truth' is apparently none other than the *alētheia* of Martin Heidegger—to whom, by the way, Lacan's references become more and more insistent, and whose 'sovereign word' begins to compete seriously with that of the 'master,' Kojève. […] The subject, in sum, heir to all the features of Heidegger's Being, is now considered to speak himself in every statement—but also to disappear in every statement, since the subject speaks himself as nothing and as pure *desire* of self. Truth/certainty, classically defined since Descartes by the statement's subject being identical to the subject of the enunciation, now becomes—once it has passed through the burning fire of *alētheia*—the non-self-identity of the 'same' subject. (Borch-Jacobsen 1991, pp. 104–108)

In effect, what Lacanian theory does is normalize the negative aspects of subjectivity, according to Borch-Jacobsen. To be alienated from one's own self-image, to be unable to articulate desire in words, to confront the impossibility of ever fulfilling that desire: these are the basic conditions of modern existence that Lacanian theory insists that we should accept as our unchangeable reality.

Borch-Jacobsen regards these philosophical conclusions as a betrayal of the therapeutic possibilities of Freudian psychoanalysis. If the analysand cannot articulate their desire through words, if repression can only express itself through lies and fictions, then the value of the analytic relationship is nullified, since any relationship between analyst and patient is rendered impossible. The analysand can speak all they want, but the breakdown of this relationship means that the process is irresolvable and therefore interminable:

> To profess, as Lacan did, that repression is the truth of desire was not only to call into question one of the most firmly anchored certainties of Freudianism; it was also, ultimately, to challenge the analytic cure itself, at least as it had been conceived until Lacan, for wasn't this fundamentally the same as promising the patient that he would never be cured and that his analysis would be endless, as 'interminable' as his neurosis? (Borch-Jacobsen 1991, p. 124)

The pertinent questions that Borch-Jacobsen thus puts to Lacanian analysis are: what is the point of providing a treatment that is effectively interminable? What is the value of a mindset that, operating on Heideggerian principles, can only imagine enjoyment in the image of death? Such a mode of thought can only conclude with madness and nihilism.

The third and final puppet master who influences Lacan is Lévi-Strauss, for the way he normalizes Saussurean structuralism. Like Tallis, Borch-Jacobsen argues that the structuralist logic which underlies Lacanian thought results in a denial of reality, so that what 'the subject must conform to is a pure and arbitrary *convention*, a pure linguistic *contract*' (Borch-Jacobsen 1991, p. 154). As such, the analytic situation, far from being a zone of neutral exchange, creates a normative space that 'represents, within society as it *is*, society as it *should be*' (Borch-Jacobsen 1991, p. 154). Lacan's skills as a charismatic performer are compared by Borch-Jacobsen to the manipulative function of the shaman in Lévi-Strauss's influential essays 'The Sorcerer and His Magic' (1949) and 'The Effectiveness of Symbols' (1949). 'The shaman, the sorcerer, and the magician [...] procure for both the sick person and the group a *myth* in which both can integrate ineffable (that is, the unsymbolizable) psychic or physical pain into a communal language,' he argues. 'Even more precisely, they procure a "zero symbol" intended to bridge the gap between what can and cannot be said within a given symbolic system' (Borch-Jacobsen 1991, p. 160). Where Lacan differs from this function, however, is his awareness that he is *playing* the role of the shaman figure, a self-conscious act of charlatanry that redefines the analytical situation as a mode of therapeutic trickery.

> Lacan [...] transformed the analyst into a *shaman conscious of being a shaman*—that is, as Lévi-Strauss would have it, into a distinguished mathematician-linguist-topologist. Is analysis a sort of trickery? Of course, Lacan essentially answers—except that it exhibits the truth of trickery, which is precisely that the truth of the subject, being purely symbolic, has a 'fictive structure.' (Borch-Jacobsen 1991, p. 161)

Borch-Jacobsen regards the mathemes, in particular, as evidence of this pseudo-mystical tendency in Lacan's work. What Lacan is creating may not be a religion as such, but his thought is nonetheless grounded in a religious mode of unaccountable authority, so that 'the symbolic pact sealed between the patient and his analyst-shaman could easily give rise to a *sect* (and who would deny that the Lacanian School was just such a sect?)' (Borch-Jacobsen 1991, p. 164). In that sense, Lacan's clownish parody of the master shaman becomes, by default, an absolute master in reality.

From Ancient to Modern

One crucial aspect of Lacan's critique of mastery that Borch-Jacobsen does not address is the historical difference that Lacan posits between its ancient and modern manifestations, in which the modern Hegelian master is contrasted to the masters of Greek antiquity. A key focus of Lacan's discourse on this topic is the pair of Socrates and Plato, whose respective positions in the philosophical tradition have established them as the archetypal master and disciple. Especially intriguing is the way that this outwardly harmonious relationship conceals a number of inherent conflicts: the disparity, for instance, between the master who speaks, like Socrates, and the disciple who writes, such as Plato; the extent to which this inscription of the master's thoughts is a faithful reproduction of his ideas, or an idiosyncratic reinterpretation by the disciple; and most vexing of all, the point at which the disciple can be considered to have broken with the master, thus establishing themselves as a master in their own right. What begins as admiration in the master/disciple relationship has a long history of transforming into bitterness and resentment, and the history of psychoanalysis is no exception to this pattern. Lacan's own conflicts with the established authorities of his discipline may be read in this light, just as his slogan of a 'return to Freud' is an implicit avowal of psychoanalytic orthodoxy. The pairing of Freud and Lacan can thus be understood as a variation on the master/disciple template established by Socrates and Plato.

Despite its familiarity, this dynamic does not, in Lacan's eyes, translate so easily into modern terms. A crucial shift has occurred that separates the ancient from the modern master, one that bars today's subject from becoming another Socrates or Plato. We have already seen Lacan use a similar historical argument in Chap. 5, when he argues in *Seminar VII* that the modern 'man of pleasure' differs in important qualitative ways from older notions of hedonism. In a similar manner, Lacan notes a crucial difference between the hierarchical context of the ancient world, which unabashedly divided masters from slaves, and the theoretical egalitarianism of the modern world, as Dominiek Hoens explains:

> Lacan, following Alexandre Kojève and Alexandre Koyré, argues throughout his seminar that Christianity meant a break with the ancient, Greek world. If we agree with Badiou that (Pauline) Christianity founded universalism, on the level of the subject this means that we are all equal. In contrast, the Greek aristocratic master's discourse was founded on inequality. Already in *Seminar II*, and in a much more developed manner in *Seminar XVII*, the model for the master's discourse is the one that divides the roles into master and slave, formalized as S_1 and S_2 respectively. The master is master only in relation to a slave. In contrast, in a Christian world, no one is anyone else's master. We are *free* and *equal* subjects and without a given 'one that divides into two.' (Hoens 2006, pp. 92–93)

In pointing to *Seminar II*, Hoens no doubt has in mind Lacan's assertion that Socrates was regarded as dangerous because he challenged the hegemony of the master:

> It is obvious that at that time, it was only the masters who made history, and that the slave who Socrates wanted to put through his paces has nothing to say. It will still take him some time to be Spartacus. For the moment he is nothing. It is precisely because only gentlemen have something to say in this story that they find the right words. And even a chap like Socrates will be turned out because he stepped a little too far out of line from the society of gentlemen. (Lacan 1988, pp. 20–21)

The logic of equality that is so central to the political and social revolutions of the Enlightenment was grounded in the notion that human beings have a universal capacity for reason. While this idea has not done away with hierarchy or inequality in material terms, Lacan argues that it nonetheless has forced a significant change in the *rhetoric* of authority. The revolution is as much a game of words and appearances as it is one of reality. The positions of the master and the slave can no longer be articulated as the reflection of a natural hierarchy but, in theory at least, must now be articulated as if they are potentially reversible.

This putative capacity for reversibility, for the slave to become a master, turns out to be more complicated than a straightforward exchange of positions. What enables this shift is a drastic revolution in the parameters of what constitutes the mastery of authority, one that mirrors the change that Lacan traces, in his critique of ethics, from the Platonic notion of the Good to the Kantian logic of rationality. The most important feature of the ancient mode of mastery is that its authority is, at base, arbitrary, a condition that springs from the fact that its legitimacy rests not on logic or reason, but on an act of power. God's responses to Job are a typical example of such mastery, in which the deity gives no rational justification for his superiority. Instead, God merely reminds Job that divine might and power are the basis for their respective positions in the order of things. Shifting the foundations of social hierarchy onto an outwardly rational basis has a revolutionary effect on how power is imagined and spoken about in a society grounded in this ancient mode of authority. Not only does it theoretically level the difference between master and slave by assuming that each of them is equally capable of rational thought, but it also forces the ancient master to justify their socially superior position.

The result of such a move is that the traditional master, whose authority is built on an arbitrary rather than a rational basis, is unable to provide a reasonable answer as to why some people are awarded the master's privileges simply because of an accident of birth. The new rational standard for social worth reveals the essential charlatanry of the aristocracy's claims to superiority. From this modern perspective, a king can only be a fake, an actor who is playing a role, as Peter Carey demonstrates in this depiction of Louis XVIII from his novel *Parrot and Olivier in America* (2009):

> I shall never forget the impression Louis XVIII made when he came out to receive us; we saw an enormous mass emerge from the king's study, shuf-

> fling and waddling; this mass was topped by a fine and noble head but the expression of the features was entirely theatrical; the king came forward with his hand over his heart, his eyes raised to heaven. He said a few perfectly well-judged words to us, delivered in the most sentimental manner. It was clear from this that he had rehearsed his performance. We retired from his presence with gratitude for the special kindness that he showed us, and with the conviction that as a king he would make a most excellent actor. (Carey 2009, p. 33)

The authority of the ancient master was grounded primarily in an arbitrary power, which ultimately proved unable to stand *openly* against the new standards of reason set by the Enlightenment. Power thus had to find a new way of speaking so as to conceal its mastery, and Lacan argues that it did so by deploying an innovative form of misdirection, the pursuit of knowledge, a strategy that would give birth to the university discourse.

Playing the Master

In the modern critique of the master, the arbitrariness of authority is undone by the expectation that the slave, now recognized as a theoretical equal, can step into the shoes of authority if proven worthy. The actual result, for Lacan, is that rationalization shifts the parameters of authority in such a way that the very notion of authority is compromised. The position of the master, in short, cannot be redeemed from the haunting shadow of charlatanry, a collapse of prestige that is signaled by the transition from the ancient master of Aristotle to the modern master in Hegel:

> At the beginning of the nineteenth century, there was the utilitarian conversion or reversion. We can define this moment [...] in terms of a radical decline of the function of the master, a function that obviously governs all of Aristotle's thought and determines its persistence over the centuries. It is in Hegel that we find expressed an extreme devalorization of the position of the master, since Hegel turns him into the great dupe, the magnificent cuckold of historical development, given that the virtue of progress passes by way of the vanquished, which is to say, of the slave, and his work. Originally, when he existed in his plenitude in Aristotle's time, the master

> was something very different from the Hegelian fiction, which is nothing more than his obverse, his negation, the sign of his disappearance. (Lacan 1992, pp. 11–12)

Passages like these show both the strength and the weakness of Borch-Jacobsen's reading of Lacan. On the one hand, they underscore the nihilism, the collapse of authority, the essential *charlatanry* that Borch-Jacobsen rightly detects in Lacan's appropriation of Kojève's reading of Hegel. On the other hand, they also reveal Borch-Jacobsen's interpretation as overly one-sided and negative. Lacan was clearly aware of how problematic his occupation of the position of master really was, and it is precisely his ambivalence toward his dual roles as master *and* charlatan, and the way in which these two notions converge in Lacan's interpretation of modern authority, that inform my analysis.

Despite Lacan's apparently affirmative reading of Hegel/Kojève, it is important to be alert to the ways in which, at the same time, there is also a counter-current of criticism that portrays Hegel, like Lacan, as walking an ambiguous line between master and charlatan. Lacan is particularly fascinated by the ignorance of the master, who is portrayed as successfully bluffing the slave into continuing to accept the master's superiority. 'A real master, as in general we used to see until a recent era, and this is seen less and less, doesn't desire to know anything at all—he desires that things work,' observes Lacan in *Seminar XVII*. 'And why would he want to know? There are more amusing things than that' (Lacan 2007, p. 24). If the ancient master is an ignorant impostor whose superiority is a kind of social bluff, the modern version that emerges in Hegel is doubly impotent, for not only can the slave see through this bluster of superiority, but the master also lacks the ability to gain the knowledge that is the new currency of the university discourse. Lacan nonetheless criticizes Hegel because, despite the insights the latter gives into the nature of mastery, Hegel continues to think of this position in psychological rather than structural terms. 'Hegel thereby remains rooted in psychology, because there is no master,' Lacan argues in 'On Comprehension and Other Themes,' a lecture he delivered in late 1971. 'There is a master signifier, and the master follows as best he can' (Lacan 2017, pp. 65–66). The master, it turns out, is not a master at all—he is an actor, a charlatan who is only ever following a script of authority that the audience mistakes for words and gestures that are his own.

Far from simply affirming the Hegelian/Kojèvian position, as Borch-Jacobsen claims, Lacan finds himself repeatedly entangled in its negative implications, since he too must tread the ambiguous line between master and charlatan whenever he speaks. There are two crucial but overlooked passages in Lacan's work dealing with this theme, both of which contain poignant criticisms of Hegel that, in turn, reflect back on Lacan's own role as a thinker and speaker. The first comes from the 'Introduction to the Names-of-the-Father,' the aborted seminar that Lacan delivered in 1963, in which he says:

> Nevertheless, regardless of the prestige of Hegel's dialectic—regardless of its effects via Marx, through whom it entered into the world, completing what Hegel signified, namely, the subversion of a political and social order founded on the *Ecclesia*, the Church—regardless of its success at this—regardless of the value of its political impact when realized, Hegel's dialectic is false. It is contradicted both by the evidence of the natural sciences and by the historical progress of the fundamental science—namely, mathematics. (Lacan 2013, p. 62)

It is tempting to read this passage as a straightforward rejection of Hegel—'Hegel's dialectic is false' sounds pretty damning, after all—but to do so is to strip Lacan's words of their proper context. In the lead-up to this quotation, Lacan has been talking about the rise of a utilitarian mindset, 'the ever more intentional undertakings of technocracy,' and 'the psychological standardization of subjects who are seeking jobs' (Lacan 2013, p. 61). The false promise of Hegel's dialectic, argues Lacan, is that knowledge, after the master's exposure as an ignorant charlatan, can satisfactorily fill the new void created by the elimination of the old model of authority. In the passage that immediately follows, Lacan clarifies that he regards Kierkegaard's critique of Hegel in *The Concept of Anxiety* (1844), together with Freud's theories on this topic—remembering that Lacan had just completed *Seminar X* on the topic of anxiety—as 'the sign or witness of an existential gap' that undoes the Hegelian (Kojèvian) solution (Lacan 2013, p. 62).

This earlier reflection on the Hegelian dialectic and its relationship to the utilitarian critique of the discourse of mastery anticipates the direction that Lacan will take several years later in *Seminar XVII*, when he gives this transition its official name: the university discourse. The university discourse would not have been possible without the movement from the ancient to the modern mode of mastery, since 'what happens between the classical master's discourse and that of the modern master, whom we call capitalist, is a modification in the place of knowledge' (Lacan 2007, p. 31). The second crucial passage about Hegel occurs toward the end of *Seminar XVII*, in which Lacan is explaining this 'mutation' that 'gives the master's discourse its capitalist style,' transforming it into the university discourse (Lacan 2007, p. 168). After berating his audience for neglecting to read *The Phenomenology of Spirit*, and praising 'my master, Alexandre Kojève' (Lacan 2007, p. 169) for his illuminating readings of that text, Lacan makes this startling pronouncement:

> *The Phenomenology of Spirit* [...] is truly the most extraordinary thing there is. It is also a cold, I won't say black, humor. There is one thing you can be absolutely convinced of, which is that he [i.e. Hegel] knows perfectly well what he is doing. What he is doing is sleight of hand and he takes the whole world in. And this, on the basis of the fact that what he says is true. There is obviously no better way to pin down the master signifier S_1 [...] than by identifying it with death. And so, what is involved? It involves showing in a dialectic, as Hegel puts it, what it is that is the zenith, the highest point, the thought of this term's function. [...] The truth of what he articulates is this—the relationship to this real insofar as it is, properly speaking, impossible. (Lacan 2007, p. 170)

Lacan is claiming here that Hegel outlines his theory of the slave triumphing in the dialectic not because he believes in it, but to show that it *cannot* work, to demonstrate that it is nothing more than a fantasy. The entire dialectic is false, a sleight of hand, but a sleight of hand in which the magician, for comic effect, does not bother to conceal what he is doing. In Lacan's interpretation, Hegel is a charlatan, a Tommy Cooper-like figure whose unexpectedly brilliant innovation is to flaunt, rather than conceal, his own fraudulence.

Whether or not we accept this extraordinary interpretation of Hegel, this situation certainly describes the paradox of Lacan's own speaking position. Reading this particular session of *Seminar XVII* carefully shows the extent to which he is not only aware of his own precarious authority, but how willing he is to test its limits. Once again, Borch-Jacobsen is correct that Lacan regards Kojève as his 'master,' a point he acknowledges at length in this session. Yet Borch-Jacobsen's reading fails to grasp that this compliment is a double-edged sword, that Lacan's homage is simultaneously an act of homage *and* derision. Just as Borch-Jacobsen sardonically places Lacan in the position of the 'Absolute Master,' so too Lacan plays a similar trick on Kojève. For what is this modern, Hegelian master if not a mockery of the traditional mode of authority, an impotent charlatan who is reduced to a laughing stock on the stage of history, a poor player who is shown to be nothing more than history's puppet? The after-effect of the Hegelian dialectic is that 'the master subsequently appears only as the instrument, the magnificent Cuckold of history' (Lacan 2007, p. 171)—how can we not read this line *also* as a reference to 'my master, Alexandre Kojève' (Lacan 2007, p. 169)? The Hegelian system is a witty game of deceptions and delusions, in which 'the cunning of reason is, he tells us, what directed the whole game' (Lacan 2007, p. 171). Hegel is an 'amusing' charlatan, for Lacan, and his most famous performance is an 'extraordinary dirty trick called *The Phenomenology of Spirit*' (Lacan 2007, p. 171).

Far from being a Kojèvian puppet, Lacan interprets Hegel, much like Sade, as an insightful but problematic villain, whose value lies in peeling away the disingenuousness of the prevailing system, but who is ultimately unable to come to overcome its limitations. This critique of Hegel is already being formulated at least a decade before *Seminar XVII*—indeed, the line about the 'magnificent Cuckold of history' is Lacan referencing himself from *Seminar VII*, as shown in the passage quoted earlier in this section. Hegel's villainy lies not in the negation of the ancient master, but in his support for the emerging capitalist paradigm of the university discourse. The ignorance of the old master having been exposed, knowledge becomes the new emblem of mastery, a commodity that can be obtained only through work. As such, 'Hegel is the sublime representative of the discourse of knowledge (*savoir*) and of university knowledge' (Lacan

1992, p. 171). The university discourse emerges in *Seminar XVII* as the treacherous new paradigm of modern, utilitarian thinking. Its duplicity lies primarily in the way that its promises of liberation are twisted back into a perverse justification of the existing mechanisms of enslavement.

The Hegelian slave, in particular, is seduced into the endless task of producing knowledge, which has been recast by the university discourse as the new means of gaining mastery. The technocratic dream is one in which the master is no longer ignorant, in which it is knowledge that drives power, not the other way around. 'In *Seminar XVII*, Lacan seems to draw the consequences of this historical shift,' explains Hoens. 'There is an old and waning master's discourse (some of us are masters), a recent, bureaucratic university discourse (all of us are slaves), the hysteric's discourse (I am the master of a master become impotent), and the analyst's discourse' (Hoens 2006, p. 93). The technocratic dream of aligning power and knowledge is beset, however, by an internal paradox. The privilege of the ancient master was to bend knowledge to their will, capable of contradicting even the most blatant reality in a testament to their own power. When this relationship is reversed and knowledge is placed in the ascendancy, there is simply no longer any place for mastery, in much the same way that Descartes effectively eliminates the function of God. The authority of an equation, for instance, does not depend on any outside subject for its validity. The technocratic fantasy of a mastery grounded in knowledge is thus an illusion: either one has the master's power to shape reality to one's own ends, or one submits to the validity of what knowledge reveals. No authentic compromise between these two positions is possible.

Lacan argues, in the first example above, that the failure of the Hegelian technocratic fantasy is signaled by the deep-seated anxiety that Kierkegaard, and later Freud, detect in the modern subject. So too in *Seminar XVII* he argues that the university discourse, far from providing a satisfactory synthesis of power and knowledge, can only activate the death drive. Instead of providing human beings with mastery over their world, knowledge instead 'cuckolds' them by demanding their submission to its findings. For Lacan, therefore, the honest psychoanalyst cannot claim to 'love' the disempowering truth that knowledge brings:

> [I]f there is something that truth must inspire you with, if you want to uphold *Analysieren*, it is certainly not love. For truth, as it happens, makes this signifier 'death' appear. And even, there is every appearance that if there is one thing that gives a completely different sense to what Hegel proposed, it is what Freud had nevertheless discovered at that time, which he characterized as best he could, as the death instinct, namely the radical character of repetition, this repetition that insists, and which characterizes the psychical reality, if there is such a thing, of this being inscribed in language. (Lacan 2007, p. 172)

The death drive arises in this situation because the human desire for mastery is stronger than the desire for knowledge and truth. It is therefore wrong to understand Lacan as expressing only a fawning admiration for his 'master' in Kojève. There is a murderous intent lurking in this session of *Seminar XVII*, in which Lacan uses his outward praise of his former teacher to conceal a vicious betrayal. Even though Kojève's philosophical assassination takes place right in front of our very eyes, no one seems to have noticed.

Why does Lacan betray his former master Kojève in this manner? Why, in particular, is such a step necessary, when Lacan himself concedes that the modern master is an impotent figure, who bears merely the shadow of its former authority? The answer can be found in Lacan's reflections on 'Hegelian murder' (Lacan 2006, p. 56), as he calls it in 'On My Antecedents' (1966), in the later sessions of *Seminar XI*, in which he contemplates a reformulation of the highwayman's well-known command '*your money or your life!*':

> It is in Hegel that I have found a legitimate justification for the term alienating *vel*. What does Hegel mean by it? To cut a long story short, it concerns the production of the primary alienation, that by which man enters into the way of slavery. *Your freedom or your life!* If he chooses freedom, he loses both immediately—if he chooses life, he has life deprived of freedom. (Lacan 1994, p. 212)

Regarded in terms of the master/slave dialectic, the obvious choice would be to choose life, even if it is a life without freedom, since the position of the slave leaves open the possibility of overcoming that condition through work—that, in essence, is the Kojèvian solution. Already in *Seminar XI*, Lacan vehemently rejects this answer: 'Curiously enough, in the conditions in which someone says to you, *freedom or death!*, the only proof of freedom that you can have in the conditions laid out before you is precisely to choose death, for there, you show that you have freedom of choice' (Lacan 1994, p. 213). The position of the master may have been reduced to an empty symbol, drained of all genuine authority, but for Lacan that is not a sufficient justification for accepting the position of the slave. Under these conditions, Lacan would still rather be a master, even an impotent one, than submit to being a disciple, a fate worse than death.

Since after Hegel it is no longer possible to be the master for real, Lacan's solution is to take up the role of the 'master charlatan' in a dual sense—as the master who is an inherent charlatan and, at the same time, as a charlatan who occupies the symbolic position of the master. In so doing, Lacan replicates the strategy he attributes to Hegel in *The Phenomenology of Spirit*, in which, according to Lacan's reading, Hegel openly plays the part of an impostor who refuses to hide his fraudulence. Lacan thus repeatedly tells the truth about the fact that he is not telling the truth, that he *cannot* tell the truth, as he states in the famous opening lines of *Television*:

> I always speak the truth. Not the whole truth, because there's no way, to say it all. Saying it all is literally impossible: words fail. Yet it's through this very impossibility that the truth holds onto the real. (Lacan 1990, p. 3)

Lacan layers irony upon irony in order to test how far he can push the credulity of his disciples. This performative fraudulence lies at the heart of Lacan's exploration of the limits of authority, especially the sham authority of the 'subject who is supposed to know,' an investigation that threatens to undermine the very core of the psychoanalytic process.

There is, as such, a note of mixed nostalgia and mockery in Lacan's references to the old symbols of mastery, such as his famous reflections, in 'Presentation on Psychical Causality,' on the fine line that separates an actual king from a madman who believes he is a king. '[I]t should be noted that if a man who thinks he is a king is mad,' Lacan observes, 'a king who thinks he is king is no less so' (Lacan 2006, p. 139). He then points, first of all, to the historical example of Ludwig II of Bavaria, whose extravagant spending on architectural and artistic projects mired him in debt. Ludwig's financial difficulties were so dire that he was accused of insanity in order to remove him from office, even though the charge was probably a political maneuver rather than an actual manifestation of madness. Lacan then turns from Ludwig II to the more poignant example of Napoleon:

> Don't think that I am being witty, [...] in the saying that Napoleon was someone who thought he was Napoleon. Because Napoleon did not think he was Napoleon at all, since he knew full well by what means Bonaparte had produced Napoleon and how Napoleon, like Malebranche's God, sustained his existence at every moment. If he ever thought he was Napoleon, it was at the moment that Jupiter had decided to bring him down; once fallen, he spent his spare time lying to Las Cases in as many pages as you could want, so that posterity would think that he had thought he was Napoleon—a necessary condition for convincing posterity that he had truly been Napoleon. (Lacan 2006, p. 140)

Lacan chooses Napoleon not only because he is one of those archetypal figures with whom madmen frequently identify, but also because Napoleon has a particularly ambiguous relationship with the new form of mastery. Napoleon came into power because of the French Revolution, at the symbolic moment when the old authority of the monarchy was swept away. Napoleon's kingly ambitions were thus thwarted by the very thing that made his ascent to power possible, his coronation as Emperor representing the contradictory pinnacle of his position as the defender of the Republic.

Napoleon can never actually become the master he longs to be, so he is forced to resign himself to playing the part of one instead. This interpretation of Napoleon is inspired, Lacan affirms one page later, by Hegel's 'analysis in his *Phenomenology of Spirit*,' in which Napoleon's advent as 'the *Welt-Seele*, the World Soul' is explicated by Hegel 'with the precise aim of revealing to Napoleon what Napoleon had the honor of thus incarnating, even though he seemed profoundly unaware of it' (Lacan 2006, p. 141). Lacan reminds the reader how for Hegel, Napoleon resembles a character from a play—in Hegel's version, Karl Moor from Friedrich Schiller's play *The Robbers* (1781), although Lacan himself prefers Molière's Alceste, from *The Misanthrope* (1666), as his point of comparison. Lacan's argument is that the modern master can never be identical with their own self, and so they can only ever occupy the position of an actor who is *playing* the character of the master. This condition is true even when that character, as is the case with Napoleon, actually *is* himself. Lacan is indebted to Kojève for this insight into the charlatanry of the master, for showing how the modern master is a puppet with only the semblance of authority. This devastating critique of the limits of Kojève's dialectical approach, in particular Lacan's exposure of the enticing myth that the puppet-slave can eventually transcend its position, transformed by knowledge into a true master, is the missing element in Borch-Jacobsen's often-brilliant analysis in *The Absolute Master*.

References

Borch-Jacobsen, M., 1991. *Lacan: The Absolute Master*. Stanford: Stanford University Press.

Borch-Jacobsen, M., 1997. Basta Così! Mikkel Borch-Jacobsen on Psychoanalysis and Philosophy. In: T. Dufresne, ed. *Returns of the 'French Freud': Freud, Lacan, and Beyond*. New York and London: Routledge, pp. 209–227.

Carey, P., 2009. *Parrot and Olivier in America*. New York: Alfred A. Knopf.

Harris, O., 2017. *Lacan's Return to Antiquity: Between Nature and the Gods*. London and New York: Routledge.

Hoens, D., 2006. Toward a New Perversion: Psychoanalysis. In: J. Clemens & R. Grigg, eds. *Jacques Lacan and the Other Side of Psychoanalysis: Reflections on Seminar XVII*. Durham NC and London: Duke University Press, pp. 88–103.

Huson, T., 2006. Truth and Contradiction: Reading Hegel With Lacan. In: S. Žižek, ed. *Lacan: The Silent Partners*. London and New York: Verso, pp. 56–78.

Lacan, J., 1988. *The Seminar of Jacques Lacan, Book II: The Ego in Freud's Theory and in the Techniques of Psychoanalysis, 1954–1955*. Cambridge: Cambridge University Press.

Lacan, J., 1990. *Television: A Challenge to the Psychoanalytic Establishment*. New York and London: W.W. Norton & Company.

Lacan, J., 1991. *The Seminar of Jacques Lacan, Book I: Freud's Papers on Technique, 1953–1954*. New York and London: W.W. Norton & Company.

Lacan, J., 1992. *The Seminar of Jacques Lacan, Book VII: The Ethics of Psychoanalysis, 1959–1960*. New York and London: W.W. Norton & Company.

Lacan, J., 1994. *The Four Fundamental Concepts of Psycho-Analysis*. Harmondsworth: Penguin.

Lacan, J., 2006. *Écrits: The First Complete Edition in English*. New York and London: W.W. Norton & Company.

Lacan, J., 2007. *The Seminar of Jacques Lacan, Book XVII: The Other Side of Psychoanalysis*. New York and London: W.W. Norton & Company.

Lacan, J., 2013. *On the Names-of-the-Father*. Cambridge UK and Malden MA: Polity.

Lacan, J., 2017. *Talking to Brick Walls: A Series of Presentations in the Chapel at Sainte-Anne Hospital*. Cambridge UK and Malden MA: Polity.

Macey, D., 1988. *Lacan in Contexts*. London and New York: Verso.

Scruton, R., 2006. The Trouble With Islam, the European Union – and Francis Fukuyama. *Open Democracy*, 31 May, p. np.

7

Lacan the Master Charlatan

The Fatal Flaw

François Roustang is, without question, the most discerning of Lacan's accusers, a brilliant thinker whose insights into mastery and discipleship have deeply influenced this book. Roustang, who was born in France in 1923 and died in 2016, was the closest to Lacan of any of the thinkers examined so far. Before becoming involved with psychoanalysis he was a priest, an active intellectual who wrote books and contributed to magazines related to the Jesuit order. In 1965 he joined the EFP, became a psychoanalyst under the supervision of Leclaire, and remained an integral part of Lacan's school until its dissolution. Roustang had all the outward signs of a faithful disciple, but he was also an active and insightful critic operating from inside the fold of Lacanian psychoanalysis. Roustang's forthright views on psychoanalysis first appear in *Un destin si funeste*, published in French in 1976 and translated into English as *Dire Mastery: Discipleship from Freud to Lacan*, a searing critique of the role that transference plays in psychoanalytic practice. Roustang followed that up with *Elle ne le lâche plus…* (*Psychoanalysis Never Lets Go*) in 1980, while in 1986 he announced his official break with Lacan by publishing *Lacan, de*

P. D. Mathews, *Lacan the Charlatan*, The Palgrave Lacan Series,
https://doi.org/10.1007/978-3-030-45204-9_7

l'équivoque à l'impasse, translated as *The Lacanian Delusion*, which begins with a chapter bearing the poignant title 'Why Did We Follow Him For So Long?'. The rest of the book consists of a complex critique of the Lacanian concept of the real, followed by a denunciation of Lacan's pretensions to scientific rigor. After *The Lacan Delusion*, Roustang shifted his therapeutic attention away from psychoanalysis to examine the possibilities of hypnosis as a mode of treatment.

In order to give context to Roustang's growing pessimism about the effectiveness of Lacanian psychoanalysis, particularly its tendency to cultivate an intellectually stifling orthodoxy and hermeticism in its ranks, it is useful to contrast his attitude with the kind of optimism that emerges around this time in Anglophone humanities departments about the liberating powers of analysis, a position well represented by Felman's *Jacques Lacan and the Adventure of Insight*. Felman ascribes this potential for emancipation, in particular, to the pedagogical style of Lacanian psychoanalysis, in which power is not invested in some outside authority, but instead centers on developing the subject's understanding of their own desires. What makes Lacan so inspiring as a thinker, for Felman, is

> *the revolutionary radicality of the very nature of the teaching* to be derived from the originality of the psychoanalytic experience. The analysand is qualified to be an analyst as of the point at which he understands his own analysis to be inherently unfinished, incomplete as of the point, that is, at which he settles into his own didactic analysis—or his own analytical apprenticeship—as fundamentally interminable. It is, in other words, as of the moment the student recognizes that *learning has no term*, that he can himself become a teacher, assume the position of teacher. But the position of the teacher is itself the position of the one who learns, of the one who teaches nothing other than the way he learns. The subject of teaching is interminably—a student; the subject of teaching is interminably—a learning. This is the most radical, perhaps the most far-reaching insight psychoanalysis can give us into pedagogy. (Felman 1987, p. 88)

This innovative pedagogical method transforms the student/analysand, not by reshaping them into the image of the master, claims Felman, but by empowering them to have the confidence and insight to become masters themselves. Nor does Lacan's pedagogy end there, with Felman emphasizing the infinitely self-reflexive process of the Lacanian master who, although no longer a student, continues to submit to the process of learning:

> Lacan's well-known polemical and controversial stance—his critique of psychoanalysis—itself partakes, then, of his understanding of the pedagogical imperative of didactic psychoanalysis. [...] Through Lacan we can understand that the psychoanalytic discipline is an unprecedented one in that its teaching does not just reflect upon itself but turns back upon itself so as to subvert itself, and truly teaches only insofar as it subverts itself. Psychoanalytic teaching is pedagogically unique in that it is inherently, interminably, self-critical. Lacan's amazing pedagogical performance thus sets forth the unparalleled example of a teaching whose fecundity is tied up, paradoxically enough, with the inexhaustibility—the interminability—of its self-critical potential. From didactic analysis, Lacan indeed derives a whole new theoretical (didactic) mode of *self-subversive self-reflection*. (Felman 1987, p. 90)

As inspiring as Felman's enthusiasm for Lacan's pedagogy may be, the real-world application of these ideas did not even produce the outcomes she describes in Lacan's own school. Lacan admitted as much when he dissolved the EFP: 'I failed—that is, got bogged down in confusion' (Lacan 1990, p. 130), he says in the official 'Letter of Dissolution.'

The difference between the radical, self-critical theory that Lacan taught was regularly eclipsed, in practice, by institutional pressures, which were only made worse by Lacan's double role as an authoritarian leader who, at the same time, wished to disavow his own place in the power structure. 'Paradoxically, this society, created in the name of freedom, became a place of dogmatism and of the recitation of catechism,' writes Marini. 'In the process, dramas, tears, solitude, and sometimes suicide took place' (Marini 1992, p. 28). Based on these experiences, Roustang, who was a member of the EFP for most of its history, would have found Felman's enthusiasm more naïve than inspiring. In the introduction to *Psychoanalysis Never Lets Go*, he writes: 'I had to dismantle this machine in order no longer to be overtaken by it' (Roustang 1983, pp. x–xi). There is a recurrent disparity between Lacanian theory and practice that, for Roustang, produces a cognitive dissonance that brings the whole psychoanalytic endeavor into question.

For an optimist like Felman, the solution to such a crisis would be more of the same, to apply the tools of psychoanalytic self-critique even more rigorously in order to correct the problem. Roustang's *Psychoanalysis Never Lets Go* is a fascinating book because it both recognizes and struggles against this self-perpetuating cycle. The title, borrowed from a remark made by the Swiss psychiatrist Ludwig Binswanger, refers to how once one enters the discourse of psychoanalysis, it becomes almost impossible to emerge from it, resulting in an analysis that never reaches any kind of satisfactory resolution. The dilemma that Roustang experiences at this stage of his career can be felt in the way his words form a prescient counterpoint to the sentiments expressed by Felman. Notice how closely his initial thoughts on the ability of psychoanalysis to perform its own self-critique anticipate hers:

> The paradox is that I am not at all opposed to psychoanalysis—if I were, how could I practice it? I wish only to retain the opportunity to ask the most radical questions of it, even those that I cannot answer, because I want to know something about what I am doing as a psychoanalyst[.] [...] Does not psychoanalysis, by its very definition, give us the opportunity to question the very foundations of our practice and our theory? (Roustang 1983, p. viii)

In contrast to Felman, who has spent her whole career studying psychoanalysis from a purely academic point of view, Roustang approaches this problem from the perspective of a hands-on practitioner. He has seen directly how psychoanalysis, despite its capacity to ask radical questions of itself, often fails to do so in practice.

> Why do analysts or those who have been analyzed have so little inclination to ask themselves what they are doing and what is at work in the treatment? To put it as plainly as I can, it is because *psychoanalysis, through its intermediary the transference, has not really disengaged itself from hypnosis*

> *and suggestion*. The result of this is that the treatment, without even being noticed, risks leading to a more or less latent form of blindness. (Roustang 1983, p. viii)

In other words, Roustang does not deny that there is a *potential* for radical self-critique in psychoanalysis—indeed, this reflexive aspect is what continues to draw him back into the Lacanian fold. However, he also becomes increasingly aware that there is a fatal flaw embedded in the logic of psychoanalysis that blocks this revolutionary aspect, a defect that is intimately related to questions of power and authority.

The Transference Trap

The core of Roustang's charge against psychoanalysis is laid out in *Dire Mastery*, a book that delves into the history of the discipline in order to gain a deeper understanding of this fatal flaw. As such, Roustang starts by examining how Freud, the founder (and thus master) of psychoanalysis, related to his disciples, and what the bitterness of those interactions can teach us about the transmission of power and authority in the context of the discipline. The obvious starting place for such an examination is the relationship between Freud and Jung. Jung was initially groomed by Freud as his obvious successor, until Jung broke with him over differing interpretations of the unconscious and the importance of sexuality. These theoretical differences were the mask for a deeper struggle for power between the two men, argues Roustang, which centered on the implicit challenge that the rebellious disciple presents to the master's authority.

> The struggle between the disciples to be acknowledged as unique by the master and thus, in some way, to see the others excluded, doubles the struggle on the part of the master to keep the disciples at bay. [...] [I]t is precisely because Jung touched the imago of the uncontested master that he must perish, and perish at the hands of all the faithful. For there is nothing better than a crime perpetuated by one and all to ensure the cohesion of the horde. (Roustang 1982, p. 3)

The acrimonious fallout of the struggle between Freud and Jung is not a singular occurrence, but rather institutes a pattern in the history of psychoanalysis that Freud goes on to replicate with every one of his major interlocutors. 'At once striking and astonishing, the same processes are repeated with every one of Freud's close collaborators, given their personal history and geographic situation,' observes Roustang. 'At work in each case were: attachment to Freud's person, demand for privileged recognition, jealousy of the others, and conflict about the inheritance' (Roustang 1982, p. 9). This repeated conflict between master and disciple, between the established authority and its challengers, is so central to the history of the psychoanalytic movement that Freud weaves its logic into the fabric of his theoretical work, so that without 'the Jung affair, we would probably have neither *Totem and Taboo* nor *On the History of the Psychoanalytic Movement*' (Roustang 1982, p. 11). Roustang is not saying that psychoanalysis does not value critique as one of the central principles of its discourse, only that struggles over power and authority have repeatedly stifled this potential.

For Roustang, the problem of authority is rooted in the way that psychoanalysis has always structured itself around the central figure of a master. This mode of organization not only leads to conflict with disciples but, in terms of its political logic, this configuration is also inherently at odds with the critical mindset of psychoanalysis. 'There is a complete contradiction between the aim of psychoanalysis, which, along with its rules, must remain an artifact,' observes Roustang, 'and the constitution of a society around an irreplaceable leader whose thinking is adopted and who is acknowledged as the master' (Roustang 1982, p. 13). The historical preference for investing authority in a master, therefore, is a practice that encourages either orthodoxy or revolution. In contrast to Felman's sanguine belief that psychoanalysis can simultaneously provide a space for intellectual autonomy and productive critique, Roustang's position is that a psychoanalytic community functioning along these lines can achieve neither.

> The group around Freud was constituted through the transference onto him—which can be seen in the statutes of the association. This involved very real things like the use of power and the circulation of money. [...]

> [A]ny group of psychoanalysts carries within it the principle of its own disintegration. If the group is stable and functions well, however, it is a proof of the contrary: it has definitely abandoned the Freudian discovery. In this sense, psychoanalysis is basically asocial, and to speak of psychoanalytic societies is a contradiction in terms. (Roustang 1982, p. 14)

The typical psychoanalytic society is thus organized around an implicit double bind. If it functions well and produces faithful disciples who follow the directions of the master, it becomes intellectually stagnant due to its overly rigid adherence to the leader's authority. In this first scenario, the critical element that made the Freudian discovery worthwhile is lost, as happened to the Vienna School in the wake of Freud's death. However, if the critical function remains alive and well, disciples have no choice but to revolt against the master, thus forfeiting their place in the hierarchy. Roustang comes to the gloomy conclusion that the history of psychoanalysis is a hopeless struggle to keep the spirit of critique alive in an institutional structure that, against its own principles, always places an authoritarian master in charge.

The inevitable result, for Roustang, is that psychoanalysis ends up being a discourse that operates on two contradictory levels. On the surface, it maintains a rhetoric of critique and subversion, the empty shell of the revolutionary spirit that brought it to life in the first place. Beneath that superficial layer, though, is a disavowed orthodoxy that bears a disquieting similarity to the authority of organized religion:

> Although he denied it, Freud was possessed by an uncontrollable need to have disciples and to surround himself with completely devoted followers. […] [A]ll this is contrary to the aims of psychoanalysis. […] The absence of dogma, ritual, or moral doctrine is therefore not enough to prevent psychoanalysis from being affected by a surreptitious revival of religion. The relation between faith and the transference must be considered. (Roustang 1982, pp. 15–18)

Roustang's reflections on the impossibility of a legitimate and vital psychoanalytic society, together with his experiences in the EFP, reveal an important contextual difference between the French experience of

Lacanian psychoanalysis, which was marked by the constant upheavals of politics and factions, and the Anglophone experience of an academic like Felman.

The institutional dilemma confronted by the revolutionary determined to throw off the chains of the master discourse is, by now, a familiar scenario. The rebellious students at Vincennes attempted to get outside the university system only to be compromised, as Lacan points out to them, by the necessity of entering it in the first place. 'To get them to leave, you enter,' he says. 'When you leave here you continue to speak, consequently you continue to be inside' (Lacan 2007, p. 205). Lacan, similarly, had a long history of conflict with the IPA, which led to his 'excommunication' from the psychoanalytic community in 1963. His own school, the EFP, was established along lines that tried (and failed) to avoid the authoritarian hierarchy of previous psychoanalytic organizations, as illustrated not only by Lacan's behavior, but also by the EFP's treatment of Luce Irigaray. Irigaray was expelled—or, to use the more appropriate and dramatic term, excommunicated—from the EFP in 1974 because of her book *Speculum of the Other Woman*, which challenged key aspects of Lacanian thought. In *Feminism and Psychoanalysis*, Gallop calls out Lacan's hypocrisy, arguing that

> it is Irigaray who is carrying on Lacan's most radical battle, the battle against the institutionalized stagnation of psychoanalysis. [...] To the extent that Lacan is the 'Master' of a psychoanalytic institution, he cannot carry on that battle. To the extent that any disciple is inscribed by his or her fidelity to the master, this cannot be that disciple's battle. [...] Irigaray, excommunicated by the Lacanian institution, is in the position Lacan occupied in the 1950s when he had been excluded from the International Psychoanalytic Association. [...] But what is also born out is that analytic work, writing, theory is always political, always involved with power structures. Psychoanalysis invokes authority and to refuse to analyze psychoanalytic politics is not to be apolitical, but to shore up the master's power, and to ensure the patients' submission to institutionalized discourse. (Gallop 1982, p. 94)

Although less pessimistic than Roustang, Gallop comes to a similar conclusion about the deleterious effects of power on the history and practice of psychoanalysis. Displaying a greater awareness than Felman about the insidiousness of dealing with a master discourse, she speaks with clarity about the dangers of mixing psychoanalysis and politics:

> The mutual incompatibility of psychoanalysis and politics leads to paralyzing representations. Power rigidly resists all criticism and becomes totalitarian. Psychoanalysis supposedly flees the exercise of power only to create psychoanalytic institutions which codify correct representations of the unconscious and become arenas for violent power struggles as well as forces of oppression over analysands and analysts who do not conform. 'Never one without the other,' knowingly, lucidly to exercise *and* criticize power is to dephallicize, to assume the phallus and unveil that assumption as presumption, as fraud. A constantly double discourse is necessary, one that asserts and then questions. (Gallop 1982, p. 122)

Gallop thus attempts to articulate a middle ground that is somewhere between Roustang and Felman, a realistic recognition of the problems of the political structure of the psychoanalytic organization around a master figure, while still holding out hope that the revolutionary critique of psychoanalysis can overcome the master's authority.

Roustang's position is that even this seemingly reasonable solution cannot work in the institutional context in which he is operating, because the problems and contradictions of psychoanalysis extend beyond the conflict inherent in the organizational structure. The penchant for this kind of master/disciple organization is also embedded in the power structure of the analytical situation, for instance, and is produced specifically to unlock the central psychoanalytic dynamic of transference. 'Here lies the paradox: the transmission of analysis is the greatest threat to analysis itself if it is assumed that that transference should be reinforced rather than dissolved,' he writes in *Dire Mastery* (Roustang 1982, p. 20). This claim is particularly important to Roustang's critique because, especially in the reflections on the 'subject who is supposed to know' in *Seminar XI*, the dissolution of the transference becomes one of the central problems of Lacan's theory. That is why examining the desire of the analyst is so crucial for Lacan, because transference can be an insidious trap for both sides of the analytical relationship. The temptation of the analyst is to take seriously the position of the master they are only supposed to *pretend* to be occupying. An unethical transition from analyst to master is what Roustang sees happening repeatedly in the EFP, where Lacan's words and theories are cited uncritically by his disciples, as though they bear the authority of scripture:

> Those who do not understand his writings assume that Lacan understands them and that if they are very studious, they will one day also understand. [...] The principle behind the use of 'Lacan said' is quite comparable to a similar use of the Scriptures, or the authorities of the Christian tradition. [...] This mania for citing Lacan reveals an imaginary identification with the master. When someone cites Lacan to settle a dispute, supposedly to clarify it, instead of explaining his position or speaking in his own name, he thinks he is a substitute for Lacan, he is Lacan's mouth for want of being his brain. (Roustang 1982, pp. 21–22)

This prevailing attitude among Lacan's disciples, this almost cultish adherence to what he has to say, signals to Roustang that Lacan's followers have no practical ability to resist the lure of mastery. They have been so enraptured by Lacan's charisma that they are unable, when placed in the analytic situation, to resist the siren song of the transference. 'They are no longer simply believers, but idolaters,' he rightly points out. 'If this endeavor were to succeed, it would be the end of analysis, for in this field the argument from authority has no place' (Roustang 1982, p. 72). The 'constantly double discourse' that Gallop envisions is not possible in this kind of environment, as far as Roustang is concerned, because the critical side of psychoanalysis is always crushed under the weight of authority, reducing it to a single discourse: that of the master.

Roustang first articulates these ideas in *Dire Mastery*, five years before Lacan's death, but they are given a new resonance when he repeats them ten years later in the opening chapter of *The Lacanian Delusion*. What changes, in particular, is the historical context, with the latter work appearing five years *after* Lacan's death, when the Lacanian movement in France had splintered into factions that were furiously at war with each other. This critical distance allows Roustang to see more clearly Lacan's manipulations, to understand how Lacan used the transference to establish himself as an authority figure.

> A limitless pretention to being custodian of the truth, already so widespread among psychoanalysts of all persuasions, was laying the groundwork for an intellectual terrorism that would stifle all those who admitted their inability to understand, and who dared not to agree with everything that was being said and done. [...] It was thus from 1968 on that an exorbitant belief in Lacan as the keeper of some great secret became widespread: He was the one who would be able to build, or rebuild, the unity of knowledge. If we followed Lacan, it was because he was a prestidigitator of genius. (Roustang 1990, pp. 6–7)

Roustang gives detailed examples of Lacan's 'intellectual terrorism,' such as his immense skill at ingratiating himself with the ideas and values of a particular follower, and then, 'once the other had been somewhat lulled into feeling secure, Lacan would exploit the authority he had acquired in order to impose his own views' (Roustang 1990, p. 5). Roustang acknowledges that in the early days of the EFP there really was a diversity of views and ideas, but that there increasingly emerged 'certain new lieutenants who were becoming intolerant of any deviation from obedience to the master' (Roustang 1990, p. 5).

Over time, in other words, Roustang observes that the mindset within Lacanian circles hardened into a kind of orthodoxy, to the point where disciples at the school harbored 'the conviction, still held by many, that, in order to master the analytic object and remain at the pinnacle of humanity, it is enough just to read Lacan, and never leave the confines of his writings' (Roustang 1990, p. 7). Far from following through on the principle of encouraging others to see through the analyst as the 'subject who is supposed to know,' revealing the master as a charlatan, Roustang accuses Lacan himself of giving in to the temptation of power and mastery: 'Lacan wanted to remain the one who was supposed to know and, to that end, he set up an entire apparatus designed to prevent his knowledge from being put to the test' (Roustang 1990, p. 8). As Roustang first perceived in *Dire Mastery*, this betrayal was predicated on the paradoxes of the transference, which makes the analytic situation possible and, perversely, encourages its own continuation: 'Maintaining the transference was the condition of possibility of his mastery, which is why good disciples today still sneer at the possibility of resolving the transference' (Roustang 1990, p. 9). Roustang thus actually does detect two conflicting discourses in Lacan, but instead of providing a healthy counterpoint to each other, they prove to be the apex of a paradoxical disconnection between Lacan the critical theorist and Lacan the authoritarian master. 'Thus, an absolute contradiction emerges between the Lacan who wanted to be the analyst *par excellence*,' concludes Roustang, 'and the Lacan who assumed the position of the master who knew and taught what he knew' (Roustang 1990, p. 10). Roustang's powerful critique rests on the argument that Lacan, like Freud before him, was ultimately unable to solve the underlying contradictions of power and authority, that even as he described the functions of the master's discourse, he was hopelessly caught up in its seductions.

Irony and the Master's Writing

As we saw at the end of Chap. 1, in *Psychoanalysis and the Future of Theory*, Bowie contends that irony is an effective way of dealing with the excesses of Lacan's disciples and the problems of mastery identified by Roustang. Consider, for instance, Lacan's use of the slogan of the 'return to Freud,' which is usually read as Lacan signaling his devotion to the Freudian tradition. Some critics, however, have expressed skepticism about its sincerity, regarding it instead as an ironic homage that conceals a deeper theoretical antagonism between the two psychoanalysts. Richard Boothby, for example, opens his essay 'The Psychical Meaning of Life and Death' (1996) by highlighting the difficulty of speaking about Freud's and Lacan's ideas together because, despite their common adherence to psychoanalysis, there are clear differences between the two thinkers:

> For how can we fail to be struck by the enormous tension in Lacan's relation to Freud, composed on the one hand by Lacan's insistence on the faithfulness of his 'return to Freud' and yet, on the other hand, by the

> compelling sense we have of the novelty and originality of Lacan's thought? Lacan's work is everywhere animated by his claim to have restored Freud's essential insights, yet at the same time it is difficult to avoid the impression that psychoanalysis is not so much restored by Lacan as it is completely reinvented. (Boothby 1996, p. 337)

In a different essay from the same book, Borch-Jacobsen pushes Boothby's point further. He argues that, in true Oedipal style, Lacan does not simply 'reinvent' Freudian psychoanalysis, but instead symbolically 'murders' his master/father:

> As Plato already remarked, parricide is the inevitable form of faithfulness. Lacan was undoubtedly thinking of that when he faced off with his rivals. Sometimes you have to kill your father to preserve his heritage. Sometimes you have to throw away the doctrine to find its 'meaning.' In the realm of thought, true faithfulness is not faithfulness to solutions but to *problems*. And from that point of view, Lacan was undoubtedly the most respectful of parricides. (Borch-Jacobsen 1996, p. 296)

This last sentence, in particular, drips with irony: Lacan betrays Freud, but at least he is 'respectful' when figuratively murdering his intellectual father-figure. Borch-Jacobsen's allusion to Plato in this passage is especially apposite, because what is at stake in the underlying tension between Freud and Lacan relates not only to the archetypal power struggle between master/father and disciple/son, but also to the *medium* by which the master's ideas are transmitted to the world. Lacan's repetition of the dynamic of Socrates and Plato in this regard is self-conscious and performative, full of an irony that, even when it fulfills the outlines of its original template, is inherently subversive.

Take Lacan's reluctance to publish his own writings, a disinclination that is captured in one of his more clever puns, the neologism '*poubellication*,' which combines the word '*publication*' and the French word for a rubbish bin, '*poubelle*'; to publish, as such, is to throw one's work in the bin, to turn it into trash. The reasons for Lacan's aversion to publishing are complex, but they are connected to his understanding of the master as the one who speaks, like Socrates, and the disciple as the one who, like

Plato, writes down these thoughts. Lacan discovered his anointed disciple in the form of Jacques-Alain Miller, who was given the task of 'editing' and publishing the seminars. In a 1991 addendum to her book, Turkle explains the central role Miller has played in the production of Lacan's texts:

> Lacan made Miller legal owner of the transcriptions of his seminars[.] [...] Miller's was no simple editorial job. He was not 'editing' but, as he put it, 'establishing' the texts of the seminars. He added language where there were gaps and removed contradictions and ambivalences. [...] On the one hand, Miller was a scribe, writing out what the *Maître* had said, or perhaps meant to say. On the other, Miller clearly revised and changed Lacan's work as he 'established' it. To some degree, Miller renounced his own voice to pledge himself to his version of Lacan's. The resulting symbiosis had fateful consequences for the history of Lacanianism. If by the 1980s, Miller seemed to feel justified in speaking for Lacan, by that point he was acting not only out of habit but out of a profound sense of Lacan's wanting and needing him in this role. (Turkle 1992, p. 255)

Miller's position led to a bitter legal struggle over the 'pirate' editions of the seminars circulating among the various Lacanian groups, with a court order announcing in late 1985 that unofficial transcripts could no longer be published. The advent of the internet has since made these alternative versions widely available.

One of the most insightful reflections on how the Socrates/Plato relationship sets the parameters for the tensions between Freud and Lacan is Oliver Harris's book *Lacan's Return to Antiquity*. Harris's interpretation is that Lacan's reluctance to publish his work originates with both his early comparison of himself to Socrates, and the example of Kojève, who likewise published little in his lifetime. Harris contends that this combination of factors particularly influenced Lacan's views on the publication of his seminars:

> Both Kojève and Lacan resisted publishing their ideas. [...] Lacan's seminars were self-consciously constructed to keep ideas 'alive and open,' and the figure of Socrates cements the association of this quality with speech rather than writing. But it is a Socrates we only know through texts.

> Ultimately, of course, Plato's overarching project is manifest not just in the Academy, but also the written dialogues that preserve his mentor. That these are literary artifacts unlike any others suggests the complexity of this transition, its dangers but also creative opportunities. Inevitably, it is a precedent on Lacan's mind as he finally accepts the transformation of his seminars into their own unique printed form. (Harris 2017, p. 32)

Harris makes it clear that Lacan learned more than a few tricks from Kojève, with the latter's influence going as deep as Borch-Jacobsen claims. The situation with regard to Socrates, however, is more complicated because, as Rabaté observes in *Jacques Lacan: Psychoanalysis and the Subject of Literature* (2001), 'Plato often occupies the position of master in Lacan's texts' (Rabaté 2001, p. 139). This assertion is qualified by Harris, who argues that there is a discernible shift in emphasis from Socrates to Plato regarding the question of mastery in Lacan's thought.

Such a transition is made possible, in part, by the advent of Miller in Lacan's life. Miller 'appears to cast himself as Plato in his simultaneous act of codifying and ventriloquism' contends Harris, even as Lacan starts to identify less and less with Socrates (Harris 2017, p. 36). Lacan prefers Socrates as an intellectual model in the earlier seminars, but as his teaching unfolds he becomes increasingly ambivalent about the template set by this ancient pairing. 'It is inevitable that Plato-Socrates will become involved in Lacan's conflicted feelings about writing, as well as teaching more broadly,' writes Harris. 'Plato's exceptionally slippery literary creations provide Lacan with another stimulating precedent in relation to how we might respond to an impasse' (Harris 2017, p. 33). The appropriation of Kojève by the university discourse again proves important to how Lacan interprets this issue:

> University discourse describes the use of supposedly 'objective', 'neutral' knowledge to acquire a position of power: power that is more often than not in the unacknowledged service of some greater ideology. But while it is fully elaborated in 1969, [...] the roles of Plato and Socrates allow Lacan to explore equivalent themes early in the seminar series. So, finally, the act of writing and publishing transforms an initiating 'master' (Kojève) into an academic. In *Seminar XVII*, Lacan considers the difficulty of translating his own theories into academic language and presents the medium not merely

as a threat but as a fundamental alteration of his message[.] (Harris 2017, p. 35)

This dilemma is heightened further by the publication of two groundbreaking texts during this period of Lacan's life: Anthony Wilden's *The Language of the Self: The Function of Language in Psychoanalysis* (1968), the first translation into English of 'The Function of Speech and Language in Psychoanalysis,' with an extensive commentary and notes by Wilden; and Anika Lemaire's *Jacques Lacan* (1970), the first academic study of Lacan's work. 'Anthony, Anika… what a sign of a new wind is insisting in these initials,' ponders Lacan in his preface to Lemaire's book (Lemaire 1977, p. vii). In the wake of these two publications, this 'new wind' portending the arrival of further academic analysis of his work, Lacan is forced for the first time to contend seriously with a public discourse generated by his disciples. 'The question becomes how one might publish without becoming university discourse,' observes Harris. 'Publication, for both Kojève and Lacan, was the work of a disciple' (Harris 2017, p. 35). Unlike Socrates and Plato, who are defined by the split between speech and writing, in Lacan's view the modern master may now both speak *and* write, because the task of the disciple has evolved into one of editing, establishing, publishing, and disseminating.

The most perceptive aspect of Harris's analysis is the gradual shift he notices in Lacan's interpretation of the respective importance of Socrates and Plato as a template for the master/disciple relationship. Initially, out of these two precursors, it is Socrates with whom Lacan tends to identify. This decision is reflected in his preference for holding seminars over writing books, which emphasizes the master's task of speaking. 'Lacan's ongoing engagement with Plato centres on this question of how knowledge relates to the society around it,' writes Harris, 'a question explored in the content (and manifest in the form) of both Plato's dialogues and Lacan's seminars' (Harris 2017, pp. 10–11). The problem with Socrates arises from the fact that, despite the ancient master's lack of knowledge, the latter nonetheless recognizes that power depends on the master *appearing* to control the flow and distribution of knowledge. The result, in both Socrates and Lacan, is a performance of mastery that bears a close resemblance to mockery. 'Mastery as a position to be exploited will inform

Lacan's thinking on both practicing and teaching analysis over the next decades,' observes Harris. 'But [...] it is an odd mastery, defined by bluff, opposition to convention and, more even than that, by not having, by definition, any fixed place amongst the authorities of society' (Harris 2017, p. 20). It is this initial reading of Socrates as an anti-authoritarian outsider that appears to drive Lacan's identification with him, relegating Plato to the lesser position of the disciple.

This view serves Lacan best in the early years of his teaching, when he is faced with the institutional problem of his membership in the IPA. Once he establishes his own school and begins to attract a loyal band of disciples, his views on mastery, and also on the Socrates/Plato relationship, begin to shift accordingly. In this context, Harris points out, the anti-authoritarian stance of Socrates suddenly seems counter-productive to the psychoanalytic cause, and so it is that Lacan glimpses new possibilities in his reading of Plato:

> Socrates ruins Athens by placing the key to universal truth within each man, instituting a rift with merely conventional morality, demanding we search for a truth beyond the truths we're given. An inevitable division opens up between this radical Socrates and a Plato who does build institutions, does write, does concern himself with the politics of society. [...] For Lacan, it is the outreaching Plato who can often smell of the mob. And this division within Plato, between the crowd-pleasing icon and the subversive iconoclast, will prove valuable to Lacan as he seeks to rescue Freud's theories from Freud himself. (Harris 2017, pp. 20–21)

The problematic consequences of this pragmatic step are felt in a number of ways, from the criticism of the 'pass,' to Lacan's frustrating reluctance to lead the EFP proactively, to Roustang's critique of the way psychoanalytic organizations maintain themselves in contradiction to the principles on which they are founded. The increasing fascination with Plato would appear to be a symptom of this growing institutionalization of the Lacanian message.

For Harris, the changing interpretation of Plato should also be understood as Lacan's response to the publication of his work, and the increasing commentary such texts are beginning to attract. In *Seminar XX*, for instance, Lacan expresses his ambivalence about Miller's preparation of the text of *Seminar XI* for publication, as well as the appearance of Nancy and Lacoue-Labarthe's *The Title of the Letter*. 'As the process gathers pace, and a quantity of published work comes to seem inevitable,' argues Harris, 'a new interest in Plato's literary style emerges, in particular his creation of texts that defend themselves' (Harris 2017, p. 38). The core of this strategy, for Lacan, lies in Plato's use of ironic humor as a way of simultaneously affirming and undermining the authority of the text:

> As Lacan's wariness over his own role grows, a very different Plato appears, one who is more cunning about his communications, sometimes a quite startling, provocatively reimagined figure. [...] Humour is now seen as a critical ingredient of the Platonic dialogue, identified with a self-reflexive irony and an aloofness. At its extreme this new Plato is an outright satirist, never more so than when his work addresses society at large such as in *The Republic*[.] [...] This ambiguous, potentially comic nature of the dialogues allows Lacan to divide a Socratic Plato from the Plato who tries to teach more straightforwardly, who reveals an unwavering, superior realm of higher values. (Harris 2017, pp. 39–41)

Lacan identifies this ironic humor as a crucial feature of the modern master: comedy is now the realm that belongs to the performance of authority. This humor further separates the master from the disciple who, from Lemaire to Miller, from Roudinesco to Fink, has the problematic tendency not only to be serious, but to be *too* serious. When Žižek appeared on the scene, it was his sense of humor that was the signal of his originality, his refusal to be just another Lacanian disciple.

Harris argues that it was Badiou who, in *Conditions* (1992), first recognized the extent to which Lacan understood the importance of humor in Plato's dialogues. Badiou argues that Lacan borrows from Plato's comic strategy in order to bypass the pitfalls he identifies in the four discourses, choosing to speak instead from a zone of performative uncertainty:

> Plato is so valuable to Lacan as he pursues his own self-deconstruction because he represents a way of communicating that lies diagonal to the four

> discourses: in Badiou's account, Plato's dialogues lie between the master's injunction, the hysteric's disruption, the reasoning of the university, and the ominous silence of the analyst. [...] The dialogues, and the seminars they inspire, allow Lacan to be both a Socrates and a Plato and to position psychoanalysis as a discipline defined by its self-consciousness with regards to the constitution of knowledge. (Harris 2017, pp. 42–43)

This insight into the self-consciously humorous tone of Lacan's work is a crucial complement to the Hegelian performance of mastery. Hegel is characterized by Lacan as possessing a 'cold' or 'black' humor (Lacan 2007, p. 170), a deadpan irony that keeps the reader guessing whether or not the speaker is actually serious. This combination of comedy and performance allows Lacan, in turn, to place his own authority in a zone of uncertainty that leaves his audience wondering if he really is a master, or just a brilliant charlatan playing the part of one, an ironic performance that provides a potential solution to Roustang's concerns.

The Meta-Charlatan

To the critics examined in the course of this book, Lacan is a charlatan because he is perceived as a fraud, a poseur who uses his rhetorical skills to cover over the contradictions (or worse still, the total emptiness) of his theories. The charges laid against him begin with a criticism of some specific shortcoming, but they all ultimately hang on the question of Lacan's authority. As I have set out to demonstrate in this book, the conclusion that Lacan is a charlatan is often rooted in misreadings and logical fallacies that limit or undermine the effectiveness of those criticisms. As such, my goal has been not only to investigate the validity of these charges against Lacan, but also to provide a rigorous reading of the questions of mastery and authority they raise. Roustang has been an invaluable antecedent in this process, not only because his critique of Lacan is a model of intellectual integrity, but also because he shines a spotlight on the general unwillingness to ask genuine, searching questions about psychoanalysis in Lacanian circles. The root of this problem lies, as Roustang points out, in the organizational investment of authority in a psychoanalytic master.

Yet what has been overlooked by critics, even by one as perceptive as Roustang, is the extent to which Lacan himself gives the issue of authority a central place in his work, an evolving, self-reflexive interrogation of the master's discourse that actually dares, through a mixture of humor and critique, to ask some uncomfortable questions about the validity of psychoanalysis. 'Discussions have flourished on true, authentic wit—in a word, good wit—and also on bad wit, that is, the wit with which charlatans entertain their audience,' says Lacan in *Seminar V*. 'How are they to be distinguished?' (Lacan 2017, p. 13). This kind of ambivalent questioning of his own authority haunts Lacan's entire oeuvre, and the weekly seminar was where he put into practice these experiments with its paradoxes and limitations. It proved to be an ideal venue, not only because as his fame escalated in the late 1960s he started to attract an audience that came to see him for reasons other than intellectual engagement, but also because this newfound celebrity allowed him to test its boundaries in ways that reflected Lacan's fascination with the power of performance.

This penchant for theatricality was a crucial aspect of Lacan's discourse, easily overlooked by a new generation that, because he is no longer alive, has no choice but to encounter him primarily through the printed word. This gap is accentuated in *Jacques Lacan: Past and Present* (2012), for instance, a conversation between Roudinesco and Badiou held to mark the thirtieth anniversary of Lacan's death, in which the two disciples recall the theatrical legacy of their master. 'Lacan was a master to the extent that he located himself at the point of convergence between two exigencies,' claims Badiou. 'This is the portrait of Lacan that I, for my part, would propose: a man of the Enlightenment who encountered the power of theater' (Badiou and Roudinesco 2014, pp. 33–34). A young Rabaté, who first began attending the weekly seminars in 1968, detected a queer sense of humor in Lacan's performance. Rabaté also noticed how, despite Lacan's bizarre style of presentation, his disciples received his lectures with unsettling gravity:

> This sounded deep, Dadaist, and hilarious, and yet no one laughed or even smiled. Here I was, facing an aging performance artist (Lacan was sixty-seven then) whose very garb had something of the cabaret comedian's outfit, with a dandiacal Mao costume, a strange shirt, and the most tortured elocution one could imagine, broken by sighs, wheezes, and sniggers, at times slowing down to a meditative halt, at times speeding up to culminate in a punning one-liner. Curiously, he was being listened to in utmost silence by an audience intent on not missing one word. (Rabaté 2003, p. 2)

Like Rabaté, Millot emphasizes the paradoxes of Lacan's presentation style. 'Theatricalization was part of Lacan's oratorical art. A mimicry of anger and ostentatious rage were its recurrent traits,' she recalls. 'They seemed to be aimed at his audience whose obtuse will to know nothing, whose deafness, in a word, doomed to failure his desire to be heard and understood' (Millot 2018, p. 35). Millot captures the radical disjunction between speaker and audience on these occasions, with Lacan engaging in a 'mimicry' of real passion, a performance of mastery concealing an undertone of mockery lost on an audience that refused to question the authority of his words.

This state of affairs caused Lacan a mixture of amusement and frustration that reached its visible pinnacle with the production of *Television* in 1973. Lacan's oratorical style in that film is an uncanny mixture of deadpan and mockery, a method designed to goad audiences with its superficial veneer of absolute seriousness. In her essay 'Lacan's Afterlife: Jacques Lacan Meets Andy Warhol' (2003), Catherine Liu identifies how this famous performance, in particular, reveals the dual roles of master and charlatan that Lacan is provocatively seeking to merge:

> Playing the master on the airwaves allowed for Lacan to perform as both charlatan and master—consider his performance in *Télévision*: his analytic attitude seemed like a posture of pure provocation of his more conservative colleagues. In his pedagogical performances, Lacan demonstrated that all forms of inter-subjectivity, whether mediated by transference or other forms of telecommunication, are based upon a bewitching mirage of reciprocity or mutual understanding. (Liu 2003, p. 253)

Copjec makes a similar observation, noting that 'in *Television*, Lacan parodies the image of himself—of his teaching—that we have, to a large extent, received and accepted' (Copjec 1994, p. 15). This image is so powerful that the audience continues to take it seriously, even when Lacan mocks and parodies it himself. 'That this proffered image is parodic, however, is almost surely to be missed,' writes Copjec, 'so strong are our misperceptions of Lacan' (Copjec 1994, p. 15). Lacan finds himself trapped by his misrecognized image to such an extent that he baffles his too-serious disciples, not by deceiving them, as his detractors claim, but by revealing his charlatanry in a way that they refuse to accept or understand.

This lack of comprehension among his disciples comes from not having learned the importance of ironic humor when interpreting Lacan. The significance of comedy is specified in *Seminar I*, for instance, when he pauses during an explanation of an optical experiment to reflect on how being too serious corrupts critical thought. 'The closer we get to psychoanalysis being funny the more it is really psychoanalysis,' observes Lacan. 'So let us rejoice, we are still doing psychoanalysis' (Lacan 1991, p. 77). In a recent essay, Nobus explores how the lighthearted camaraderie of those early years of the seminar gradually transmuted into the intellectually stifling atmosphere of the 1970s, when Lacan's reputation was at its zenith:

> Those who did take him seriously, so seriously that they were prepared to follow him, demonstrated both their captivation by what they perceived to be the image of the unassailable master, and their unwillingness to allow this image to fall from the superior position it was held to occupy. They may have gone so far as to laugh *with* him, but they would never have dared to laugh *at* him. In Rome in 1974, Lacan in a sense complained about the fact that too many psychoanalysts were lacking in humor, despite his best intentions to make them laugh or, better still, despite his consistent attempts at presenting himself as a risible figure. (Nobus 2016, pp. 38–39)

Lacan tried to use comedy to liberate his disciples from their slavish devotion to him, hoping that humor would reawaken their capacity for critical thought. 'I am a clown,' he tells the audience in 'La troisième' (1974).

'Take that as an example, and don't imitate me!' (Lacan in Nobus 2016, p. 37). Of course, this injunction is still caught up in Lacan's irony—the disciple who takes Lacan's advice and refuses to imitate him is, in a sense, still following the master's orders.

This comic situation is not just a game that Lacan is playing with his audience, but must be read, as Nobus urges, as an essential part of his exploration of the limits of authority. If, as Lacan argues, there is no master, only a master signifier, then the matter of who gets to occupy the place of the master is ultimately arbitrary. The position of intellectual leadership afforded by the weekly seminar provides Lacan with the opportunity to put this theory, self-reflexively, into practice. 'So Lacan imitates "the voice of the master,"' observes Juliet Flower MacCannell in *Figuring Lacan* (1986). 'Why not? since a master's voice is the only one we deem worthy of listening to' (MacCannell 1986, p. 75). The stakes of this experiment rise with the advent of the 'subject who is supposed to know,' a figure that is placed in the position of the master, but whose obscurity means they could equally be a fraud or a charlatan. This self-reflexive critique, notes Althusser, places Lacan in the strange position of revealing that authority is a bluff, yet a bluff that, somehow, is still taken seriously: 'Lacan was thus playing a double game. To philosophers he brought the guarantee of the master who is "supposed to know" what Freud thought. To psychoanalysts he brought the guarantee of the master who is "supposed to know" what thinking (philosophically) means. He duped everybody, and quite plausibly, despite his extreme trickiness, he duped himself as well' (Althusser 1996, p. 91). It is too straightforward, therefore, to say that Lacan is a charlatan and nothing more. The self-reflexive way he reveals that he is imitating the voice of the master makes him not just a charlatan, but a meta-charlatan. Lacan is ultimately a fraudulent master whose duplicity is enacted not for the sake of tricking us, but in order to open our eyes to the fact that authority is *always* a deceit that only succeeds when we fall for the would-be master's bluff.

The ultimate aim of this book is to help readers realize this crucial point in a way that, I hope, reframes their interpretation of what Lacan is doing. The repeated error has been to place the burden of understanding on him, as a master, to guarantee the transmission of knowledge, an intellectual bad habit that needs to be broken. One of Lacan's great insights is that such transmissions are an illegitimate fantasy of the university discourse, an illusion of objectivity that is caught up in the repressed power game that insidiously promises the slave access to mastery through knowledge. Lacan requires us always to acknowledge the doubleness of mastery's appearance of power. Napoleon, as the Emperor of France, had access to a certain kind of power, for instance, but Hegel shows the extent to which Napoleon was also, in another sense, powerless, a plaything of the *Zeitgeist*. Once this doubleness of power has been grasped, the grandiose proclamations of the master can only be read ironically, and Lacan's evident self-consciousness of this situation stretches the joke to its very limits.

Roustang's tortured question as to why people followed Lacan for so long thus needs to be supplemented by another: why did his followers (and indeed, his critics) fail to acknowledge that Lacan was telling them a joke, that his discourse was undercut by a paradoxical irony? Lacan cannot be made to bear the responsibility for the refusal of his audience to understand what he was trying to do, for their stubborn adherence to seriousness in the midst of his clown act. Is this not the same error that Chomsky committed when he stubbornly refused to believe that Lacan was not serious when, at their 1975 meeting, Lacan claimed that he thought with his feet? Lacan shows up the doubleness of the master's power, its essential charlatanry, because he has come to understand the paradox of authority, its inherent death drive, a contradiction that Roustang so perceptively detects in the conflicting desires of psychoanalysis about its own preservation as a discourse. The ultimate contradiction of Lacan is that, by strategically positioning himself as the master charlatan, he aims both to perpetuate his discourse *and* to dissolve it, just as he did with the EFP. It is in this sense that Roustang's gesture of turning his back on Lacan is also an inherently Lacanian gesture, for it is only by ending the transference, by turning in disillusionment away from the sham authority of the master, that we exit the vicious cycle of the death drive. The only way to be genuinely true to Lacan, in the end, is to break with him, an ironic truth that, because of the inherent paradoxes of mastery, he could only communicate through the ambiguous medium of humor. Lacan has done his part: now, it is up to us to put it into practice by getting up, standing on our own two feet, and walking away from him in order to do some real thinking.

References

Althusser, L., 1996. *Writings on Psychoanalysis*. New York: Columbia University Press.

Badiou, A. & Roudinesco, É., 2014. *Jacques Lacan: Past and Present*. New York: Columbia University Press.

Boothby, R., 1996. The Psychical Meaning of Life and Death: Reflections on the Lacanian Imaginary, Symbolic, and Real. In: D. Pettigrew & F. Raffoul, eds. *Disseminating Lacan*. Albany (NY): State University of New York Press, pp. 337–363.

Borch-Jacobsen, M., 1996. The Oedipus Problem in Freud and Lacan. In: D. Pettigrew & F. Raffoul, eds. *Disseminating Lacan*. Albany (NY): State University of New York Press, pp. 295–314.

Copjec, J., 1994. *Read My Desire: Lacan Against the Historicists*. Cambridge MA and London: The MIT Press.

Felman, S., 1987. *Jacques Lacan and the Adventures of Insight: Psychoanalysis in Contemporary Culture*. Cambridge (MA): Harvard University Press.

Gallop, J., 1982. *Feminism and Psychoanalysis: The Daughter's Seduction*. Basingstoke and London: Macmillan.

Harris, O., 2017. *Lacan's Return to Antiquity: Between Nature and the Gods*. London and New York: Routledge.

Lacan, J., 1990. *Television: A Challenge to the Psychoanalytic Establishment*. New York and London: W.W. Norton & Company.

Lacan, J., 1991. *The Seminar of Jacques Lacan, Book I: Freud's Papers on Technique, 1953–1954*. New York and London: W.W. Norton & Company.

Lacan, J., 2007. *The Seminar of Jacques Lacan, Book XVII: The Other Side of Psychoanalysis*. New York and London: W.W. Norton & Company.

Lacan, J., 2017. *The Seminar of Jacques Lacan, Book V: Formations of the Unconscious*. Cambridge UK and Malden MA: Polity.

Lemaire, A., 1977. *Jacques Lacan*. London, Henley, and Boston: Routledge & Kegan Paul.

Liu, C., 2003. Lacan's Afterlife: Jacques Lacan Meets Andy Warhol. In: J. Rabaté, ed. *The Cambridge Companion to Lacan*. Cambridge: Cambridge University Press, pp. 254–271.

MacCannell, J. F., 1986. *Figuring Lacan: Criticism and the Cultural Unconscious*. London and Sydney: Croom Helm.

Marini, M., 1992. *Jacques Lacan: The French Context*. New Brunswick (NJ): Rutgers University Press.

Millot, C., 2018. *Life With Lacan*. Cambridge UK and Medford MA: Polity.
Nobus, D., 2016. Psychoanalysis as gai saber: Toward a New Episteme of Laughter. In: P. Gherovici & M. Steinkoler, eds. *Lacan, Psychoanalysis, and Comedy*. New York: Cambridge University Press, pp. 35–59.
Rabaté, J.-M., 2001. *Jacques Lacan: Psychoanalysis and the Subject of Literature*. Basingstoke and New York: Palgrave.
Rabaté, J.-M., 2003. Lacan's Turn to Freud. In: J. Rabaté, ed. *The Cambridge Companion to Lacan*. Cambridge (MA): Cambridge University Press, pp. 1–24.
Roustang, F., 1982. *Dire Mastery: Discipleship from Freud to Lacan*. Baltimore and London: The Johns Hopkins University Press.
Roustang, F., 1983. *Psychoanalysis Never Lets Go*. Baltimore and London: The Johns Hopkins University Press.
Roustang, F., 1990. *The Lacanian Delusion*. Oxford: Oxford University Press.
Turkle, S., 1992. *Psychoanalytic Politics: Jacques Lacan and Freud's French Revolution*. 2nd ed. New York & London: The Guilford Press.

References

Althusser, L., 1996. *Writings on Psychoanalysis*. New York: Columbia University Press.

Badiou, A., 2006. Lacan and the Pre-Socratics. In: S. Žižek, ed. *Lacan: The Silent Partners*. London and New York: Verso, pp. 7–16.

Badiou, A. & Roudinesco, É., 2014. *Jacques Lacan: Past and Present*. New York: Columbia University Press.

Bérubé, M., 2006. *Rhetorical Occasions: Essays on Humans and the Humanities*. Chapel Hill: University of North Carolina Press.

Boothby, R., 1996. The Psychical Meaning of Life and Death: Reflections on the Lacanian Imaginary, Symbolic, and Real. In: D. Pettigrew & F. Raffoul, eds. *Disseminating Lacan*. Albany (NY): State University of New York Press, pp. 337–363.

Borch-Jacobsen, M., 1991. *Lacan: The Absolute Master*. Stanford: Stanford University Press.

Borch-Jacobsen, M., 1996. The Oedipus Problem in Freud and Lacan. In: D. Pettigrew & F. Raffoul, eds. *Disseminating Lacan*. Albany (NY): State University of New York Press, pp. 295–314.

Borch-Jacobsen, M., 1997. Basta Così! Mikkel Borch-Jacobsen on Psychoanalysis and Philosophy. In: T. Dufresne, ed. *Returns of the 'French Freud': Freud, Lacan, and Beyond*. New York and London: Routledge, pp. 209–227.

P. D. Mathews, *Lacan the Charlatan*, The Palgrave Lacan Series,
https://doi.org/10.1007/978-3-030-45204-9

Borch-Jacobsen, M., 2005. A Zero Theory. *Butterflies and Wheels*, 5 November, p. np.

Borch-Jacobsen, M. & Shamdasani, S., 2012. *The Freud Files: An Inquiry Into the History of Psychoanalysis*. Cambridge (MA): Cambridge University Press.

Bougnoux, D., 1997. Lacan, Sure – And Then What?. In: T. Dufresne, ed. *Returns of the 'French Freud': Freud, Lacan, and Beyond*. New York and London: Routledge, pp. 91–106.

Bowie, M., 1987. *Freud, Proust and Lacan: Theory as Fiction*. Cambridge: Cambridge University Press.

Bowie, M., 1991. *Lacan*. London: Fontana.

Bowie, M., 1993. *Psychoanalysis and the Future of Theory*. Oxford: Blackwell.

Campbell, K., 2004. *Jacques Lacan and Feminist Epistemology*. London and New York: Routledge.

Carey, P., 2009. *Parrot and Olivier in America*. New York: Alfred A. Knopf.

Chomsky, N., 1989. An Interview. *Radical Philosophy*, Volume 53, pp. 31–40.

Chomsky, N., 2000. *The Architecture of Language*. New Delhi: Oxford University Press.

Clément, C., 1983. *The Lives and Legends of Jacques Lacan*. New York: Columbia University Press.

Copjec, J., 1994. *Read My Desire: Lacan Against the Historicists*. Cambridge MA and London: The MIT Press.

Copjec, J., 2006. May '68, The Emotional Month. In: S. Žižek, ed. *Lacan: The Silent Partners*. London and New York: Verso, pp. 90–114.

Crews, F., 2017. *Freud: The Making of an Illusion*. New York: Metropolitan Books.

David-Menard, M., 1982. Lacanians Against Lacan. *Social Text*, Volume 6, pp. 86–111.

Dawkins, R., 1998. Postmodernism Disrobed. *Nature*, 9 July, Volume 394, p. 141.

de Kesel, M., 2009. *Eros and Ethics: Reading Jacques Lacan's Seminar VII*. Albany (NY): State University of New York Press.

De Kesel, M., 2009. *Eros and Ethics: Reading Jacques Lacan's Seminar VII*. Albany (NY): State University of New York Press.

Derrida, J., 2005. 'Sokal and Bricmont Aren't Serious'. In: *Paper Machine*. Stanford: Stanford University Press, pp. 70–72.

Descartes, R., 2003. *Meditations and Other Metaphysical Writings*. London: Penguin.

Dor, J., 1996. The Epistemological Status of Lacan's Mathematical Paradigms. In: D. Pettigrew & F. Raffoul, eds. *Disseminating Lacan*. Albany (NY): State University of New York Press, pp. 109–121.
Dufresne, T., 1997. Beyond the French Freud. In: T. Dufresne, ed. *Returns of the 'French Freud': Freud, Lacan, and Beyond*. New York and London: Routledge, pp. 1–10.
Dufresne, T., 2003. *Killing Freud: Twentieth Century Culture and the Death of Psychoanalysis*. London and New York: Continuum.
Dufresne, T., 2014. The Making of a 'Freud Basher,' or Reflections of a 'Supercilious Neurotic…'. *The European Legacy: Toward New Paradigms*, 19(1), pp. 72–82.
Durand, A., 1996. Lacan and Lévi-Strauss. In: R. Feldstein, B. Fink & M. Jaanus, eds. *Reading Seminars I and II: Lacan's Return to Freud*. Albany (NY): State University of New York Press, pp. 98–108.
Evans, D., 2004. *Placebo: Mind Over Matter in Modern Medicine*. Oxford: Oxford University Press.
Evans, D., 2005. From Lacan to Darwin. In: J. Gottschall & D. S. Wilson, eds. *The Literary Animal: Evolution and the Nature of Narrative*. Evanston (IL): Northwestern University Press, pp. 38–55.
Evans, D., 2014. *Atheism: All That Matters*. London: Hodder & Stoughton.
Evans, D., 2015. *The Utopia Experiment*. London: Picador.
Feldstein, R., 1996. Introduction I. In: W. Apollon & R. Feldstein, eds. *Lacan, Politics, Aesthetics*. Albany (NY): State University of New York Press, pp. xi–xviii.
Felman, S., 1987. *Jacques Lacan and the Adventures of Insight: Psychoanalysis in Contemporary Culture*. Cambridge (MA): Harvard University Press.
Felman, S., 2003. *Madness and Literature: Literature/Philosophy/Psychoanalysis*. Palo Alto (CA): Stanford University Press.
Fink, B., 2004. *Lacan to the Letter: Reading Écrits Closely*. Minneapolis: University of Minnesota Press.
Fink, B., 2018. The Master Signifier and the Four Discourses. In: D. Nobus, ed. *Key Concepts of Lacanian Psychoanalysis*. New York: Routledge, pp. 29–47.
Forrester, J., 1991. *The Seductions of Psychoanalysis: Freud, Lacan and Derrida*. Cambridge (MA): Cambridge University Press.
Foucault, M., 1984. What is Enlightenment?. In: P. Rabinow, ed. *The Foucault Reader*. New York: Pantheon, pp. 32–50.
Gallop, J., 1982. *Feminism and Psychoanalysis: The Daughter's Seduction*. Basingstoke and London: Macmillan.

Gallop, J., 1985. *Reading Lacan*. Ithaca, NY and London: Cornell University Press.
George, F., 1979. *L'Effet 'Yau de poêle: De Lacan et des lacaniens*. Paris: Hachette.
Glynos, J., 2002. Theory and Evidence in the Freudian Field: From Observation to Structure. In: J. Glynos & Y. Stavrakakis, eds. *Lacan and Science*. London and New York: Karnac, pp. 13–50.
Glynos, J. & Stavrakakis, Y., 2002. Postures and Impostures: On Lacan's Style and Use of Mathematical Science. In: J. Glynos & Y. Stavrakakis, eds. *Lacan and Science*. London and New York: Karnac, pp. 207–229.
Goshgarian, G., 1999. Review of *Impostures Intellectuelles*. *Rethinking Marxism*, 11(1), pp. 120–131.
Grosz, E., 1990. *Jacques Lacan: A Feminist Introduction*. London and New York: Routledge.
Harris, O., 2017. *Lacan's Return to Antiquity: Between Nature and the Gods*. London and New York: Routledge.
Hoens, D., 2006. Toward a New Perversion: Psychoanalysis. In: J. Clemens & R. Grigg, eds. *Jacques Lacan and the Other Side of Psychoanalysis: Reflections on Seminar XVII*. Durham NC and London: Duke University Press, pp. 88–103.
Homer, S., 2006. *Jacques Lacan*. London and New York: Routledge.
Huson, T., 2006. Truth and Contradiction: Reading Hegel With Lacan. In: S. Žižek, ed. *Lacan: The Silent Partners*. London and New York: Verso, pp. 56–78.
Ian, M., 1997. Freud, Lacan, and Imaginary Secularity. *American Imago*, 54(2), pp. 123–147.
Klepec, P., 2016. On the Master in the Four 'Discourses'. In: S. Tomšič & A. Zevnik, eds. *Jacques Lacan: Between Psychoanalysis and Politics*. London and New York: Routledge.
Kordela, A. K., 2007. *$urplus: Spinoza, Lacan*. Albany (NY): State University of New York Press.
Kordela, A. K., 2013. *Being, Time, Bios: Capitalism and Ontology*. Albany (NY): State University of New York Press.
Kordela, A. K., 2018. Marx and Psychoanalysis. In: *Epistemontology in Spinoza-Marx-Freud-Lacan*. New York and London: Routledge, pp. 151–165.
Lacan, J., 1988. *The Seminar of Jacques Lacan, Book II: The Ego in Freud's Theory and in the Techniques of Psychoanalysis, 1954–1955*. Cambridge: Cambridge University Press.
Lacan, J., 1990. *Television: A Challenge to the Psychoanalytic Establishment*. New York and London: W.W. Norton & Company.
Lacan, J., 1991. *The Seminar of Jacques Lacan, Book I: Freud's Papers on Technique, 1953–1954*. New York and London: W.W. Norton & Company.

Lacan, J., 1992. *The Seminar of Jacques Lacan, Book VII: The Ethics of Psychoanalysis, 1959–1960*. New York and London: W.W. Norton & Company.

Lacan, J., 1993. *The Seminar of Jacques Lacan, Book III: The Psychoses, 1955–1956*. London: Routledge.

Lacan, J., 1994. *The Four Fundamental Concepts of Psycho-Analysis*. Harmondsworth: Penguin.

Lacan, J., 1999. *The Seminar of Jacques Lacan, Book XX: Encore: On Feminine Sexuality, The Limits of Love and Knowledge, 1972–1973*. New York and London: W.W. Norton & Company.

Lacan, J., 2006. *Écrits: The First Complete Edition in English*. New York and London: W.W. Norton & Company.

Lacan, J., 2007. *The Seminar of Jacques Lacan, Book XVII: The Other Side of Psychoanalysis*. New York and London: W.W. Norton & Company.

Lacan, J., 2013a. *On the Names-of-the-Father*. Cambridge UK and Malden MA: Polity.

Lacan, J., 2013b. *The Triumph of Religion, preceded by Discourse to Catholics*. Cambridge UK and Malden MA: Polity.

Lacan, J., 2014. *The Seminar of Jacques Lacan, Book X: Anxiety*. Cambridge UK and Malden MA: Polity.

Lacan, J., 2016. *The Seminar of Jacques Lacan, Book XXIII: The Sinthome*. Cambridge UK and Malden MA: Polity.

Lacan, J., 2017a. *Talking to Brick Walls: A Series of Presentations in the Chapel at Sainte-Anne Hospital*. Cambridge UK and Malden MA: Polity.

Lacan, J., 2017b. *The Seminar of Jacques Lacan, Book V: Formations of the Unconscious*. Cambridge UK and Malden MA: Polity.

Lacan, J., 2018. *The Seminar of Jacques Lacan, Book XIX: …or Worse*. Cambridge UK and Malden MA: Polity.

Lemaire, A., 1977. *Jacques Lacan*. London, Henley, and Boston: Routledge & Kegan Paul.

Liu, C., 2003. Lacan's Afterlife: Jacques Lacan Meets Andy Warhol. In: J. Rabaté, ed. *The Cambridge Companion to Lacan*. Cambridge: Cambridge University Press, pp. 254–271.

MacCannell, J. F., 1986. *Figuring Lacan: Criticism and the Cultural Unconscious*. London and Sydney: Croom Helm.

Macey, D., 1988. *Lacan in Contexts*. London and New York: Verso.

Marini, M., 1992. *Jacques Lacan: The French Context*. New Brunswick (NJ): Rutgers University Press.

McGowan, T., 2004. *The End of Dissatisfaction?: Jacques Lacan and the Emerging Society of Enjoyment*. Albany (NY): State University of New York Press.

Mellard, J. M., 2006. *Beyond Lacan*. Albany (NY): State University of New York Press.

Melville, S., 1987. Psychoanalysis and the Place of 'Jouissance'. *Critical Inquiry*, 13(2), pp. 349–370.

Michelman, S., 1996. Sociology Before Linguistics: Lacan's Debt to Durkheim. In: D. Pettigrew & F. Raffoul, eds. *Disseminating Lacan*. Albany (NY): State University of New York Press, pp. 123–150.

Miller, J.-A., 1996a. A Discussion of Lacan's 'Kant with Sade'. In: R. Feldstein, B. Fink & M. Jaanus, eds. *Reading Seminars I and II: Lacan's Return to Freud*. Albany (NY): State University of New York Press, pp. 212–237.

Miller, J.-A., 1996b. An Introduction to Seminars I and II. In: R. Feldstein, B. Fink & M. Jaanus, eds. *Reading Seminars I and II: Lacan's Return to Freud*. Albany (NY): State University of New York Press, pp. 3–14.

Millot, C., 2018. *Life With Lacan*. Cambridge UK and Medford MA: Polity.

Nancy, J.-L. & Lacoue-Labarthe, P., 1992. *The Title of the Letter: A Reading of Lacan*. Albany (NY): State University of New York Press.

Newman, S., 2010. *The Politics of Postanarchism*. Edinburgh: Edinburgh University Press.

Nobus, D., 2003. Lacan's Science of the Subject: Between Linguistics and Topology. In: J. Rabaté, ed. *The Cambridge Companion to Lacan*. Cambridge: Cambridge University Press, pp. 50–68.

Nobus, D., 2016. Psychoanalysis as gai saber: Toward a New Episteme of Laughter. In: P. Gherovici & M. Steinkoler, eds. *Lacan, Psychoanalysis, and Comedy*. New York: Cambridge University Press, pp. 35–59.

Nobus, D., 2018a. Life and Death in the Glass: A New Look at the Mirror Stage. In: D. Nobus, ed. *Key Concepts of Lacanian Psychoanalysis*. New York: Routledge, pp. 101–138.

Nobus, D., 2018b. Preface. In: D. Nobus, ed. *Key Concepts of Lacanian Psychoanalysis*. New York: Routledge, pp. v–viii.

Phillips, J., 1996. Lacan and Merleau-Ponty. In: D. Pettigrew & F. Raffoul, eds. *Disseminating Lacan*. Albany (NY): State University of New York Press, pp. 69–106.

Rabaté, J.-M., 2001. *Jacques Lacan: Psychoanalysis and the Subject of Literature*. Basingstoke and New York: Palgrave.

Rabaté, J.-M., 2003. Lacan's Turn to Freud. In: J. Rabaté, ed. *The Cambridge Companion to Lacan*. Cambridge (MA): Cambridge University Press, pp. 1–24.

Rapaport, H., 2016. Transference Love in the Age of 'Isms'. In: S. M. Wortham & C. Alfano, eds. *Desire in Ashes: Deconstruction, Psychoanalysis, Philosophy*. London: Bloomsbury, pp. 73–92.

Roudinesco, É., 1997. *Jacques Lacan: Outline of a Life, History of a System of Thought*. New York: Columbia University Press.

Roudinesco, É., 2014. *Lacan: In Spite of Everything*. London and Brooklyn: Verso.

Roustang, F., 1982. *Dire Mastery: Discipleship from Freud to Lacan*. Baltimore and London: The John Hopkins University Press.

Roustang, F., 1983. *Psychoanalysis Never Lets Go*. Baltimore and London: The Johns Hopkins University Press.

Roustang, F., 1990. *The Lacanian Delusion*. Oxford: Oxford University Press.

Schneiderman, S., 1983. *Jacques Lacan: The Death of an Intellectual Hero*. Cambridge MA and London: Harvard University Press.

Schneiderman, S., 2002. That Night At Elaine's. *The Reading Room*, 4, pp. 205–222.

Schneiderman, S., 2014. *The Last Psychoanalyst*. self-pub: CreateSpace.

Schneiderman, S., 2015. *Who Was Jacques Lacan?*. [Online] Available at: http://stuartschneiderman.blogspot.com/2015/06/who-was-jacques-lacan.html [Accessed 2 December 2019].

Schneiderman, S., n.d. *About Stuart Schneiderman*. [Online] Available at: http://www.stuartschneiderman.com/about-stuart-schneiderman/ [Accessed 2 December 2019].

Schopenhauer, A., 1969. *The World as Will and Representation*. Mineola (NY): Dover Publications.

Scruton, R., 2006. The Trouble With Islam, the European Union – And Francis Fukuyama. *Open Democracy*, 31 May, p. np.

Scruton, R., 2015. *Fools, Frauds and Firebrands: Thinkers of the New Left*. London: Bloomsbury Continuum.

Sokal, A. & Bricmont, J., 1998. *Fashionable Nonsense: Postmodern Intellectuals' Abuse of Science*. New York: Picador.

Soler, C., 2006. *What Lacan Said About Women: A Psychoanalytic Study*. New York: Other Press.

Tallis, R., 1988a. *In Defence of Realism*. Lincoln NE and London: University of Nebraska Press.

Tallis, R., 1988b. *Not Saussure: A Critique of Post-Saussurean Literary Theory*. Basingstoke and London: Macmillan.

Tallis, R., 1997. The Shrink From Hell. *The Times Higher Education Literary Supplement*, 31 October, p. 20.

Tallis, R., 1999a. Sokal and Bricmont: Is this the beginning of the end of the dark ages in the humanities?. *PN Review*, Volume 128, pp. 35–42.

Tallis, R., 1999b. *Theorrhoea and After*. Basingstoke and London: Macmillan.

Timpanaro, S., 2011. *The Freudian Slip: Psychoanalysis and Textual Criticism*. New York: Verso.

Tomšič, S., 2015. *The Capitalist Unconscious: Marx and Lacan*. London and New York: Verso.

Turkle, S., 1992. *Psychoanalytic Politics: Jacques Lacan and Freud's French Revolution*. 2nd ed. New York & London: The Guilford Press.

Tverdek, E., 2003. Review: Fool Me Once. *Science and Society*, 67(1), pp. 87–99.

Weber, S., 1990. Psychoanalysis, Literary Criticism, and the Problem of Authority. In: R. Feldstein & H. Sussman, eds. *Psychoanalysis And....* London and New York: Routledge, pp. 21–32.

Žižek, S., 1989. *The Sublime Object of Ideology*. London and New York: Verso.

Žižek, S., 1990. The Limits of the Semiotic Approach to Psychoanalysis. In: R. Feldstein & H. Sussman, eds. *Psychoanalysis And....* London and New York: Routledge, pp. 89–110.

Žižek, S., 1991. The Truth Arises from Misrecognition. In: E. Ragland-Sullivan & M. Bracher, eds. *Lacan and the Subject of Language*. London and New York: Routledge, pp. 188–212.

Žižek, S., 1996. Hegel With Lacan, or The Subject and Its Cause. In: R. Feldstein, B. Fink & M. Jaanus, eds. *Reading Seminars I and II: Lacan's Return to Freud*. Albany (NY): State University of New York Press, pp. 397–413.

Žižek, S., 2008. *Enjoy Your Symptom! Jacques Lacan in Hollywood and Out*. New York: Routledge.

Žižek, S., 2016. Divine Ex-sistence: Theology Between Politics and Psychoanalysis. In: S. Tomšič & A. Zevnik, eds. *Jacques Lacan: Between Psychoanalysis and Politics*. London and New York: Routledge, pp. 253–267.

Zupančič, A., 2006. When Surplus Enjoyment Meets Surplus Value. In: J. Clemens & R. Grigg, eds. *Jacques Lacan and the Other Side of Psychoanalysis: Reflections on Seminar XVII*. Durham NC and London: Duke University Press, pp. 155–178.

Index[1]

[1] Note: Page numbers followed by 'n' refer to notes.

P. D. Mathews, *Lacan the Charlatan*, The Palgrave Lacan Series,
https://doi.org/10.1007/978-3-030-45204-9

The manufacturer's authorised representative in the EU is Springer Nature Customer Service Centre GmbH, Europaplatz 3, 69115 Heidelberg, Germany. If you have any concerns regarding our products, please contact ProductSafety@springernature.com

Printed and bound by CPI Group (UK) Ltd, Croydon, CR0 4YY
30/09/2026
02225460-0002